AF763240

Casual laborers waiting to be hired.

Occupational Mobility in Contemporary India

This book analyses the magnitude of the relationship between family background and adult occupational and educational outcomes and provides a comprehensive view of intergenerational mobility in the context of religious and caste dynamics in India.

Based on nationally representative data sets, the book tracks educational and occupational mobility experiences of different socio-religious groups in contemporary India. Examining primary and secondary data to comprehend the macro picture and the micro details, the book offers insights into intra-generational occupational mobility and the perceptions and expectations of Muslim households. The book presents a classification of jobs and mobility analysis that is built on solid foundations of stratification theories. Moreover, it identifies data and presents evidence on the neighborhood effects in India.

Offering an analysis of intergenerational advancement, this book is aimed at researchers in the field of economics, sociology, labor studies, development studies, minority and subaltern studies as well as those interested in the socio-economic issues of disadvantaged socio-religious groups in India.

Nawazuddin Ahmed received his PhD from IIT Roorkee, India, and is currently Assistant Professor of Economics at the Symbiosis School of Economics, Pune, Symbiosis International (a Deemed University), Pune, India. His research focuses on development and labor, and he has published on the impact of family background, occupational shifts and mobility.

D.K. Nauriyal is Senior Professor of Economics at the Indian Institute of Technology, Roorkee, India. He has published widely, and his recent publication includes *Migration, Gender and Home Economics in Rural North India* (co-authored with Nalin S. Negi and Rahul K. Gairola, Routledge, 2020).

Routledge/Asian Studies Association of Australia (ASAA) South Asian Series

Edited by Rahul K. Gairola, Murdoch University, Australia.

Published in association with the Asian Studies Association of Australia (ASAA), represented by Alexander E. Davis, Chair of the ASAA Publications Committee, University of Western Australia.

International Editorial Advisory Board

Meera Ashar, Australian National University; Nandi Bhatia, University of Western Ontario, Canada; Chandan Bose, Indian Institute of Technology Hyderabad, India; Priya Chacko, University of Adelaide, Australia; Assa Doron, Australian National University; Bina Fernandez, The University of Melbourne, Australia; Rashmi Gaur, Indian Institute of Technology Roorkee, India; Amanda Gilbertson, The University of Melbourne, Australia; Michael Gillan, University of Western Australia; Rachita Gulati, Indian Institute of Technology Roorkee, India; Ramaswami Harindranath, UNSW Australia; Nalini Iyer, Seattle University, USA; Ritu Khanduri, University of Texas at Arlington, USA; Ketu Katrak, University of California, Irvine, USA; Suvir Kaul, University of Pennsylvania, USA; Kama Macelan, UNSW Australia; Irfan Nooruddin, Georgetown University, USA; Geeta Patel, University of Virginia, USA; Jasbir Puar, Rutgers University, USA; Dibyadyuti Roy, University of Leeds, UK; Debjani Sengupta, University of Delhi, India; Sunera Thobani, University of British Columbia, Canada; Asha Varadharajan, Queen's University, Canada; Anand Yang, University of Washington, USA.

This series is published in cooperation with the ASAA to support and promote outstanding scholarship in the humanities, arts, and social sciences on South Asia, here widely understood as work emerging from or dealing with Bangladesh, Bhutan, India, Nepal, Pakistan, Sri Lanka, the Maldives, the Indian Ocean region, and comparative work on South Asia and its diasporas with and in other countries. The series publishes excellent, innovative research across a wide range of disciplines including history, politics and political economy, anthropology, geography, literature, sociology and social sciences, the fields of cultural studies, communication studies, security and surveillance studies, studies of religion and ethnicity, and women, gender, and sexuality studies. Interdisciplinary and comparative research is encouraged, and the Editor is also interested in work that stretches the interstices of area studies, identity studies, and technology studies in/ of South Asia into the 21st century.

Works in the series are published simultaneously in UK/ US and India editions, as well as in e-book format. Publications include single-authored monographs and edited volumes by authors based anywhere in the world.

Islam and Egalitarianism in Colonial Bengal
The Making of a Moral Community
Ananya Dasgupta

Occupational Mobility in Contemporary India
Beyond One Generation Into the Future
Nawazuddin Ahmed and D.K. Nauriyal

For more information about this series, please visit: https://www.routledge.com/RoutledgeAsian-Studies-Association-of-Australia-ASAA-South-Asian-Series/book-series/ASAASAS

Occupational Mobility in Contemporary India

Beyond One Generation Into the Future

Nawazuddin Ahmed and D.K. Nauriyal

Routledge
Taylor & Francis Group
LONDON AND NEW YORK

First published 2023
by Routledge
4 Park Square, Milton Park, Abingdon, Oxon OX14 4RN

and by Routledge
605 Third Avenue, New York, NY 10158

Routledge is an imprint of the Taylor & Francis Group, an informa business

© 2023 Nawazuddin Ahmed and D.K. Nauriyal

The right of Nawazuddin Ahmed and D.K. Nauriyal to be identified as author[/s] of this work has been asserted in accordance with sections 77 and 78 of the Copyright, Designs and Patents Act 1988.

All rights reserved. No part of this book may be reprinted or reproduced or utilised in any form or by any electronic, mechanical, or other means, now known or hereafter invented, including photocopying and recording, or in any information storage or retrieval system, without permission in writing from the publishers.

Trademark notice: Product or corporate names may be trademarks or registered trademarks, and are used only for identification and explanation without intent to infringe.

British Library Cataloguing-in-Publication Data
A catalogue record for this book is available from the British Library

Library of Congress Cataloging-in-Publication Data
Names: Ahmed, Nawazuddin, author. | Nauriyal, D. K., author.
Title: Occupational mobility in contemporary India: beyond one generation into the future / Nawazuddin Ahmed, D.K. Nauriyal.
Description: Abingdon, Oxon; New York, NY: Routledge, 2023. | Includes bibliographical references and index.
Identifiers: LCCN 2022061608 (print) | LCCN 2022061609 (ebook) | ISBN 9781032421247 (hardback) | ISBN 9781032421230 (paperback) | ISBN 9781003361299 (ebook) Subjects: LCSH: Occupational mobility—India. | Social mobility—India. | Social classes—India. | Caste—India.
Classification: LCC HD5717.5.I4 A46 2023 (print) |
LCC HD5717.5.I4 (ebook) | DDC 305.5/130954—dc23/eng/20230126
LC record available at https://lccn.loc.gov/2022061608
LC ebook record available at https://lccn.loc.gov/2022061609

ISBN: 978-1-032-42124-7 (hbk)
ISBN: 978-1-032-42123-0 (pbk)
ISBN: 978-1-003-36129-9 (ebk)

DOI: 10.4324/9781003361299

Typeset in Times New Roman
by Deanta Global Publishing Services, Chennai, India

Dedicated to…

My Parents (Mrs Shahnaz & Mr Naimuddin) and My Wife (Dr Rukhsar Ahmed)

Dr Nawazuddin Ahmed

Indian Institute of Technology, Roorkee, India for providing me the learning environment, support and all that made me what I am today.

Prof D.K. Nauriyal

Contents

Figures and Tables

Figures

Tables

Preface

This book provides a comprehensive view of India's religious and caste dynamics on the matter of intergenerational mobility. Based on nationally representative data sets, it tracks the educational and occupational mobility experiences of different socio-religious communities in contemporary India. It also offers a critical view of the combination of occupational and educational mobility and argues that Muslims' backwardness is more educational than occupational, in sharp contrast to the Scheduled Castes and Tribes, for whom progress is more on the educational than on the occupational front. This study is a sharp departure from the mainstream studies on intergenerational mobility in developing nations, which are mostly concerned with aggregate mobility patterns and rarely address the factors influencing such movements. Micro-level exploration of work processes in the form of primary data is expected to be very useful as secondary data-based evidence is insufficient to capture the processes of mobility and associated barriers. This primary data-based study yields two key contributions to the scholarly community and policymakers: insights into intra-generational occupational mobility and the perceptions and expectations of Muslim households. The classification of jobs and mobility analysis are built on the solid foundations of stratification theories. The book identifies data and presents evidence on neighborhood effects in India's sparse literature on neighborhood effects.

Readers will find all the aspects of IG mobility in one place. This book includes the evolution of the Indian labor market over the years and a comprehensive review of the socio-economic conditions of Indian Muslims. This book addresses many research curiosities, such as: who works in India's prominent and well-paying jobs? Where do Muslim, Dalit and tribal people stand? What is the impact of one of the largest affirmative action programs on the educational and economic conditions of marginalized communities? Additionally, what effects do individual, household and geographic factors have on occupational mobility? This work also addresses the most intriguing subject in the research on inequality: who attends higher education. Has mobility increased or decreased in the post-liberalization era? Who is reaping the benefits of a freer economy? What is the feature of Indian society: mobility or immobility?

The modeling strategy to capture the parent-child occupational movements in the MNL framework (multinomial logit models) falls short when it comes to dealing with the multiple socio-religious communities (SRCs). The existing methodology, on the one hand, brings complexities (with relative risk ratios), and on the other, it produces misleading results (in ratio-based analysis, a weaker community appears stronger just because of a relatively low base). This problem is solved by this study, which comes up with some changes to the way social group-wise estimates are made.

Further, this is the only study that calculates the intercept coefficients of education OLS literature. By presenting intercept coefficients of IG educational mobility, this study adds empirical evidence to the sparse literature in developing countries. In developing nations, where a sizable proportion of parents have little or no formal education, the intercept coefficient offers information about children's educational attainment whose parents did not acquire formal education. Furthermore, neighborhood effects play a significant role in the educational mobility of various SRCs.

The observations on intra-generational mobility are quite helpful in comprehending intergenerational mobility, which contributes to this work. This book brings to the fore that without data on how people move within their own generations, it will be harder to understand how people move between generations.

Acknowledgments

This book is the result of a collective effort stretching across many months. A special thanks goes to Professor D.K. Nauriyal for his leading role in the creation of this book. It was a mammoth task that was professionally carried out by him. While Dr Nawazuddin Ahmed's participation in the writing of a book was a first-hand experience, on the other hand, Professor Nauriyal has significantly contributed to a number of academically acclaimed books. His experience and expertise certainly resulted in this eight-chapter book on such an important issue. Professor Nauriyal also handled correspondence with Routledge, UK. The editors at Routledge, United Kingdom, have been incredibly helpful and patient. We would like to thank Dr Rahul K. Gairola, Editor of the Routledge/ASAA South Asia Book Series, for his persistent support and wise counsel whenever we needed it. We would also like to thank the reviewers for their insightful comments on the prior draft. We have benefited from the writings and thoughts of an array of scholars who have written on intergenerational mobility and other issues that are the subject matter of the current book. We extend our sincere thanks to all such scholars. We have also drawn extensively on the data produced by the National Sample Survey Office, India (now known as the National Statistical Organization, India), earlier as the National Sample Survey and now as the Periodic Labour Force Survey rounds. We also want to take this opportunity to thank all of the people who took part in the primary survey. We acknowledge the locals who helped make one of the author's visits possible in their respective localities.

1 Introduction

1.1 Introduction

Several studies in recent years have indicated that peers, school environment, parents' occupational status, parental expectations and attitudes all play a critical role in determining children's occupational goals and, subsequently, actual choices (Kniveton, 2004; Young & Friesen, 1992). Low parental education, low family income, and socio-economic poverty, on the other hand, have been identified as limiting factors that contribute to low offspring aspirations and achievements (Andersen, 2019; Checchi, 2006; Reardon, 2016). Sociologists and economists have examined and continue to analyze intergenerational mobility, including an examination of opportunity inequity (Bowles & Gintis, 2002; Breen & Jonsson, 2005; Brunori et al., 2013; Lefranc et al., 2008; Levine & Mazumder, 1999). All of these studies have identified outcomes such as education, money, profession, status and social standing as the most powerful predictors of intergenerational mobility and persistence for subsequent generations. It is worth emphasizing that past research on inequality and mobility disparities has largely focused on the developed North, most likely owing to a lack of comparable data for the developing South. Consider India, where more than half of the workforce lives in rural areas and where disparities in opportunity and outcomes are contentious issues for all socio-religious groups, particularly marginalized groups like Scheduled Castes and Scheduled Tribes and minorities. It is no surprise that intergenerational mobility is a little-discussed topic in Indian studies and academic journals (Asher et al., 2018; Azam & Bhatt, 2015; Iversen et al., 2017; Majumder, 2010; Reddy & Swaminathan, 2014). This void is what draws attention to the subject, and this work is a modest attempt to bridge, at least partially, this gap. This study will attempt to address a few of them, such as how family background affects adult outcomes; whether the connecting mechanism has changed over time; and whether there are significant differences across various socio-religious communities.

It is notable that the United States, the United Kingdom and some Nordic countries exhibit high intergenerational occupational mobility (Breen, 2004; Long & Ferrie, 2013; Modalsli, 2017). This shows that in these countries, the offspring's career trajectory does not tie with their parents' socio-economic status.

DOI: 10.4324/9781003361299-1

In the case of developing countries, intergenerational mobility is low and still, the issue is focused on farm-to-non-farm mobility as many such developing countries employ a large workforce on farm fields. Since education is the primary prerequisite for higher income achievement in a knowledge economy, IG mobility studies in developed countries are shifting their focus from the analysis of IG occupational mobility to the analysis of educational mobility (Chetty, 2019, 2021). The same approach to data analysis has been used by some researchers in developing nations (Asher et al., 2018).

There is an increasing need for a highly educated workforce due to the technological advancements sweeping the globe, especially in developing nations. Developing countries have a low proportion of such workers relative to total employment despite the growing need for them, as a result of lower educational attainment and a lack of necessary skills. As a result of an ever-expanding educational infrastructure, it is suggested that the increase in children's educational attainment may not translate into increased occupational mobility because the levels of education and skills necessary for higher-paying jobs may have been overlooked for a variety of reasons. This study specifically takes into account both educational and occupational mobility in order to address the complex issue at hand.

In India, some studies have backed up the widely held perception that Muslims fare poorly in terms of educational mobility (Asher et al., 2018; Azam & Bhatt, 2015). While these findings are crucial for policymakers, they also highlight a slew of other challenges. Among them are the following: what is the occupational mobility of Muslims as compared to other marginalized caste groups, such as scheduled tribes and scheduled castes? How do the occupational and educational mobility experiences of Muslims differ from national trends in different regions? Additionally, can we obtain more insight into intra-generational mobility and intergenerational goals by conducting primary surveys rather than relying solely on secondary data?

As this study focuses on population diversity in terms of caste, class and religion, it is critical to examine what percentage of the workforce is skilled and educated, as well as the degree to which each socio-religious community has access to such employment. How do household variables, as well as the traits of parents and individuals, affect the ability of people from different socio-religious groups to move into skilled and education-based jobs?

1.2 Work and Labor Force Participation of Various Socio-Religious Categories: Trends

In this section, work participation and labor force trends are discussed among different socio-religious communities in India and at the all-India level. The different socio-religious communities (SRCs) are as follows: Among Hindus, SRCs are classified as STs (Scheduled Tribes), SCs (Scheduled Castes), OBCs (Other Backward Classes), and Others. Among Muslims, there are OBCs and Others. Other religious minorities are grouped together under the heading "Other

Minorities". Hindus account for 79.8 percent of India's total population. Muslims constitute India's second-largest community, accounting for 14.23 percent of the population. Other minorities and those who have not declared their faith account for 5.97 percent of the population (Census, 2011). There are no caste-based census figures available. However, based on estimates from the Periodic Labour Force Survey (2017–18), STs account for 7.73 percent, SCs 17.78 percent, OBCs 35.03 percent, and Others 21.05 percent of the total Hindu population. Similarly, survey approximation indicates that half of the Indian Muslim population is OBC.[1] The analysis in this chapter is based on the National Sample Employment-Unemployment Survey (NSS EUS) quinquennial rounds of 1999–00 (55th), 2004–05 (61st), 2011-12 (68th), and the Periodic Labour Force Survey (PLFS) 2018–19. The standard weight procedure was applied in consonance with the NSS estimation strategy (NSSO Sixty-Eighth Round Report, 2012, pp. 394–400). The employment for the age group 15–65 years, based on UPS (Usual Principal Status), which refers to a person's engagement during the majority of the year preceding the date of the survey (NSS Sixty-Eighth Round Report 2011–2012, p. 11), has been adopted.

The labor force comprises those who are working and those who are actively seeking employment. The workforce includes only those working because it is the labor force minus involuntarily unemployed people. In Table 1.1, the work participation rate (WPR) also shows a similar trend to the labor force participation rate (LFPR) for all socio-religious communities. As can be seen from Table 1.1, between 2000 and 2005, maximum employment (45.22 million) was generated. In 2012, despite sustaining a high growth rate, the Indian economy experienced a drastic decline in job creation. In 2019, job creation was modest at 29.48 million. Many researchers have reported a net reduction in job creation in 2019 over 2012. However, our estimates do not reflect that case. It is noticeable that employment statistics reported on Usual Status (Principal and Subsidiary Status) figure out a net loss of employment in 2019 compared to 2012 (Nath & Basole, 2020).[2] Once we shift the calculation from usual status to principal status, there is a modest increment in job creation. It reflects that mainly part-time workers lost their jobs (as WPR indicates) or withdrew their labor from the market (as LFPR indicates). Job creation or job loss depends on the methodology of calculations, such as mid-point time, population projection method, age bracket, educational level, and, most importantly, status (principal vs usual). Given all these considerations, the best strategy is to focus on the gap between LFPR (supply-side) and WPR (demand-side), which is the unemployment rate (UR).

In 2019, the gap rose exceptionally, and in absolute terms, it is 28.41 million. This figure is way higher than the 11.09 million of 2012 and the 12.34 million of 2005. Many arguments have been given about this new trend in the labor market, such as changes in methodology, technological changes, more students going for higher studies, jobless growth and job-loss growth (Kannan & Raveendran, 2019; Kerswell & Pratap, 2019; Mitra & Singh, 2019). In such a weak labor market, it is difficult to prove demand for methodological changes or rising educational demand (Kannan & Raveendran, 2019). The series of economic shocks like the

Table 1.1 Population, Labor Force and Working Population Across SRCs

NSS EUS	*2000*	*2005*	*2012*	*2019*
Population (15–65 age)	579.61	649.08	759.09	887.74
Labor Force in Millions (15–65 age)				
All (% figures in bracket)	341.33 (58.89)	389.39 (60.01)	403.46 (53.16)	450.26 (50.71)
LFPR Among SRCs in % (15–65 age)				
Hindu ST	74.04	74.24	64.75	58.93
Hindu SC	62.93	62.59	54.90	52.05
Hindu OBC	61.55	62.50	53.94	51.24
Hindu Others	52.39	54.38	49.39	48.22
Muslim OBC	51.97	50.53	47.96	44.86
Muslim Others	52.15	52.74	49.43	47.32
Other Minorities	55.67	58.07	52.10	52.38
Work Force in Millions (15–65 age)				
All (% figures in bracket)	331.83 (57.25)	377.05 (58.12)	392.37 (51.70)	421.85 (47.52)
WPR Among SRCs in % (15–65 age)				
Hindu ST	73.22	73.30	63.92	56.31
Hindu SC	61.49	60.74	53.41	48.44
Hindu OBC	60.28	60.88	52.66	48.17
Hindu Others	50.20	52.13	47.79	45.08
Muslim OBC	49.77	48.07	46.37	41.27
Muslim Others	50.40	51.10	47.55	44.59
Other Minorities	53.28	54.67	49.82	48.56

Source: Calculations are based on unit-level data of NSS EUS Rounds (2000, 2005, 2012) and PLFS 2019.

Note: By multiplying the workforce participation rate (WPR) and labor force participation rate (LFPR) from the NSS data by the projected population estimates for the corresponding year taken from Census India, one can determine the size of the workforce and labor force in absolute terms (in any year).

poor performance of agriculture in the fiscal year 2014–15, the implementation of Goods and Service Tax (GST), Demonetization, and the slow growth of the world economy could be a potential explainer of this mass unemployment (Kannan & Raveendran, 2019; Mehrotra & Parida, 2019; Subramanian, 2019).

Examining the individual share of different socio-religious communities, it is evident from Table 1.2 that Hindu OBCs have a 36.32 percent share of the total employment in the year 2019. There is a decline in the share of Hindu Others in the year 2019 compared to 2000, but there is an increment in the share of Hindu OBCs in the same period. Similarly, there is a decline in the share of Muslim Others and a rise in the share of Muslim OBCs.

As is evident from Figure 1.1, which depicts workforce participation and educational attainments,[3] a large part of the workforce, i.e., over 44 percent in 2000, was without any formal education. A significant proportion of the population without formal education comes from Hindu STs (around 68 percent) and Hindu SCs (around 58 percent). Other socio-religious communities (SRC), such as

Table 1.2 Share of Each SRC in Overall Employment during Selected Years

Years	*Total Volume of Employment (in Millions)*	*Percentage Share of Each Community in the Total Employment*						
		Hindu ST	*Hindu SC*	*Hindu OBC*	*Hindu Others*	*Muslim OBC*	*Muslim Others*	*Other Minorities*
2000	331.83	9.62	18.79	33.09	23.25	3.13	6.72	5.41
2005	377.05	8.91	18.43	36.70	20.45	3.86	6.29	5.36
2012	392.37	9.04	17.88	36.68	19.80	5.94	5.80	4.85
2019	421.85	8.74	18.12	36.32	19.8	6.17	5.03	5.82

Source: Calculations are based on unit-level data of NSS EUS Rounds (2000, 2005, 2012) and PLFS 2019.

Hindu OBCs, Muslim OBCs, and Muslim Others, on the other hand, were closer to the national average. In contrast, Hindus and Other Minorities had most of their workforce participants with some formal levels of education. Interestingly, there appeared to be a sharp reduction in the labor force without any formal education, from 44 percent in 2000 to 23.2 percent by 2019. And this reduction was substantive for all communities, with the largest contributors being the Hindu STs and Hindu SCs.

Figure 1.1 highlights that among all, graduates appear to be much fewer among Hindu STs and Hindu SCs in 2019, followed by Muslim OBCs and Muslim

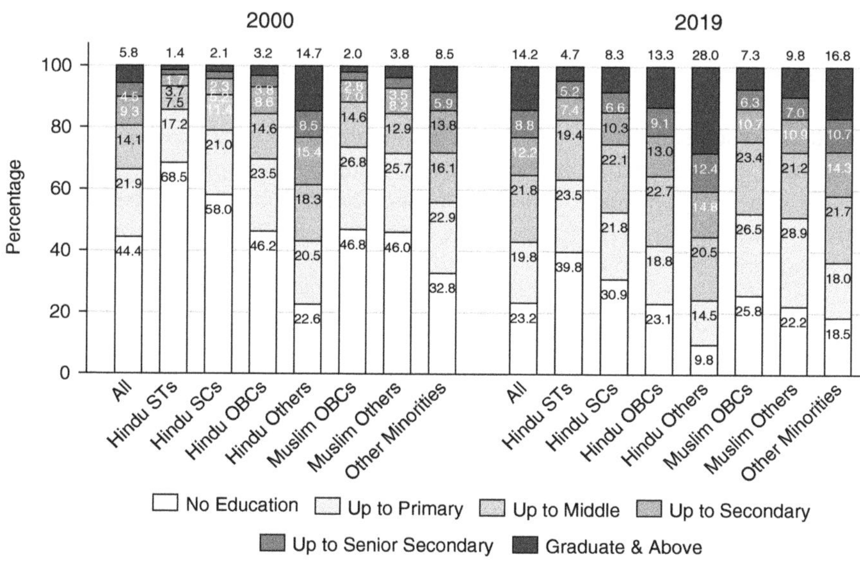

Figure 1.1 Work Force at Different Levels of Education. Note: Read Other Mino. as Other Minorities; Source: Calculations are based on unit-level data of NSS Employment-Unemployment Survey (EUS) Rounds (2000, 2005, 2012) and Periodic Labour Force Survey (PLFS 2019).

Others. The largest proportion of graduates comes from Hindu Others and Other Minorities.

Figure 1.2 brings to the fore that there has been a reduction in labor force participation in 2019 over 2000 across all socio-religious communities and genders. It also indicates the existence of a formidable gender gap in labor force participation. If female labor force participation is dropped from the analysis, there is not much difference in male labor force participation, especially in 2019, across socio-religious communities. The Muslim community has the lowest female labor force participation, followed by Hindu Others. Much of the increase in the labor force took place in the period from 2000 to 2005. After 2005, the labor force increment has shown signs of slowing down for various reasons, a prominent one being the withdrawal of women from the labor market (Bhalla & Kaur, 2011; Chowdhury, 2011; Klasen & Pieters, 2012). It has been reported that the percentage of women who work has declined from 36 percent in 2005–05 to 24 in 2015–16 (Economic Survey 2017–18 Volume 1, p. 108), which is very low when compared to the global average of 49 percent (Klasen et al., 2021). The dwindling work participation of women is a matter of serious concern, especially in the face of strong economic growth, because the rising work participation of women drives growth (Volart-Esteve, 2004). The low female LFPR can also be attributed to the increasing enrolment of young girls and women in education. Another view is that higher work participation of women in developing countries does not always indicate women's empowerment but could be a signal of a higher level of poverty as the labor force participation of women in such countries is generally found to be in low-productivity and low-paid jobs (Gaddis & Klasen, 2014).

Unfortunately, the gender gap in labor force participation is greatest in South Asian nations, the Middle East and North Africa, in stark contrast to the Southeast Asian, East Asian and Pacific regions (Verick, 2014), most likely due to historically defined societal gender roles and continuing stereotypes with minimal education and income effects, structural transformation of economic effects, and a rising gap between much-desired and much-needed labor force participation geared toward women (Abraham, 2013; Kapsos et al., 2014; Rangarajan et al., 2011; Sanghi et al., 2015).

1.3 Occupational Changes at a Glance

1.3.1 Overall Changes

Table 1.3 highlights the distribution of jobs in the 9-division occupational classification. It should be noted that, despite accounting for a small proportion of total jobs, four occupational classes (1+2+3+4), which are considered to be education and skill-intensive, have shown steady growth over the study period. The share of these four occupations, for example, rose from 10.04 percent in 2000 to 19.21 percent by 2019. There was also a modest rise in jobs in these four occupational classes from 2012 to 2019, when the labor market suffered a sharp slowdown. It is worth noting that the share of employment in these four occupations,

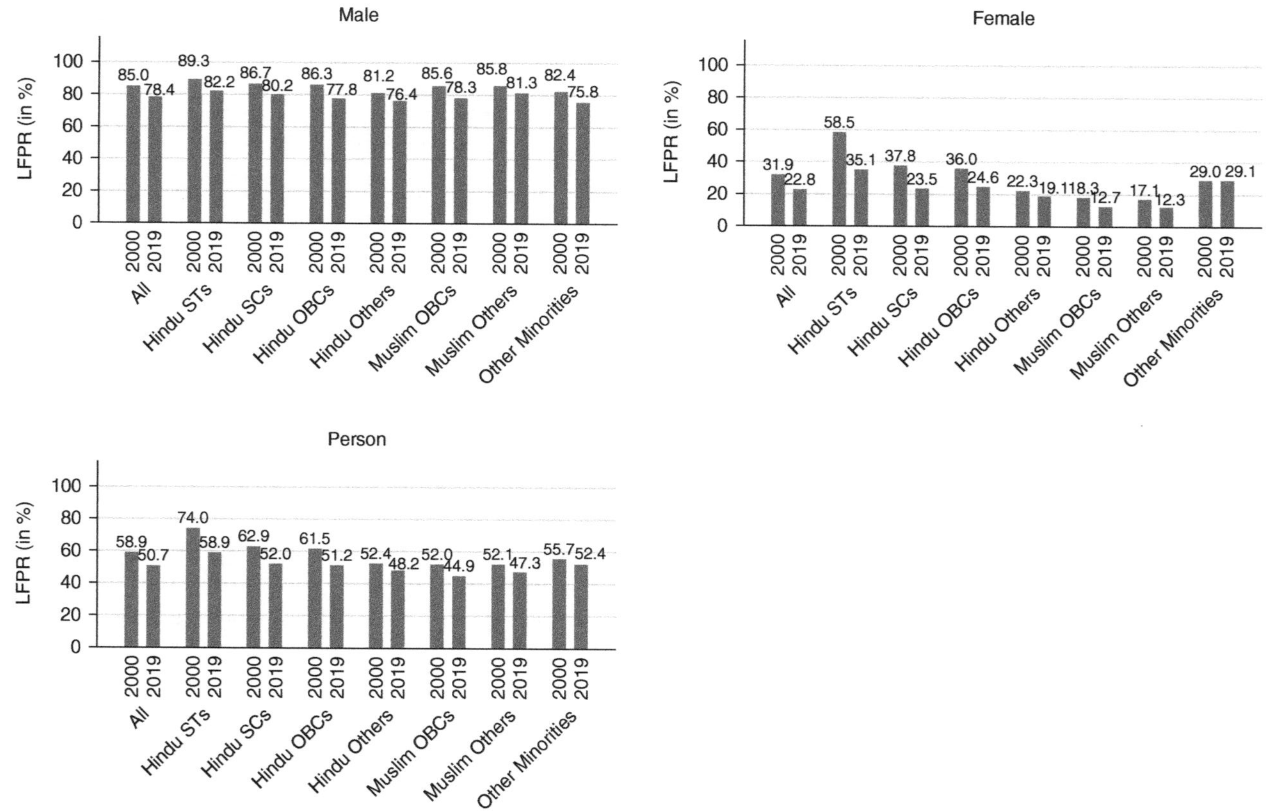

Figure 1.2 Labor Force Participation across Socio-Religious Communities and the Genders. Note: All figures have the same Y-axis. Source: Calculations are based on unit-level data of NSS EUS Rounds (2000, 2005, 2012) and PLFS 2019.

comprising Officials and Managers (1), Professionals (2), Associate Professionals (3) and Clerks (4), has changed significantly over the course of different years. For instance, while engagement of people as officials and managers increased by 239 percent in 2019 over 2000, it has also increased significantly for professionals by about 184 percent and for associate professionals by 88.56 percent.

There are 90.02 million new entrants in the workforce in 2019 compared to 2000, and there is a rise in employment in certain occupations, such as officials and managers, professionals and associate professionals (Ramaswamy & Agrawal, 2012). The share of agriculture in percentage terms has sided down as there seems to be a movement out of agriculture. In absolute terms, the number of laborers has decreased by about 10 million in 2019 compared to 2000, 2005 and 2012. In terms of percentage growth, it has witnessed a constant decline since the year 2000. Since the service sector has been growing faster, a rise can be witnessed in trade-related activities in both percentage and absolute terms. The largest increment in employment has been registered majorly by two occupations, i.e., officials and managers and crafts and trade (Table 1.3). One point that piques our interest is that the absolute number of jobs in skilled agriculture and related fields increased between 2000 and 2005, despite a decline in relative terms. The general convention is that agriculture is shrinking. The issue is that here the occupation (skilled agriculture and allied) is considered and not the agriculture and agricultural labor per se. If we measure employment in terms of agriculture and agricultural labor put together, we find that people moving out of the "agriculture

Table 1.3 Occupational Distribution in the 9-Division Occupational Categorization

9-division occupations	*In Millions*				*In Percentage*			
	2000	*2005*	*2012*	*2019*	*2000*	*2005*	*2012*	*2019*
1. Officials & Managers	10.45	13.65	28.13	35.44	3.15	3.62	7.17	8.40
2. Professionals	6.40	7.62	14.60	18.18	1.93	2.02	3.72	4.31
3. Associate Professionals	9.62	11.27	13.30	18.14	2.90	2.99	3.39	4.30
4. Clerks	6.84	6.90	8.16	9.28	2.06	1.83	2.08	2.20
1+2+3+4	**33.31**	**39.44**	**64.19**	**81.04**	**10.04**	**10.46**	**16.36**	**19.21**
5. Service Workers, Shop, Market Sales	28.11	34.58	30.76	41.43	8.47	9.17	7.84	9.82
6. Skilled Agri & Fishery	107.78	128.84	114.14	123.01	32.48	34.17	29.09	29.16
7. Craft-Related Trades	32.35	40.16	50.69	50.92	9.75	10.65	12.92	12.07
8. Plant-Machine Operators	15.60	19.08	20.05	24.34	4.70	5.06	5.11	5.77
9. Laborers	114.65	114.96	112.53	101.08	34.55	30.49	28.68	23.96
Total (1:9)	**331.80**	**377.06**	**392.36**	**421.82**	**100**	**100**	**100**	**100**

Note: Agri shows Agriculture. Source: Calculations are based on unit-level data of NSS EUS Rounds (2000, 2005, 2012) and PLFS 2019.

industry" include cultivators, laborers and fishery workers. Some studies, however, reported a decline in employment in "agriculture and allied" occupations. Such studies are based on an inappropriate measure of occupation, "agriculture and allied". Until 2005, NSS reports occupation on NCO-1968, which has "agriculture and allied" occupation with agriculture and plantation labor information. In the years 2012 and 2019, survey data used NCO-2004, which separated occupations "agriculture and allied" from agriculture and plantation labor.

NCO-2004 classifies agriculture and plantation labor as elementary occupations (division 9). Studies based on up to 2005 data considered NCO-1968 where "agriculture and allied" was merged with "agriculture and plantation labor". Multiple studies that include 2005 onwards NSS rounds establishing concordance of NCO-2004 to NCO-1968 appeared to have made inaccurate estimations. In this study, concordance was established from NCO-1968 (older) to NCO-2004 (recent). If we do the reverse, then we are treating labor and cultivators together. In this study on the NCO-2004 scheme, the cultivator and fishery workers (Division-6) and agricultural laborers (Division-9) are treated differently. The observation of an increment in "skilled agriculture and allied" and a reduction in agriculture labor in absolute terms is also supported by Mehrotra (2019) (see table 2, p. 13, Mehrotra, 2019).

The participation of female workers has increased in professional and associate professional occupations (Table 1.4). In the "plant-machine operators"

Table 1.4 The Gender Distribution of Occupations in the 9-Division Occupational Classification

9-division occupations	*2000*		*2005*		*2012*		*2019*	
	Male	*Female*	*Male*	*Female*	*Male*	*Female*	*Male*	*Female*
1. Officials & Managers	86.59	13.41	86.06	13.94	86.96	13.04	85.43	14.57
2. Professionals	82.81	17.19	79.78	20.22	77.42	22.58	74.38	25.62
3. Associate Professionals	73.52	26.48	70.81	29.19	71.28	28.72	66.84	33.16
4. Clerks	86.93	13.07	83.83	16.17	83.13	16.87	79.05	20.95
5. Service Workers, Shop, Market Sales	86.58	13.42	84.89	15.11	85.14	14.86	82.17	17.83
6. Skilled Agri & Fishery	70.92	29.08	67.40	32.60	73.91	26.09	73.90	26.10
7. Craft-Related Trades	79.6	20.4	78.92	21.08	81.58	18.42	82.33	17.67
8. Plant-Machine Operators	86.27	13.73	88.00	12.00	94.82	5.18	96.25	3.75
9. Laborers	66.22	33.78	66.84	33.16	72.99	27.01	73.09	26.91
Total	73.33	26.67	72.40	27.60	77.75	22.25	77.62	22.38

Source: Calculations are based on unit-level data of NSS EUS Rounds (2000, 2005, 2012) and PLFS 2019.

Note: The figures are in percentage.

occupation, women's participation has declined from 13.73 percent to 3.75 percent. Since 2012, the number of female workers has also declined. Since 2000, the number of women working as officials and managers has stayed almost the same.

The educational attainment of workers also appeared to have registered an upward trend (Table 1.5). For instance, the occupational groups such as professionals, associate professionals and clerks have witnessed a rise in their educational profile in terms of graduation and above. On the contrary, very small percentages of graduate and above manpower are engaged in agriculture and fisheries, which suggests the possibility of a knowledge deficit in this very important sector of the Indian economy that employs the largest chunk of employable manpower.

1.3.2 Occupational Distribution of Various Socio-Religious Communities

The distribution of the first four occupations among different SRCs in the 9-division occupational classification is shown in Table 1.6. When we look at the four professions as a whole, we find that Hindu OBCs and Hindu Others hold the bulk of these employment among SRCs. For instance, they continued to claim 81.38 percent of the jobs in these four occupations in 2019, compared to 82.6 percent in 2000. Muslim OBCs are the other major gainers, rising from 2.53 percent in 2000 to 6.68 percent in 2019. The STs and SCs have also marginally gained, but Muslim Others have lost in the process. From the data in Table 1.6 on the first four occupations, it can be discerned that there has been a perceptible change in the relative shares of different communities in the job pie. Although Hindu Others still lead by sharing almost one-third of such jobs in 2019, they have mainly lost ground to Hindu OBCs. In relative terms, the least gainers are Muslims, both OBCs and Others, and Hindu SCs. The Muslim OBCs that appeared to have made remarkable inroads into this job market in 2012 did not see any noticeable change six years later, i.e., in 2019, while Muslim Others lost during this time.

In order to further probe into the job market, employment was subdivided into three categories, viz., Self-Employed (SE), Regular Wage/Salaried (RWS), and Casual Labor (CL).[4] Among the three, work tends to be more beneficial in the RWS category, as this category is likely to be entitled to benefits such as social security, old-age pension, health insurance, etc. In the case of self-employed and casual labor, such incentives are not available. As could be discerned from Table 1.7, almost all the communities have made an appreciable rise in the RWS category, most notably the Hindu SCs and Hindu OBCs, with almost the same percentage point, followed by Muslim Others, Hindu STs, Hindu Others, Other Minorities, and Muslim OBCs in 2019 over 2000.

Although there has been an increase in self-employment for Hindu STs, followed by Hindu SCs and Other Minorities, there has been a decrease for Hindu Others, followed by Muslim OBCs, Muslim Others and Hindu OBCs. In the case of the "Self-employed" category, while there has been a rise in self-employment for Hindu STs, followed by Hindu SCs, and Hindu OBCs, there has been a reduction for Hindu Others, followed by Muslim OBCs, Muslim Others and Other

Table 1.5 Distribution of Occupations within the 9-Division Occupational Categorization by Level of Education

	Within Occupations							
	% Senior Secondary Completed				*% Graduates & Above*			
9-division occupations	*2000*	*2005*	*2012*	*2019*	*2000*	*2005*	*2012*	*2019*
1. Officials & Managers	26.87	28.24	32.32	27.54	23.05	25.57	23.14	27.90
2. Professionals	20.14	22.86	20.90	15.69	65.22	63.73	64.49	71.55
3. Associate Professionals	48.36	48.13	37.72	26.22	37.60	39.67	49.96	63.38
4. Clerks	45.05	43.37	41.56	31.15	40.46	43.03	48.60	58.55
5. Service Workers, Shop, Market Sales	25.28	28.19	32.84	32.53	7.92	8.84	12.27	14.50
6. Skilled Agricultural & Fishery	11.50	12.40	18.72	18.68	2.05	2.28	3.31	5.18
7. Craft-Related Trades	17.06	16.53	21.61	23.09	2.51	2.28	2.86	7.17
8. Plant and Machine Operators	22.43	23.56	32.05	28.89	3.52	2.73	4.50	9.07
9. Laborers	4.62	4.96	10.32	12.99	0.38	0.40	0.78	1.86
Total	13.76	15.01	20.65	21.01	5.79	6.28	9.51	14.21
	Between Occupations							
	% Senior Secondary Completed				*% Graduates & Above*			
9-division occupations	*2000*	*2005*	*2012*	*2019*	*2000*	*2005*	*2012*	*2019*
1. Officials &Managers	6.15	6.82	11.22	11.01	12.54	14.75	17.45	16.49
2. Professionals	2.83	3.08	3.76	3.22	21.75	20.52	25.23	21.70
3. Associate Professionals	10.20	9.60	6.19	5.37	18.85	18.90	17.81	19.18
4. Clerks	6.75	5.28	4.18	3.27	14.39	12.51	10.62	9.08
5. Service Workers, Shop, Market Sales	15.57	17.22	12.47	15.20	11.60	12.90	10.12	10.02
6. Skilled Agricultural & Fishery	27.14	28.26	26.38	25.92	11.53	12.41	10.13	10.62
7. Craft-Related Trades	12.09	11.73	13.53	13.26	4.23	3.87	3.89	6.09
8. Plant and Machine Operators	7.66	7.95	7.94	7.93	2.85	2.20	2.42	3.68
9. Laborers	11.61	10.07	14.33	14.81	2.26	1.94	2.34	3.13
Total	100.0	100.0	100.0	100.0	100.0	100.00	100.0	100.0

Source: Calculations are based on unit-level data of NSS EUS Rounds (2000, 2005, 2012) and PLFS 2019.

Note: Row sum does not equal 100 because only high school completed and graduation and above data are presented.

Table 1.6 Distribution of the First Four Occupations across SRCs

SRCs	*Number of people of each SRC employed in the first four occupations (Figures are in %)*				*SRC-wise break-up of the share of four occupations in the total employed people of each community (Figures are in %)*			
	2000	*2005*	*2012*	*2019*	*2000*	*2005*	*2012*	*2019*
All	100.00	100.00	100.00	100.00	10.04	10.46	16.35	19.21
Hindu ST	3.14	2.62	3.17	3.20	3.28	3.08	5.73	7.04
Hindu SC	9.17	9.04	10.13	11.24	4.9	5.13	9.26	11.92
Hindu OBC	22.38	26.10	30.49	32.43	6.79	7.44	13.59	17.15
Hindu Others	47.91	42.99	37.44	34.51	20.69	21.99	30.92	33.48
Muslim OBC	2.53	3.13	5.91	6.68	8.11	8.48	16.27	20.79
Muslim Others	6.71	5.98	5.93	5.37	10.03	9.94	16.72	20.49
Other Minorities	8.05	8.17	6.92	6.63	14.94	15.94	23.34	21.88

Source: Calculations are based on unit-level data of NSS EUS Rounds (2000, 2005, 2012) and PLFS 2019.

Minorities. With regard to the "Casual Labor" group, Hindu STs and SCs, followed by Hindu OBCs, and Other Minorities, Muslim Others, reported a major decrease in terms of percentage points over 2000 in 2019. A fall, followed by Hindu Others, has also been reported by Muslim OBCs. Thus, a massive restructuring of the job market for the communities is taking place, albeit at a different pace for each one of them, where all of them are moving away from the "Casual Labor" category to other categories. This, however, is not upward mobility within the same generation but rather intergenerational job market restructuring.

1.4 An Overview of the Literature and the Need for This Book

Intergenerational mobility is an important indicator of the available opportunities in society. Higher mobility indicates that the occupational and educational success of people does not depend on their parental background. In simple words, higher mobility ensures that the younger generation does not face barriers to attaining their desired career path and educational accomplishments due to their parental background. In reality, inequality persists, and some people who are not born into fortunate socio-economic families face many difficulties. Their success is closely tied to the success of their predecessors. Again, such inequalities may be higher or lower in some castes and religious groups. The majority of the studies in India on intergenerational mobility were conducted in this decade only. Prior to that, there were not so many attempts to look for intergenerational mobility. There are limited studies on this subject in India. However, the available literature has contributed immensely to developing the conceptual framework and innovation in data and findings. These studies are mainly descriptive and were carried out to study the differences in the mobility outcomes of SCs, STs and forward castes. The mobility pattern among other social groups, like Muslims, is largely ignored.

Table 1.7 Activity Status of Workers within and across SRCs

Year	*2000*			*2005*			*2012*			*2019*		
Within (Row Sum)												
SRCs	SE	RWS	CL	SE	RWS	CL	SE	RWS	CL	SE	RWS	CL
Hindu ST	44.41	6.76	48.83	49.06	6.72	44.22	49.94	8.55	41.51	53.80	12.28	33.92
Hindu SC	31.98	11.08	56.94	36.57	13.31	50.12	34.17	16.41	49.41	37.21	21.32	41.46
Hindu OBC	54.54	12.32	33.14	58.39	13.25	28.36	53.52	17.08	29.39	55.33	23.24	21.42
Hindu Others	57.00	26.43	16.57	59.84	26.36	13.80	54.85	31.72	13.42	53.60	36.73	9.67
Muslim OBC	53.90	13.94	32.16	61.68	12.48	25.84	50.90	17.07	32.02	50.57	21.42	28.01
Muslim Others	54.59	14.99	30.42	56.67	14.99	28.34	55.12	17.83	27.05	50.04	25.25	24.71
Other Minorities	46.15	21.79	32.06	50.70	21.96	27.34	47.93	27.64	24.43	45.29	29.40	25.31
All	49.42	15.58	35.00	53.43	15.91	30.66	49.67	19.65	30.68	50.43	24.95	24.62
Between (Column Sum)												
SRCs	SE	RWS	CL	SE	RWS	CL	SE	RWS	CL	SE	RWS	CL
Hindu ST	8.65	4.18	13.44	8.20	3.77	12.87	9.10	3.94	12.25	9.33	4.30	12.05
Hindu SC	12.19	13.39	30.66	12.64	15.45	30.18	12.32	14.96	28.84	13.37	15.49	30.52
Hindu OBC	36.57	26.19	31.37	40.17	30.61	34.00	39.59	31.94	35.19	39.85	33.83	31.60
Hindu Others	26.93	39.59	11.05	22.93	33.92	9.22	21.90	32.02	8.67	21.05	29.15	7.78
Muslim OBC	3.15	2.59	2.66	4.29	2.92	3.13	5.95	5.04	6.05	6.18	5.29	7.02
Muslim Others.	7.44	6.48	5.86	6.68	5.93	5.82	6.45	5.27	5.12	4.99	5.09	5.05
Other Minorities	5.06	7.58	4.96	5.09	7.40	4.78	4.69	6.83	3.87	5.22	6.85	5.98

Note: Figures are in percentage; SE: Self-employment, RWS: Regular wage/salaried, CL: Casual Labor; Source: Calculations are based on unit-level data of NSS EUS Rounds (2000, 2005, 2012) and PLFS 2019.

Also, some findings, like Asher et al. (2018) about the poor performance of Muslims in the last two decades in IG educational mobility, do not tell us anything about the actual picture of backwardness among Muslims. Are Muslims also performing poorly in terms of IG occupational mobility? This research question allows us to think about conducting an analysis of education and occupation together. There is a growing argument favoring IG educational mobility due to the importance of education in the skill and knowledge-based economy. Does the success of educational mobility translate into occupational mobility among some regional pockets or population sub-groups? The rapid expansion of education in recent decades may give an impression that marginalized segments of society are also catching up fast with the forward population. In reality, occupational accomplishments may remain low.

Previous studies made the assumption that Muslims were underachievers when building education-occupation switch regression models but did not examine their performance. (Hnatkovska et al., 2013; Iversen et al., 2016; Majumder, 2010; Motiram & Singh, 2012). The research by Asher et al. (2018) makes an effort to discuss the patterns of Muslim mobility in India. According to the study's findings, Muslims in India have lower levels of educational mobility than STs and SCs. The second-largest population in India is Muslims, who have a population percentage similar to that of the scheduled castes. Leaving such a large population group out of the study is a source of future mobility knowledge deprivation. The current study fills this gap by looking at a larger group with a broader range of socio-religious diversity. According to the literature, Muslims struggle in the educational domain. Muslims have the greatest labor force participation rate (LFPR) across all religious groups and the national average for those who are between the ages of 15 and 19 (NSSO Sixty-Eighth Round Report for Religious Groups, 2012, p. A-56). The high LFPR in the age group of 15–19 is a matter of concern because these participants are early entrants into the labor market and dropouts. It is clear that if a community has relatively high labor market participation in the age group of 15–19, most of them are push participants due to a low level of investment in education. It creates a cycle of underdevelopment. A low level of investment in education results in a low return in the labor market, which again hinders the next generation's growth. The low quality of the Muslim labor force is also visible in the category of secondary and above education. About 23 percent of Muslim males are participating in the labor market with an education higher than the secondary level compared to their Hindu counterparts, who stand with a 35.3 percent endowment of at least secondary education. Nearly half of Christian males in the labor force have secondary or higher education (NSS EUS 2011–12). The high share of the Muslim labor force in the illiterate and up to primary category and the low share in the secondary and above categories confirms the early entrant and dropout positions.

The ground reporting of such an important topic is necessary to capture true sentiments and for a unique, different reason. The literature addressed the issues of Muslims in India while considering them the second-largest minority group. This notion has created an identity for Muslims as a homogeneous group that is in the minority. However, the truth lies in specific details, like how Muslims in India cut across the different regions, castes and schools of thought of Islam. Muslims are frequently addressed as a collective nationwide community in literature. While ignoring the fact that the Muslims of Gujrat are very different from the Muslims of Bengal in terms of language, food habits, caste composition, employment opportunities, etc., the same is true for India. The labor market composition of Muslims in India is also not unique and identical throughout India; it has many differences. This study chose to look into the employment conditions of Muslims by collecting ground sentiments from the field of Western UP. Western UP is one of the densely Muslim-populated regions in the northern state of Uttar Pradesh, India. The details of the Muslim population in different states and regions of India are given in the methodology section in Chapter 6.

In Chapter 2, there is a detailed look at the idea, the sources and availability of data, the method, the major international and national trends, the trends in the Indian labor market, and writings about the socio-economic situation of Muslims in India.

1.5 The Objectives of the Book

This book aims at examining the trends and patterns of intergenerational occupational mobility among different socio-religious groups in India. Furthermore, it aims at identifying the differences in the impact of individual, parental, household and locational factors on intergenerational occupational mobility among different socio-religious groups in India. Finally, it analyses intergenerational occupational mobility among Muslims in India with a special reference to the West Uttar Pradesh region.

1.6 Contribution of the Study

This work adds to the literature on the disparities in socio-economic outcomes among India's diverse socio-religious communities. The current study examines intergenerational occupational mobility in India using a broader socio-religious group population. With a larger demographic base, it is possible to compare the mobility outcomes of two constitutionally protected marginalized groups, SCs and STs, with Muslims. Additionally, the analysis of educational mobility provides a comprehensive picture of the progress made by each of the communities in Indian society during the study period. This study elucidates shreds of evidence on the differing impacts of household, individual-level and locational characteristics on occupational attainment among socio-religious groups. This study adds evidence to the limited literature on neighborhood effects and their impact on educational mobility. This primary and secondary data-based study yields two key contributions to the scholarly community and policymakers: insights into intra-generational occupational mobility and the expectations of Muslim households.

1.7 Organization of the Book

This book has been organized in eight chapters in the following way:

This chapter analyses the labor force and workforce participation skill and educational attainment, and activity status of workers from different socio-religious groups. National Sample Survey employment-unemployment data from 2000 to 2012 and recently concluded Periodic Labour Force Survey data for 2019 were used for this purpose. The National Classification of Occupations (NCO 2004) allows us to classify employment into nine different occupational categories.

In Chapter 2, the concept, data, measurement and national-international trends of IG mobility are reviewed under the title "What Is Already Researched and Documented". It also carries statements on research gaps.

Chapter 3 includes trends in occupational mobility among socio-religious groups. A Multinomial Logit Model (MNL) was also estimated for a more in-depth look at the directions of mobility, in addition to the aggregated mobility measures.

In Chapter 4, we examine the distribution of jobs among India's various socio-religious groups, given the growth and position of professionals, associate professionals, officials, and managers and clerks. The mobility of these four occupations is investigated using logit models. This chapter addresses the question of interest about who is employed in these jobs and to what extent parental history and household characteristics play a role. In this chapter, there is also an interesting question about how the effects of household and locational factors on occupational mobility vary between SRCs.

In Chapter 5, we examine the trends and patterns of IG educational mobility at all-India levels and among socio-religious communities. The OLS father-son education equations are used for this purpose. The secondary or more level of educational attainment of the sons and possible factors are analyzed with the help of logit models. The neighborhood effects on intergenerational educational mobility are also examined.

Chapter 6: Survey design and study area.

Chapter 7: Primary Survey-Based Evidence on Muslim Occupational and Educational Mobility.

Chapter 8: Furthermore, the impact of affirmative actions (AAs) is discussed in light of the available literature on the subject.

1.8 Conclusion

This chapter explains the aims and objectives of the present study. The detailed analysis of the Indian labor market in this chapter gives a broader idea of India's existing occupational structure and its dynamics. It gives a fair understanding of India's occupational structure and major labor market trends to international and domestic readers who are not from this field.

Notes

1 Marginalized groups STs and SCs are protected by the constitution, and Others include forward castes. OBCs are backward classes that are inferior to forward castes in terms of social standing and educational attainment but higher in the social hierarchy than STs and SCs. In the public sector, public educational institutions, and private medical and engineering colleges, STs and SCs have quotas that are protected by the constitution. The federal and state legislatures both have seats set aside for SCs and STs. A number of educational affirmative action initiatives, including scholarships, fee waivers, and hostels, among others, also cover them. Affirmative actions for OBCs are essentially the same, with the exception of the availability of reserved seats in the national parliament and state legislative assemblies. Muslim OBCs are given the same legal protections as Hindu OBCs. The way that these benefits are actually realized can differ. The same constitutional protections that Hindu, Sikh and Neo-Buddhist SCs enjoy are not available to Muslim SCs. The terms "Muslim Others" and "Hindu Others" respectively refer to the Muslim and Hindu forward castes.

2 According to PLFS (2019, p. 18), "the activity status in which a person spent a relatively long time (major time criterion) during the 365 days preceding the date of the survey was considered the 'usual principal activity status' of the person. Such people might have also pursued, in addition to their usual principal status, some economic activity for 30 days or more during the reference period of 365 days preceding the date of the survey. The status in which such economic activity was pursued during the reference period of 365 days preceding the date of the survey was the 'subsidiary economic activity status' of the person". The summation of usual principal and subsidiary status is known as usual status.

3 The "Primary School Stage" includes classes from 1 to 5 years of education; the "Middle School Stage" includes classes from 6 to 8 years of education; the "Secondary School Stage" includes classes from 9 and 10 years of education; and the "Senior Secondary Stage" includes classes from 11 and or 12 years of education, according to the Indian Standard Education Classification (Ministry of Human Resources Development, 2015). The three levels of qualifications in higher education are a Bachelor's degree or graduation, a Master's degree or post-graduation, and pre-doctoral and doctoral programmes. A bachelor's degree in India typically requires three years of study after "Secondary School Level" (Agarwal, 2006).

4 According to PLFS Report, 2019 (p. 16), various occupational categories are defined as follows:

Self-employed: People who operate their own farm or non-farm enterprises or are independently engaged in a profession or trade on their own account or with one or a few partners are considered self-employed in household enterprises.

Regular wage/salaried employees: These were people who worked on other people's farms or non-farm businesses (both household and non-household) and were paid a regular salary or salary on a regular basis (rather than on a daily or periodic basis).

Casual labor: An individual who is employed on a temporary basis by another person's farm or non-farm enterprise (both household and non-household) and is paid according to the terms of a regular or periodic work contract.

References

Abraham, V. (2013). Missing labor or consistent "de-feminization"? *Economic and Political Weekly*, *48*(31), 99–108.

Andersen, T. M. (2019). Social background, education, and inequality. *Economic Inquiry*, *57*(3), 1441–1459.

Asher, S., Novosad P., & Rafkin, C. (2018). Intergenerational mobility in India: Estimates from new methods and administrative data (Working Paper No. 560). World Bank. http://barrett.dyson.cornell.edu/NEUDC/paper_560.pdf
Azam, M., & Bhatt, V. (2015). Like father, like son? Intergenerational educational mobility in India. *Demography*, *52*(6), 1929–1959. https://doi.org/10.1007/s13524-015-0428-8
Bhalla, S. S., & Kaur, R. (2011). *Labor force participation of women in India: Some facts, some queries* (Asia Research Centre Working Paper No. 40; London School of Economics, London). http://eprints.lse.ac.uk/38367/
Bowles, S., & Gintis, H. (2002). The inheritance of inequality. *Journal of Economic Perspectives*, *16*(3), 3–30. https://doi.org/10.1257/089533002760278686
Breen, R. (2004). *Social mobility in Europe*. OUP Oxford.
Breen, R., & Jonsson, J. O. (2005). Inequality of opportunity in comparative perspective: Recent research on educational attainment and social mobility. *Annual Review of Sociology*, *31*(1), 223–243. https://doi.org/10.1146/annurev.soc.31.041304.122232
Brunori, P., Ferreira, F. H. G., & Peragine, V. (2013). *Inequality of opportunity, income inequality and economic mobility: Some international comparisons* (IZA Discussion Papers, No. 7155; Institute for the Study of Labor, Bonn). https://doi.org/10.1596/1813-9450-6304
Census. (2011). *Census*. Registrar General of India, Ministry of Home Affairs, Government of India. https://censusindia.gov.in/Census_and_You/religion.aspx
Checchi, D. (2006). *The economics of education: Human capital, family background and inequality*. Cambridge University Press.
Chetty, R. (2019). *Using big data to solve economic and social problems*. Opportunity insights. Harvard University Press. https://doi.org/10.1145/2487575.2491135
Chetty, R. (2021). *Improving equality of opportunity – An Infosys prize lecture*. https://www.infosys-science-foundation.com/lectures/videos.asp#equality
Chowdhury, S. (2011). Employment in India: What does the latest data show? *Economic and Political Weekly*, *46*(32), 23–26.
Economic Survey. (2017–18). *Economic Survey, Volume I, (2017–2018)*. Economic Division, Department of Economic Affairs, Ministry of Finance, Government of India, New Delhi. https://www.indiabudget.gov.in/economicsurvey/allpes.php
Gaddis, I., & Klasen, S. (2014). Economic development, structural change, and women's labor force participation: A reexamination of the feminization U hypothesis. *Journal of Population Economics*, *27*(3), 639–681. https://doi.org/10.1007/s00148-013-0488-2
Hnatkovska, V., Lahiri, A., & Paul, S. B. (2013). Breaking the caste barrier: Intergenerational mobility in India. *Journal of Human Resources*, *48*(2), 435–473. https://doi.org/10.1353/jhr.2013.0012
Iversen, V., Krishna, A., & Sen, K. (2016). *Rags to riches? Intergenerational occupational mobility in India*, 1–24. http://hummedia.manchester.ac.uk/institutes/gdi/publications/workingpapers/GDI/GDI_WP2016004_Iversen_Krishna_Sen.pdf
Iversen, V., Krishna, A., & Sen, K. (2017). Rags to riches? Intergenerational occupational mobility in India. *Economic and Political Weekly*, *52*(44), 107–114. https://www.epw.in/journal/2017/44/special-articles/rags-riches-intergenerational-occupational-mobility-india.html?0=ip_login_no_cache%3Dd7897b90ac2de4a99546e1e0b51d2eac
Kannan, K. P., & Raveendran, G. (2019). From jobless to job-loss growth: Gainers and losers in India's employment performance during 2012–2018. *Economic and Political Weekly*, *54*(44), 38–44.

Kapsos, S., Silberman, A., & Bourmpoula, E. (2014). Why is female labor force participation declining so sharply in India? *ILO Research Paper*, *10*, 1–51. https://ideas.repec.org/p/ilo/ilowps/994949190702676.html

Kerswell, T., & Pratap, S. (2019). Liberalization in India: Does it resolve or aggravate employment problems? *Journal of Contemporary Asia*, *49*(4), 626–649. https://doi.org/10.1080/00472336.2018.1545916

Klasen, S., & Pieters, J. (2012). *Push or pull? Drivers of female labor force participation during India's economic boom* (IZA DP No. 6395; Institute of Labor Economics, Bonn).

Klasen, S., Le, T. T. N., Pieters, J., & Santos Silva, M. (2021). What drives female labour force participation? Comparable micro-level evidence from eight developing and emerging economies. *The Journal of Development Studies*, *57*(3), 417–442.

Kniveton, B. H. (2004). The influences and motivations on which students base their choice of career. *Research in Education*, *72*(1), 47–59. https://doi.org/10.7227/rie.72.4

Lefranc, A., Pistolesi, N., & Trannoy, A. (2008). Inequality of opportunities vs. inequality of outcomes: Are western societies all alike? *Review of Income and Wealth*, *54*(4), 513–546. https://doi.org/10.1111/j.1475-4991.2008.00289.x

Levine, D. I., & Mazumder, B. (1999). *Choosing the right parents: Changes in the intergenerational transmission of inequality between 1980 and the early 1990s*. (IRLE Working Paper No. 72; Institute for Research on Labor and Employment UC Berkeley). https://doi.org/10.2139/ssrn.323881

Long, J., & Ferrie, J. (2013). Intergenerational occupational mobility in Great Britain and the United States since 1850. *American Economic Review*. https://doi.org/10.1257/aer.103.4.1109

Majumder, R. (2010). Intergenerational mobility in educational and occupational attainment: A comparative study of social classes in India. *Margin*, *4*(4), 463–494. https://doi.org/10.1177/097380101000400404

Mehrotra, S. (2019). *Informal employment trends in the Indian economy: Persistent informality, but growing positive development* (Employment Working Paper No. 254; Employment Policy Department, ILO, Issue 254). https://www.ilo.org/employment/Whatwedo/Publications/working-papers/WCMS_734503/lang--en/index.htm

Mehrotra, S., & Parida, J. K. (2019). *India's employment crisis: Rising education levels and falling non-agricultural job growth*. October, 1–22.

Mitra, A., & Singh, J. (2019). Rising unemployment in India: A statewise analysis from 1993–94 to 2017–18. *Economic and Political Weekly*, *54*(50), 12–16.

Modalsli, J. (2017). Intergenerational mobility in Norway, 1865–2011. *Scandinavian Journal of Economics*, *119*(1), 34–71. https://doi.org/10.1111/sjoe.12196

Motiram, S., & Singh, A. (2012). How close does the apple fall to the tree? Some evidence from India on intergenerational occupational mobility. *Economic and Political Weekly*, *47*(40), 56–65. http://www.jstor.org/stable/41720217

Nath, P., & Basole, A. (2020). *Did employment rise or fall in India between 2011 and 2017? Estimating absolute changes in the workforce* (CSE Working Paper 29; Issue 29). https://cse.azimpremjiuniversity.edu.in/wp-content/uploads/2020/08/Nath_Basole_Employment_Trends_2011-2017_August_2020.pdf

NCO. (2004). National Classification of Occupation. Directorate General of Employment, Ministry of Labour & Employment, Government of India, New Delhi. https://labour.gov.in/sites/default/files/CodeStructure.pdf

NSSO Sixty Eighth Round Report. (2012). *Employment and unemployment Situation in India, (July 2011–June 2012)*. http://microdata.gov.in/nada43/index.php/catalog/EUE

NSSO Sixty Eighth Round Report for Religious Groups. (2012). *Employment and unemployment situation among major religious groups in India, (July 2011–June 2012).* http://mospi.nic.in/sites/default/files/publication_reports/nss_report_568_19feb16.pdf

PLFS. (2019). "Periodic Labour Force Survey (July 2018– June 2019)", Ministry of Statistics and Programme Implementation, Government of India, New Delhi. http://microdata.gov.in/nada43/index.php/catalog/EUE

Ramaswamy, K. V., & Agrawal, T. (2012). *Services-led growth, employment and job quality: A study of manufacturing and service-sector in Urban India* (WP-2012-007; Indira Gandhi Institute of Development Research, Mumbai, Issue March). http://www.igidr.ac.in/pdf/publication/WP-2012-007.pdf

Rangarajan, C., Kaul, P. I., & Seema. (2011). Where is the missing labor force? *Economic and Political Weekly*, *46*(39), 68–72.

Reardon, S. F. (2016). Racial academic achievement gaps. *Russell Sage Foundation Journal of the Social Sciences*, *2*(5), 34–57.

Reddy, A. B., & Swaminathan, M. (2014). Intergenerational occupational mobility in Rural India: Evidence from ten villages. *Review of Agrarian Studies*, *4*(1), 95–134. Retrieved from http://www.ras.org.in/intergenerational_occupational_mobility_in_rural_india

Sanghi, S., Srija, A., & Vijay, S. S. (2015). Decline in rural female labor force participation in India: A relook into the causes. *Vikalpa*, *40*(3), 255–268. https://doi.org/10.1177/0256090915598264

Subramanian, A. (2019). *Validating India's GDP growth estimates* (CID Faculty Working Paper No. 357; Center for International Development at Harvard University, Issue 357). https://growthlab.cid.harvard.edu/files/growthlab/files/2019-07-cid-wp-357-india-gdp.pdf

Verick, S. (2014). Female labor force participation in developing countries. *IZA World of Labor*, September, 1–10. https://doi.org/10.15185/izawol.87

Volart-Esteve, B. (2004). *Gender discrimination and growth: Theory and evidence from India* (DEDPS 42; The Suntory Centre Suntory and Toyota International Centres for Economics and Related Disciplines). http://eprints.uanl.mx/5481/1/1020149995.PDF

Young, R. A., & Friesen, J. D. (1992). The intentions of Parents in influencing the career development of their children. *Career Development Quarterly*, *40*(3), 198–206. https://doi.org/10.1002/j.2161-0045.1992.tb00326.x

2 What is Already Known and Documented

2.1 Introduction

The researchers in the field of intergenerational mobility have contributed significantly. The studies on this subject have evolved from rudimentary matrix analysis to complex modeling to answer some of the pertinent questions related to mobility in society. While the sizable literature on this issue focuses on what is (positive part), there are exemplary attempts that address the normative questions. Sociologists and economists have contributed equally to the development of intergenerational mobility. In this chapter, the concept, methodological issues, data and major trends that are related to mobility have been discussed. For developing nations, there is a dearth of literature on this issue; however, some studies have contributed significantly. To understand more about mobility in India, this book comes up with certain knowledge gaps, methodological contributions and empirics. However, to read India's IG mobility experiences, it is important to know about the labor market structure and trends. In this chapter, a review of the same has also been provided. Further, the reporting on the socio-economic conditions of an important socio-religious group of this study, Muslims, has also been provided.

2.2 Concept

The term "mobility" refers to movement from one location to another. Research in economics and sociology has mostly focused on intergenerational and intra-generational mobility (Iversen et al., 2017). Intergenerational mobility is the phenomenon that occurs when children occupy different positions in their generation's distribution of economic or social status than their parents did in their generation (Dearden et al., 1997; McMurrer et al., 1997). Concurrently, intra-generational mobility refers to mobility within the same generation (Burkhauser & Couch, 2009, p. 254). The subsequent researchers examined economic mobility, social mobility and income mobility, in addition to occupation, industry, job and organizational mobility (Blanden, 2013). Income mobility assessment is difficult precisely because permanent and lifelong income might vary, and it is critical to capture both simultaneously (Grawe, 2006). The mobility of any individual

DOI: 10.4324/9781003361299-2

within various industry groups is also a subject that has attracted much attention in the academic literature (Parrado et al., 2007). Industrial mobility has flaws. For example, if a person shifts from one industry to another, such as from agriculture to construction, it does not offer the full picture because it is entirely possible that the same person previously worked as an agricultural laborer and is now employed as a construction laborer.

Occupation remains largely steady during an individual's life cycle, making occupation mobility relatively easier to measure (Blanden, 2013). Occupational information represents the status of a class in itself, since occupation reflects the status of a person in society. Therefore, social and economic mobility are reflected in occupational mobility (Breen, 2010). Occupation has also been identified as a proxy indicator of social status (Domanski & Sawinski, 1987). Another factor driving the preference for occupational mobility over income mobility is the reflection of social status in occupation. Even if a person's earnings are quite great, she or he cannot compete with a lawyer or professor in terms of social standing (McMurrer et al., 1997).

Researchers have examined intergenerational mobility from both descriptive and normative perspectives. The descriptive approach focuses on quantifying the level of social mobility or transition. A second approach is normative and focuses on goals such as the proportion of people in society with equal chances of success and the degree of (in)equality of opportunity (McMurrer et al., 1997).

Intergenerational mobility studies are particularly popular among Western economists and sociologists concerned with the (in)equality of opportunities in society (Bowles & Gintis, 2002; Breen & Jonsson, 2005; Brunori et al., 2013; Lefranc et al., 2008; Levine & Mazumder, 1999). In India, research is predominantly descriptive and societal mobility is evaluated. Few studies have investigated intergenerational mobility in terms of inequality and differences in access to opportunities. These studies, on the other hand, have key measurement issues.

Apparently, two factors have the most influence on intergenerational mobility. The first is the transfer or circulation of a parent's profession, money or income to their children. The second is the economy's growth factor, or the rate at which it advances through time, which is referred to as structural mobility (mobility induced by structural changes in the economy) (Marks, 1996; Sobel, 1983). Changes in the occupational structure are essential for occupational mobility across generations. The literature appears to be focused more on intergenerational occupational mobility in terms of occupation transfer from parents to children. To accomplish this objective, researchers investigate the association or degree of association between parents' occupation and their offspring's occupation in order to eliminate the effect of a shift in occupational structure (Long & Ferrie, 2013). These investigations appear to be primarily concerned with determining how a person's family past influences his adult occupational success. The majority of this research in industrialized nations examines how parents actively transmit their values to their children. The familial background is also related to the endowment and investments made in the human capital of children.

When social mobility research peaked in the 1970s and 1980s, scholars examined it through the prism of social stratification theories (Blau & Duncan, 1967; Featherman & Hauser, 1978; Hout, 1988). The theoretical understanding was gradually reinforced by facts and descriptions of the mobility process through time (Kerbo, 2006). In the past ten to twenty years, there has been a revival of interest in social mobility studies as a means of comprehending social stratification. In mobility analysis, social stratification is restricted to a functionalist perspective in which occupational categories are the primary focus (Domanski & Sawinski, 1987). Typically, such occupational categories are ranked using education, skills, income, tasks, wages and status.

2.3 Data Sources and Types of Data Used for Mobility Analysis

In developed nations, longitudinal data sets are important sources for the data side of IG mobility because they allow researchers to track parents and children from the same families through time (Biblarz et al., 1996; Dearden et al., 1997; Fortin & Lefebvre, 1998; Solon, 1992). Using the census as a secondary source, attempts were made to build longitudinal data in regions where panel surveys are unavailable, some organizations or researchers undertake surveys at a certain moment in time that include retrospective questions on the parents' employment or socio-economic status. Due to the fact that the traditional concept of intergenerational mobility entails information on the whereabouts of individuals from two consecutive generations at nearly the same phases of their lives, the survey conducted at a single point in time with retrospective questions is flawed (Fortin & Lefebvre, 1998). In addition, there are issues with surveys that include retrospective questions, as respondents' answers to queries regarding their parents' condition on a backdated basis may be unreliable because they rely on memory recall.

In India, researchers rely on NSS rounds and primary surveys (Hnatkovska et al., 2013; Majumder, 2010; Reddy, 2015a; Reddy & Swaminathan, 2014). The NSS rounds do not provide data for two separate times, necessitating a shared definition of intergenerational mobility, but they do provide data for parents and their offspring at a single point in time. The biggest problem with the NSS data sets is that, although parents declare their occupation, they may be retired while their children are just entering the workforce. For the mobility notion to work, parents and their children must be compared at the same age.

Recent studies in India have explored intergenerational mobility using Indian Human Development Survey—IHDS (2005, 2011–12) data sets (Azam & Bhatt, 2015; Motiram & Singh, 2012). The IHDS data sets report parental information as the child grows up, but it is also provided retrospectively. IHDS has one advantage over NSS in that it captures information from parents while their children are still young.

2.4 Measurement

Measures of intergenerational mobility range from simple descriptive statistics such as the mobility ratio and inflow-outflow rate to more complex log-linear modeling and regression techniques (Hauser, 1978). The regression-based methodology is typically used in developed economies to examine regression in the mean earnings of sons relative to those of their fathers in order to measure intergenerational economic mobility. A sizable body of literature also suggests that researchers have also employed regression analysis to quantify intergenerational occupational mobility. Both Hnatkovska et al. (2013) and Majumder (2010) used regression models to track how people moved between jobs in India over the course of two generations.

Another extensively used tool is transition matrices, which quantify mobility in several categories typical of fathers and sons. The model displays the sons' occupations in rows and the fathers' occupations in columns of matrices. Despite the fact that basic mobility matrices and matrix-based indices were commonly employed until the 1960s, log-linear modeling eventually took over as the industry standard, thanks to the pioneering work of Hauser (1978) and Goodman (1970, 1972), among others. In contrast to regression analysis, log-linear models focus on association rather than causality.

The Altham index was popularized by the work of Ferrie (2005) and Altham and Ferrie (2007) which was developed using Altham's transition matrix (1970). Nevertheless, Hout and Guest (2013) presented serious concerns about the validity of the Altham index and demonstrated that log-linear modeling is superior to the Altham index. The Altham index, according to Hout and Guest (2013), has a measurement flaw in that it cannot assess "structural mobility". They presented five additional explanations for using log-linear transformed multinomial logit models (MNL) rather than the Altham index. This regression approach, as opposed to the Altham index, can be used to foresee patterns that span both time and space. When considering the relative distances between jobs, a regression-based technique is acceptable. Additionally, unlike the Altham index, the MNL can be expanded to include additional variables such as gender, race, geography and educational attainment. Finally, readers are familiar with regression-based analysis. It is easy to use and comparable across disciplines.

2.5 Mobility Trends across the World

Studies of IG mobility have traditionally concentrated on variations between black and white people, males and women, native-born citizens and immigrants, ethnic minorities and the majority in the United States and other parts of the world. Similarly, every study carried out in India investigates caste-related variations in mobility. In IG mobility research, another difference between economists and sociologists is that the former are more concerned with income mobility, whereas the latter are more interested in social status and occupational mobility (Blanden, 2013; Checchi et al., 1999). As the significance of education has expanded in society, economists and sociologists have begun to place greater emphasis on educational mobility. Emran and Shilpi (2019) found that few studies compare the experiences of developing and South Asian countries to those of developed countries.

It is critical to emphasize that the United States has historically had high levels of occupational mobility, which is a fundamental indicator of opportunity equality. In 1972–73, 56.7 percent of American sons, compared to 45.3 percent of British sons, reported disinterest in their father's line of work (Long & Ferrie, 2013). The differences in mobility between the United States and the United Kingdom were mostly attributable to differences in the occupational structures of the two economies. When structural changes were taken into account, the mobility gap was reduced to 3 percent. An important finding in the research on IG mobility is that structural changes must be considered when comparing two mobility tables. The British labor market saw significant changes in the twentieth century, including skill-biased technological breakthroughs and an increase in the demand for skilled, educated and professional workers (Oesch & Rodriguez, 2011; Sloane et al., 1999). According to Breen (2004), the difference in occupational mobility of 11 countries, comprising Britain, France, Ireland, West Germany, the Netherlands, Italy, Sweden, Norway, Poland, Hungary and Israel, decreased as the agricultural sector became less important and economies underwent structural changes between the early or mid-1970s and the mid- or late 1990s. The important point is that, despite certain differences, industrialized countries have comparable rates of mobility. Breen (2004) found that the main reason why people move around more in countries like Hungary and Poland is because more women are working in white-collar jobs.

A comprehensive OECD report (OECD, 2019) on the mobility experiences of European Union (EU) member states draws on recent data (2011 and 2014). According to the findings of this study, children of illiterate parents from within the EU and those from outside the EU have equal career prospects. However, the employment gap between children of native and non-EU descent grew wider as parental education levels rose. The report also asserts that the children's educational attainment is the most significant factor in bridging the gap, suggesting that education is a key component of integrating the offspring of non-EU immigrants into the local labor market. That is true for European countries like Austria, Switzerland, Spain, France, Norway and the United Kingdom, where the gap between people with native ancestry and those from outside the EU has significantly shrunk after accounting for factors such as education, age and gender. The disparity in Belgium persists even after control.

The mobility pattern in the Dutch province of Zeeland differs from that in other developed countries. Between 1811 and 1915, the father's status improved in the more industrialized parts, in sharp contrast to Zeeland as a whole. The impact of a father's employment on his son's occupation has been stronger despite macro-level advancements including industrialization, educational progress, mass communication, urbanization, geographical mobility and mass transportation (Zijdeman, 2009). Cheng and Dai (1995) present a similar argument for China. In China, even after economic openness and agricultural diversification, in 1988, 33 percent of men and 30 percent of women had not taken up their fathers' occupation. Another aspect of Chinese mobility is that women's class allocation is more closely tied to their social class origins than men's.

During the 1990–2000 observation period, approximately 70 percent of the population in Brazil and 50 percent in Colombia, Mexico and Peru were immobile, compared to 35 percent in the United States, indicating that there are notable differences in mobility between Latin America and the United States as well as significant differences within Latin America (Behrman et al., 2001).

Mobility studies in South Asian and African nations are limited by the two-sector approach. Because agriculture engages a large portion of the population, such research primarily focuses on farm-to-non-farm interactions. In 2006–07, 33 percent of males in Africa continued to work on their fathers' farms, while 43 percent continued to work on their mothers' farms. In the case of daughters, 33 percent reported that their mother was working in agriculture (Lambert et al., 2014). Intergenerational mobility between agricultural and non-farm occupations was explored by Bossuroy and Cogneau (2013) in five countries: Côte d'Ivoire, Ghana, Guinea, Madagascar and Uganda. In order to explain the observed variation in intergenerational occupational mobility across the countries, the authors cited educational immobility in Madagascar and pronounced duality in the spatial distribution of employment in other countries, which they attribute to the countries' respective colonial histories. Dorosh et al. (2018) examined IG mobility in Bangladesh using the Household Income Expenditure Survey (HIES) cycles of 1995–96 and 2010. Based on age cohorts from 1995 to 2010, their findings indicate that the 12.6 percentage point decline in the proportion of younger adult males working in agriculture is primarily attributable to a sharp drop in the percentage of youth who begin their careers in agriculture, rather than a shift in individuals' employment from agricultural to non-agricultural over time. The results indicate that intergenerational preferences for non-farm over farm sectors explain the observed shift from farm to non-farm sectors across time. In a study of IG mobility in Pakistan, Muhammad & Jamil (2017) reported that 45.56 percent of sons managed to migrate from their fathers' occupation in the survey year 2012–13. In addition to demonstrating severe immobility, the study demonstrates that downward mobility is larger than upward mobility. It indicates that people are constrained by their status and may observe a decline in the status of their sons' generation. When compared to those born into high-status homes, the sons of impoverished fathers tend to stay poor.

2.6 Trends in IG Mobility in India

It is challenging to compare aggregate mobility estimates produced by different research due to differences in the data, methodology and occupational-educational classification (Xie & Killewald, 2013). The broader trends are discussed in this section in the context of India. Several studies have noted that compared to urban areas, rural areas have poorer intergenerational occupational mobility (Iversen et al., 2017; Motiram & Singh, 2012) and educational mobility (Asher et al., 2018). In terms of mobility, studies suggest that SCs and STs have stronger persistence in elementary occupations than non-SCs and STs. However, SCs and STs exhibit less tenacity in professional employment than non-SCs and

STs (Motiram & Singh, 2012; Hnatkovska et al., 2013; Iversen et al., 2017). In the case of educational mobility, it has been reported that the gap between the upper and lower castes is converging or would be converging (Majumder, 2010; Hnatkovska et al., 2013). In the case of intergenerational occupational mobility, contradictory evidence suggests that the gap between STs and SCs and non-STs and SCs grew between 1983 and 2011. There are three explanations why SCs and STs perform poorly: financial constraints; schooling opportunities; and caste and religion-based endogamous clustering (Motiram & Singh, 2012). There is further evidence of stickier occupational mobility compared to educational mobility (Reddy, 2015a; Majumder, 2010; Sinha, 2018). Occupational mobility among older adults has been found to be greater than that of the younger generation. Majumder (2010) offers two explanations that are worth highlighting: first, sons between the ages of 20 and 40 have parents with higher employment levels, while sons between the ages of 40 and 50 have lower parental employment levels. Since younger generations are already aligned with their parents' high-level employment, their opportunities for upward mobility are constrained compared to those of their parents. Second, in the post-economic reform era of 1991, the "stricter labor market scenario" encouraged horizontal migration among similar occupations while restricting vertical mobility. The lack of professional mobility could also be caused by differences in how well people do in school, quality of the credit markets, prejudice based on caste, and a high number of marriages between people of the same caste (Reddy, 2015a).

2.7 Trends in the Indian Labor Market

It is widely reported that the Indian economy has changed in the last 70 years, and it is no longer an agricultural-based economy. In terms of GDP, the share of agriculture declined from 90 percent to 12 percent in 2020. However, in terms of employment, agriculture still accounts for 42 percent of the total workforce. In the last 20 years, there has been a rapid decline in the employment share of agriculture, and workers are moving out of agriculture (Reddy, 2015b; Thomas, 2014). Until 2011, the construction sector absorbed the majority of the freed-up agricultural labor force. The newly created jobs were mainly in the service sector, like trade, hotels, restaurants, etc. (Chowdhury, 2011; Rath, 2018). The high-tech industry, telecommunication, software, IT and computer hardware led the share of GDP and created high-skill based jobs with high wages (Mehrotra et al., 2014; Mukherjee & Majumder, 2011; Ramaswamy & Agrawal, 2012). However, the robust GDP growth rate observed in the post-reform period was not uniform, and India's regional development has also been uneven (Trivedi & Rajmal, 2011). Unfortunately, high GDP growth has resulted in an increase in inter-personal, inter-social and inter-state inequality. Mukherjee and Majumder (2011) analyzed the wage structure from 1993–94 to 2004-05 and found that there is a clear hierarchy between different occupations according to wages and earnings. He explained that administrative, professional and technical work are at the top of the wage ladder; clerical, sales, and service occupations are in the middle; and production, transport and other unclassified workers are at the bottom. While it is quite obvious that the earnings of regular workers will be higher than those of casual workers, what is alarming is that regular workers earn a daily wage rate of about three times that of casual workers. Anant et al. (2006) report that from 1983 to 1999–00, the wage difference between the 90th and 10th percentile increased sharply in urban areas. However, his further claim about the reduction in poverty rates for the same period has some positive aspects. Anant et al. (2006) explain that in any economy, high poverty rates simply reflect the fact that available employment cannot deliver even a minimally acceptable standard of living for the worker and the worker's family. The reduction in poverty shows the increasing standard of living of workers. However, Patnaik (2018) holds a different view and proves that poverty reduction is only a mathematical number. He argued that there is a continuous decline in per-person food availability. He further argued that people are not in a position to afford the basic items in the food basket; in this scenario, poverty would not go down.

The Indian labor market underwent significant changes between 2012 and 2019. With India's unemployment rate at its highest in three decades and its labor force participation rate at its lowest in the same period, concerns have been raised about the sustainability of the Indian economy (Kannan & Raveendran, 2019; Mitra & Singh, 2019). Other patterns seen between 2012 and 2019 include a significant slowdown in manufacturing employment growth, a loss of manufacturing jobs, an increase in education-skilled jobs, and a rise in the workforce aged 15 to 59 years (Kannan & Raveendran, 2019; Mehrotra & Parida, 2019; Thomas, 2020). Because enrollment rates were lower at the time, the significant drop in labor force participation between 2012 and 2019 cannot be entirely attributable to a rise in the number of those pursuing higher education (Kannan & Raveendran, 2019). However, up until 2012, rising school enrollment was one of the most widely cited reasons for the declining labor force, which was primarily composed of women (Afridi et al., 2018; Bhalla & Kaur, 2011; Chaudhary & Verick, 2014; Kannan & Raveendran, 2012; Kapsos et al., 2014; Klasen & Pieters, 2012; Mehrotra et al., 2014; Rangarajan et al., 2011). A review of the research from the 1990s and 2000s also reveals that the decline of the female labor force has been occurring since the implementation of economic reform. For male employees, one could say the same thing. At the time, researchers attributed these losses primarily to increased education (Anant et al., 2006). Now, an increase in education cannot explain the precipitous decline in the labor force.

Until 2012, the released labor force from agriculture was absorbed into the construction sector and other low-wage jobs; now, even the construction sector is contracting. Furthermore, other firms working in a variety of fields are looking for workers with a minimum of secondary education (Kannan & Raveendran, 2019). In this situation, either a sizable reserve army of unskilled labor is taking place, or workers are willing to work for lower wages (Mehrotra & Parida, 2019). Not to mention that rural-to-urban migration and out-of-agriculture worker movements are both forced and non-voluntary (Mehrotra & Parida, 2019). Studies have suggested that the marginalized sections of society have been disproportionately impacted by the Indian economy's structural transformation, as the highest decline in the labor force (2012–19) was recorded among women, less educated men, and among women, less educated women (Kannan & Raveendran, 2019; Mehrotra & Parida, 2019). Additionally, new technology's consequences are not confined to the abolition of low-wage jobs, they are also displacing certain clerical and professional jobs (Upadhyay, 2015).

Since the economic reforms of 1991, in addition to the reported jobless economic growth, analysts have also been concerned about the scarcity of "good jobs" creation (Anant et al., 2006; Ramaswamy & Agrawal, 2012; Choudhury & Chatterjee, 2015). Anant et al. (2006) suggest that whereas average GDP growth was around 5 percent between 1993–94 and 1999–00, the organized sector's share of total employment declined from 7.3 percent to 7.1 percent during the same period. Simultaneously, the organized sector underwent a substantial change called "casualization". This process involves replacing full-time regular jobs with contract jobs, which usually last for a day, a week or a month.

Since the economic reforms, there has been a drop in public sector employment, and between 2005 and 2012, the public sector lost roughly 8 percent of jobs (Ghose, 2016). Between 2012 and 2019, employment in the public sector fell by 4.5 percent (3.5 million in absolute terms). The manufacturing sector's ability to absorb additional labor is hampered by skill-biased technical advancements that favor skilled workers (Kannan & Raveendran, 2019; Kerswell & Pratap, 2019; Mitra & Singh, 2019). Furthermore, the shift from labor-intensive crops to capital-intensive crops is one factor contributing to the migration of workers from the agricultural to non-agricultural sectors (Afridi et al., 2023; Kannan & Raveendran, 2019).

2.8 The Socio-Economic Condition of Muslims in India

The first attempt to learn about the socio-economic status of Muslims in India was the Sachar Committee Report (2006). No other research on Muslims in India comes close to the lucidity of this report (Islam, 2012). The three fundamental challenges that any minority worldwide must address are identity, equity and security. Due to a paucity of data on identity and security issues, the committee concentrated on equity and attempted to explain how the three equity indicators interacted. The committee proposed a number of initiatives without first considering their viability (Wilkinson, 2007). Also, the Sachar report (2006) failed to identify specific Muslim-related subjects and provided no explanation for why Muslims appear to be less engaged in education. Wilkinson (2007) argued that the committee's data is unsuitable for determining whether Muslims perform poorly as a result of economic backwardness, levels of perceived Muslim political inclusion or exclusion, alleged anti-minority discrimination, cultural factors affecting the community, access to education or healthcare, or any other state-or community-specific factors. Researchers also criticized the committee for depicting Muslims in India as a monolithic group (Ahmed, 2019). Contrary to common belief, Muslims in India are a diverse population that spans many regions, castes, socio-economic classes, languages, nutritional preferences and clothing styles. Because this diversity is so visible in the Hindi heartland, Western UP was purposely chosen for the collection and analysis of primary data.

The study conducted by Duraisamy and Duraisamy (2017) reveals that Muslim workers earn much less in the mean and across the wage distribution than Hindus and other religious minorities. It is important to note that, excluding Muslims, religious minorities account for only 1.7 percent of the labor force, and their median income is comparable to that of upper-caste Hindus. Furthermore, between 1994 and 2005, Muslims and STs witnessed higher income growth rates (2.6 and 3.1 percent, respectively) than SCs and upper-caste Hindus (2.3 and 2.2 percent, respectively). However, the Indian labor market saw the highest wage growth rate of almost 3.9 percent between 2005 and 2012, with the exception of Muslims, for whom it was just 2.4 percent. In terms of poverty incidence, Muslims trail substantially behind other socio-religious groups. Panagariya and Mukim (2014) demonstrate that poverty rates decreased dramatically between 1993–94 and 2004–05. All religious groups in rural and urban India suffered a progressive decline, with the exception of the Sikhs in rural India. Furthermore, during 2004–05 and 2009–10, Muslims in rural and urban regions saw a poor rate of poverty reduction in comparison to other religious groups. Borooah and Iyer (2005) discovered evidence of a shrinking difference in school enrollment rates between Hindus and Muslims, particularly for children whose parents are illiterate. Borooah et al. (2007) discover that the probability of becoming a regular paid employee is substantially lower for Muslim laborers than for upper-caste Hindus, based on a single round of employment survey data (1999) from India. Bhaumik and Chakrabarty (2009) claim that the bulk of variations in average (log) earnings over time may be traced to educational inequalities between Hindu and Muslim wage employees, notably differences in the share of wage workers with university degrees. Differences in educational returns, however, do not explain the aforementioned disparity in average (log) incomes. These findings offer a solid basis for programs targeted at improving the access of ordinary Muslims to education. Sanghi and Srija (2014) reported that the Muslim population lags behind other religious groups in terms of educational attainment, labor force participation and workforce involvement, with Muslim females trailing even more. Due to religious beliefs and stereotypes, Sengupta and Das (2014) observed that Muslim women were worse off than Hindu female employees.

Using existing literature, Kamat (1981) identified three explanations for the educational underachievement of Muslims in India: first, religious tradition; second, the negative effects of partition and the ensuing severe identity crisis; and third, willful neglect and discrimination against Muslims. Alam and Raju (2007) provided a summary of two scholarly arguments for poor Muslim education. The first category is "specific theological hypotheses", which refers to a theological belief system that determines behavior and life direction, as well as values, norms and attitudes. The second hypothesis is the "characteristics hypothesis", which explains variances in educational attainment among socio-religious groups with varying degrees of socio-economic status and how this influences the demand for education across social classes. Or, to put it another way, a group or sub-segment of the population's educational level depends on the size of the strata that typically pursue education. If this is the case, the small fraction of Muslims who prioritize education may be used to explain why Muslims lag behind in education. Kingdon also analyzes the reasons behind Muslims' lower educational attainment (2002). He demonstrates how having a Muslim upbringing has a detrimental impact on a man's years of education. He goes on to explain his findings by arguing that Muslims value education less and face workplace discrimination, with support from Muzammil (1994). He further claims that Muslim families make only intermittent efforts to increase their children's educational standards because they inherited their forefathers' manual labor jobs (the lower caste argument by Muzammil, 1994). The majority of Muslims in India are converts from lower-caste Hindus, particularly the artisans and working classes, who provide everyday services such as barbers and washermen. This explains why Muslims have a tradition of manual labor jobs (Ahmed, 2019; Bhaumik & Chakrabarty, 2009; Mistry, 2005). Furthermore, Muslims own less farmland than non-Muslims (Mondal, 2000).

2.9 Conclusion

The objective of this comprehensive review of the literature was to comprehend the concept, statistics, measurements and patterns of IG mobility in India and globally. Despite the fact that experts across several disciplines have made substantial contributions to the advancement of IG mobility research, the field is constantly evolving. This study is unique in that it examines both trends in the Indian labor market and the socio-economic condition of Muslims in India. For overseas readers who are unfamiliar with local dynamics, the examined patterns provide context for the Indian labor market. Additionally, Muslims constitute a significant social group in this study; a thorough examination of Muslims sheds light on the socio-economic circumstances of India's largest minority community. Though research on IG mobility in India looks to be moving forward and scholars are making significant contributions, there are still gaps in the conversion of descriptive statistics into judgments and in linking occupational and educational mobility to explain IG mobility holistically.

References

Afridi, F., Dinkelman, T., & Mahajan, K. (2018). Why are fewer married women joining the work force in rural India? A decomposition analysis over two decades. *Journal of Population Economics*, *31*(3), 783–818. https://doi.org/10.1007/s00148-017-0671-y

Afridi, F., Bishnu, M., & Mahajan, K. (2023). Gender and mechanization: Evidence from Indian agriculture. *American Journal of Agricultural Economics*, *105*(1), 52–75.

Ahmed, H. (2019). *Siyasi Muslims: A story of political Islams in India*. Penguin Random House India Private Limited.

Alam, M. S., & Raju, S. (2007). Contextualising inter-, intra-religious and gendered literacy and educational disparities in rural Bihar. *Economic and Political Weekly*, *42*(18), 1613–1622.

Altham, P. (1970). The measurement of association of rows and columns for an r × s contingency table. *Journal of the Royal Statistical Society: Series B (Methodological)*, *32*(1), 63–73. https://doi.org/10.1111/j.2517-6161.1970.tb00816.x

Altham, P. M. E., & Ferrie, J. P. (2007). Comparing contingency tables: Tools for analyzing data from two groups cross-classified by two characteristics. *Historical Methods*, *40*(1), 3–16. https://doi.org/10.3200/HMTS.40.1.3-16

Anant, T. C. A., Hasan, R., Mohapatra, P., Nagaraj, R., & Sasikumar, S. K. (2006). Labor markets in India: Issues and perspectives. *Labor Markets in Asia, October 2005*, 205–300. https://doi.org/10.1057/9780230627383_5

Asher, S., Novosad, P., & Rafkin, C. (2018). Intergenerational mobility in India: Estimates from new methods and administrative data (Working Paper No. 560). World Bank. http://barrett.dyson.cornell.edu/NEUDC/paper_560.pdf

Azam, M., & Bhatt, V. (2015). Like father, like son? Intergenerational educational mobility in India. *Demography*, *52*(6), 1929–1959. https://doi.org/10.1007/s13524-015-0428-8

Behrman, J. R., Gaviria, A., Székely, M., Birdsall, N., Economía, S., & Fall, N. (2001). Intergenerational mobility in Latin America [with comments]. *Economía*, *2*(1), 1–44. http://www.jstor.org/stable/20065412

Bhalla, S. S., & Kaur, R. (2011). *Labor force participation of women in India: Some facts, some queries* (Asia Research Centre Working Paper No. 40; London School of Economics, London). http://eprints.lse.ac.uk/38367/

Bhaumik, S. K., & Chakrabarty, M. (2009). Is education the panacea for economic deprivation of Muslims?. Evidence from wage earners in India, 1987–2005. *Journal of Asian Economics*, *20*(2), 137–149. https://doi.org/10.1016/j.asieco.2008.09.014

Biblarz, T. J., Bengtson, V. L., & Bucur, A. (1996). Social mobility across three generations. *Journal of Marriage and Family*, *58*(1), 188–200. http://www.jstor.org/stable/353387

Blanden, J. (2013). Cross-country rankings in intergenerational mobility: A comparison of approaches from economics and sociology. *Journal of Economic Surveys*, *27*(1), 38–73. https://doi.org/10.1111/j.1467-6419.2011.00690.x

Blau, P. M., & Duncan, O. D. (1967). *The American occupational structure*. John Wiley & Sons Inc.

Borooah, V. K., Dubey, A., & Iyer, S. (2007). The effectiveness of jobs reservation: Caste, religion and economic status in India. *Development and Change*, *38*(3), 423–445. https://doi.org/10.1111/j.1467-7660.2007.00418.x

Borooah, V. K., & Iyer, S. (2005). Vidya, Veda, and Varna: The influence of religion and caste on education in rural India. *Journal of Development Studies*, *41*(8), 1369–1404. https://doi.org/10.1080/00220380500186960

Bossuroy, T., & Cogneau, D. (2013). Social mobility in five African countries. *Review of Income and Wealth*, *59*(Suppl.1). https://doi.org/10.1111/roiw.12037

Bowles, S., & Gintis, H. (2002). The inheritance of inequality. *Journal of Economic Perspectives*, *16*(3), 3–30. https://doi.org/10.1257/089533002760278686

Breen, R. (Ed.). (2004). *Social mobility in Europe*. Oxford University Press.

Breen, R. (2010). Social mobility and equality of opportunity geary lecture spring 2010. *Economic and Social Review*, *41*(4), 413–428.

Breen, R., & Jonsson, J. O. (2005). Inequality of opportunity in comparative perspective: Recent research on educational attainment and social mobility. *Annual Review of Sociology*, *31*(1), 223–243. https://doi.org/10.1146/annurev.soc.31.041304.122232

Brunori, P., Ferreira, F. H. G., & Peragine, V. (2013). *Inequality of opportunity, income inequality and economic mobility: Some international comparisons* (IZA Discussion

Papers, No. 7155; Institute for the Study of Labor, Bonn). https://doi.org/10.1596/1813-9450-6304

Burkhauser, R. V., & Couch, K. A. (2009). *Intragenerational inequality and intertemporal mobility* (B. Nolan, W. Salverda, & T. M. Smeeding, Eds.) (Vol. 996, No. 522–546, pp. 1–60). Oxford University Press.

Chaudhary, R., & Verick, S. (2014). *Female labor force participation in India and beyond* (ILO Asia-Pasific Working Paper; International Labor Organization, ILO DWT for South Asia and Country Office for India). http://www.ilo.org/wcmsp5/groups/public/@asia/@ro-bangkok/@sro-new_delhi/documents/publication/wcms_324621.pdf

Checchi, D., Ichino, A., & Rustichini, A. (1999). More equal but less mobile? Education financing and intergenerational mobility in Italy and in the US. *Journal of Public Economics, 74*(3), 351–393. https://doi.org/10.1016/S0047-2727(99)00040-7

Cheng, Y., & Dai, J. (1995). Intergenerational mobility in modern China. *Source: European Sociological Review European Sociological Review, 11*(1), 17–35. http://www.jstor.org/stable/522844

Chowdhury, S. (2011). Employment in India: What does the latest data show? *Economic and Political Weekly, 46*(32), 23–26.

Dearden, L., Machin, S., & Reed, H. (1997). Intergenerational mobility in Britain. *Economic Journal, 107*(440), 47–66.

Domanski, H., & Sawinski, Z. (1987). Dimensions of occupational mobility: The empirical invariance. *European Sociological Review European Sociological Review, 3*(1), 39–53. http://www.jstor.org/stable/522529

Dorosh, P. A., Sen, B., Van Asselt, J., & Ahmed, M. (2018). *Farm-nonfarm labor mobility in rural Bangladesh: Intersectoral shift or intergenerational occupational choice?* (IFPRI Discussion Paper 01767; International Food Policy Research Institute). http://ebrary.ifpri.org/cdm/ref/collection/p15738coll2/id/132926

Duraisamy, P., & Duraisamy, M. (2017). Social identity and wage discrimination in the Indian labor market. *Economic and Political Weekly, 52*(4), 51–60.

Emran, M. S., & Shilpi, F. (2019). *Economic approach to intergenerational mobility: Measures, methods, and challenges in developing countries*. https://doi.org/10.35188/UNU-WIDER/2019/734-7

Featherman, D. L., & Hauser, R. M. (1978). *Opportunity and change: Studies in population.* Academic Press.

Ferrie, J. P. (2005). History lessons: The end of American exceptionalism? Mobility in the United States since 1850. *Journal of Economic Perspectives, 19*(3), 199–215. https://doi.org/10.1257/089533005774357824

Fortin, N. M., & Lefebvre, S. (1998). Intergenrational income mobility in Canada. In M. Corak (Ed.), *Labor markets, social institutions, and the future of Canada's children* (p. 51). Ministry of Industry. http://dsp-psd.tpsgc.gc.ca/Collection/Statcan/89-553-XIB/0009889-553-XIBe.pdf#page=105

Ghose, A. K. (2016). *India employment report challenges and the imperative of manufacturing-led growth.* Oxford University Press.

Goodman, L. A. (1970). The multivariate analysis of qualitative data: Interactions among multiple classifications. *Journal of the American Statistical Association, 65*(329), 226–256. https://www.jstor.org/stable/2283589

Goodman, L. A. (1972). Some multiplicative models for the analysis of cross classified data. In *Proceedings of the sixth Berkeley symposium on mathematical statistics and probability* (pp. 649–696). University of California.

Grawe, N. D. (2006). Lifecycle bias in estimates of intergenerational earnings persistence. *Labor Economics*, *13*(5), 551–570. https://doi.org/10.1016/j.labeco.2005.04.002

Hauser, R. M. (1978). A structural model of the mobility table. *Social Forces*, *56*(3), 919–953. https://doi.org/10.1093/sf/56.3.919

Hnatkovska, V., Lahiri, A., & Paul, S. B. (2013). Breaking the caste barrier: Intergenerational mobility in India. *Journal of Human Resources*, *48*(2), 435–473. https://doi.org/10.1353/jhr.2013.0012

Hout, M. (1988). More universalism, less structural mobility: The American occupational structure in the 1980s. *American Journal of Sociology*, *93*(6), 1358–1400. https://doi.org/10.1086/228904

Hout, M., & Guest, A. M. (2013). Intergenerational occupational mobility in Great Britain and the United States since 1850: Comment. *American Economic Review*, *103*(5), 2021–2040. https://doi.org/10.1257/aer.103.5.2021

Islam, M. (2012). Rethinking the Muslim question in post-colonial India. *Social Scientist*, *40*(7), 61–84.

Iversen, V., Krishna, A., & Sen, K. (2017). Rags to riches? Intergenerational occupational mobility in India. *Economic and Political Weekly*, *52*(44), 107–114.

Kamat, A. A. R. (1981). Literacy and education of Muslims : A note literacy and education of Muslims. *Economic and Political Weekly*, *16*(23), 1031–1033.

Kannan, K. P., & Raveendran, G. (2012). Counting and profiling the missing labor force. *Economic and Political Weekly*, *47*(6), 77–80.

Kannan, K. P., & Raveendran, G. (2019). From jobless to job-loss growth: Gainers and losers in India's employment performance during 2012–2018. *Economic and Political Weekly*, *54*(44), 38–44.

Kapsos, S., Silberman, A., & Bourmpoula, E. (2014). Why is female labor force participation declining so sharply in India? *ILO Research Paper*, *10*, 1–51. https://ideas.repec.org/p/ilo/ilowps/994949190702676.html

Kerbo, H. R. (2006). *Social stratification*. McGraw-Hill.

Kerswell, T., & Pratap, S. (2019). Liberalization in India: Does it resolve or aggravate employment problems? *Journal of Contemporary Asia*, *49*(4), 626–649. https://doi.org/10.1080/00472336.2018.1545916

Kingdon, G. G. (2002). The gender gap in educational attainment in India: How much can be explained? *Journal of Development Studies*, *39*(2), 25–53. https://doi.org/10.1080/00220380412331322741

Klasen, S., & Pieters, J. (2012). *Push or pull? Drivers of female labor force participation during India's economic boom* (IZA DP No. 6395; Institute of Labor Economics, Bonn).

Lambert, S., Ravallion, M., & van de Walle, D. (2014). Intergenerational mobility and interpersonal inequality in an African economy. *Journal of Development Economics*, *110*, 327–344. https://doi.org/10.1016/j.jdeveco.2014.05.007

Lefranc, A., Pistolesi, N., & Trannoy, A. (2008). Inequality of opportunities vs. inequality of outcomes: Are western societies all alike? *Review of Income and Wealth*, *54*(4), 513–546. https://doi.org/10.1111/j.1475-4991.2008.00289.x

Levine, D. I., & Mazumder, B. (1999). *Choosing the right parents: Changes in the intergenerational transmission of inequality between 1980 and the early 1990s* (IRLE Working Paper No. 72; Institute for Research on Labor and Employment UC Berkeley). https://doi.org/10.2139/ssrn.323881

Long, J., & Ferrie, J. (2013). Intergenerational occupational mobility in Great Britain and the United States since 1850. *American Economic Review*, *103*(4), 1109–1137. https://doi.org/10.1257/aer.103.4.1109

Majumder, R. (2010). Intergenerational mobility in educational and occupational attainment: A comparative study of social classes in India. *Margin*, *4*(4), 463–494. https://doi.org/10.1177/097380101000400404

Marks, G. N. (1996). Structural changes and association in mobility tables: an integration and extension of existing approaches. *Quality and Quantity*, *30*, 61–86.

McMurrer, D. P., Condon, M., & Sawhill, I. V. (1997). *Intergenerational Mobility in the United States* (Companion Piece to Number 4 in Series, "Opportunity in America"; Urban Institute). https://www.urban.org/

Mehrotra, S., & Parida, J. K. (2019). *India's employment crisis: Rising education levels and falling non-agricultural job growth. October*, 1–22.

Mehrotra, S., Parida, J., Sinha, S., & Gandhi, A. (2014). Explaining employment trends in the Indian economy: 1993–94 to 2011–12. *Economic and Political Weekly*, *49*(32), 49–57. https://www.researchgate.net/publication/286723590

Mistry, M. B. (2005). Muslims in India: A demographic and socio-economic profile. *Journal of Muslim Minority Affairs*, *25*(3), 399–422.

Mitra, A., & Singh, J. (2019). Rising unemployment in India: A statewise analysis from 1993–94 to 2017–18. *Economic and Political Weekly*, *54*(50), 12–16.

Motiram, S., & Singh, A. (2012). How close does the apple fall to the tree? Some evidence from India on intergenerational occupational mobility. *Economic and Political Weekly*, *47*(40), 56–65. http://www.jstor.org/stable/41720217

Mondal, S. R. (2000). Muslim population in India: Some demographic and socio-economic features. *International Journal of Anthropology*, *15*(1–2), 91–107.

Muhammad, M., & Jamil, M. (2017). Intergenerational mobility in occupational status. *Forman Journal of Economic Studies*, 135–159. https://doi.org/10.32368/fjes.20170007

Mukherjee, D., & Majumder, R. (2011). Occupational pattern, wage rates and earning disparities in India: A decomposition occupational pattern, wage rates and earning disparities in India: A decomposition analysis. *Indian Economic Review*, *46*(1), 131–152. https://doi.org/10.2307/23266420

Muzammil, M. (1994). *Education and employment: A study of Muslims in UP (India)*. South Asia Visiting Scholar's Programme.

OECD. (2019). *Intergenerational mobility in the labor market*. https://www.oecd-ilibrary.org/sites/9789264288041-6-en/index.html?itemId=/content/component/9789264288041-6-en

Oesch, D., & Rodriguez, M. (2011). Upgrading or polarization? Occupational change in Britain, Germany, Spain and Switzerland, 1990–2008. *Socio-Economic Review*, *9*(3), 1–29.

Panagariya, A., & Mukim, M. (2014). A comprehensive analysis of poverty in India. *Asian Development Review*, *31*(1), 1–52. https://doi.org/10.1162/ADEV_a_00021

Parrado, E., Caner, A., & Wolff, E. N. (2007). Occupational and industrial mobility in the United States. *Labor Economics*, *14*(3), 435–455. https://doi.org/10.1016/j.labeco.2006.01.005

Patnaik, P. (2018). Economic liberalisation and working poor. In *Quarter century of liberalisation in India* (Quarter Ce). Oxford University Press.

Ramaswamy, K. V., & Agrawal, T. (2012). *Services-led growth, employment and job quality: A study of manufacturing and service-sector in Urban India* (WP-2012-007; Indira Gandhi Institute of Development Research, Mumbai, Issue March). http://www.igidr.ac.in/pdf/publication/WP-2012-007.pdf

Rangarajan, C., Kaul, P. I., & Seema. (2011). Where is the missing labor force? *Economic and Political Weekly*, *46*(39), 68–72.

Rath, B. N. (2018). Productivity growth and efficiency change: Comparing manufacturing and service-based firms in India. *Economic Modelling*, *70*(September 2017), 447–457. https://doi.org/10.1016/j.econmod.2017.08.024

Reddy, A. B. (2015a). Changes in intergenerational occupational mobility in India: Evidence from national sample surveys, 1983–2012. *World Development*, *76*, 329–343. https://doi.org/10.1016/j.worlddev.2015.07.012

Reddy, A. A. (2015b). Growth, structural change and wage rates in rural India. *Economic and Political Weekly*, *50*(2), 56–65.

Reddy, A. B., & Swaminathan, M. (2014). Intergenerational occupational mobility in rural India: Evidence from ten villages. *Review of Agrarian Studies*, *4*(1), 95–134. http://www.ras.org.in/intergenerational_occupational_mobility_in_rural_india

Roy Choudhury, P., & Chatterjee, B. (2015). Analyzing "jobless growth" in post-liberalisation India: A decomposition approach. *Indian Journal of Labor Economics*, *58*(4), 577–608. https://doi.org/10.1007/s41027-016-0037-0

Sachar Committee Report. (2006). Social: Economic and educational status of the Muslim community of India. In *A Report, Government of India*. http://minorityaffairs.gov.in/reports/sachar-committee-report

Sanghi, S., & Srija, A. (2014). Employment trends among religious communities of India. *Economic and Political Weekly*, *XLIX*(17), 22–24.

Sengupta, A., & Das, P. (2014). Gender wage discrimination across social and religious groups in India: Estimates with unit level data. *Economic and Political Weekly*, *XLIX*(21), 71–76.

Sinha, R. (2018). Closer, but No Cigar: Intergenerational Mobility across Caste Groups in India. In Policy Research Working Paper WPS8401, World Bank Group, Development Research Group (Issue April). https://doi.org/https://doi.org/10.1596/1813-9450-8401

Sloane, P. J., Battu, H., & Seaman, P. T. (1999). Overeducation, undereducation and the British labor market. *Applied Economics*, *31*(11), 1437–1453. https://doi.org/10.1080/000368499323319

Sobel, M. E. (1983). Structural mobility, circulation mobility and the analysis of occupational mobility: A conceptual mismatch. *American Sociological Review*, *48*(5), 721–727.

Solon, G. (1992). Intergenerational income mobility in the United States. *American Economic Review*, *82*(3), 393–408.

Thomas, J. J. (2014). The demographic challenge and employment growth in India. *Economic and Political Weekly*, *49*(6), 15–17. http://www.jstor.org/stable/24479252

Thomas, J. J. (2020). Labour Market Changes in India, 2005–18: Missing the demographic window of opportunity? *Economic and Political Weekly*, *55*(34), 57–63.

Trivedi, P., & Rajmal. (2011). Growth effects of fiscal policy of India States. *Millennial Asia*, *2*(2), 141–162. https://doi.org/10.1177/097639961100200201

Upadhyay, V. (2015). Can capitalism survive high degree of automation? A comparison with Thomas Piketty's argument. *SSRN Electronic Journal*, 1–9. https://doi.org/10.2139/ssrn.2558989

Wilkinson, S. (2007). A comment on the analysis in Sachar report. *Economic and Political Weekly*, *42*(10), 832–836.

Xie, Y., & Killewald, A. (2013). Intergenerational occupational mobility in Great Britain and the United States since 1850: Comment. *American Economic Review*, *103*(5), 2003–2020. https://doi.org/10.1257/aer.103.5.2003

Zijdeman, R. (2009). Like my father before me: Intergenerational occupational status transfer during industrialization (Zeeland, 1811–1915). *Continuity and Change*, *24*(3), 455. https://doi.org/10.1017/S0268416009990166

3 Intergenerational Occupational Mobility among Socio-religious Communities

3.1 Introduction

This chapter addresses two major issues: has mobility decreased or increased over time? And how does mobility vary over time across socio-religious communities (SRCs). If enough people manage to leave their parental occupational position, the labor market is flexible. There is equality of opportunity, and people can manage to choose their desired career paths (Bowles & Gintis, 2002; Breen & Jonsson, 2005; Levine & Mazumder, 1999). It has been debatable to what extent indicators of (in)equality of outcomes (like educational and occupational attainment) can be interpreted as (in)equality of opportunity (Corak, 2013). Still, sizable studies rely on such estimates to infer the equality of opportunity in society. In this case, it is highly desirable to probe more about the mobility process than measuring gross mobility rates alone. In this chapter, the occupational mobility rate (M1) is calculated for various SRCs and survey years. A relative mobility rate (M2) is estimated to account for marginal distributions based on changes in occupational distributions between fathers' and sons' generations. To probe deeper into the occupational movements, a multinomial logit model (MNL) was also estimated. As a result, this chapter is divided into five sections: Section 3.2 to 3.4 (Data, Occupational Classification, and Methodology); Section 3.5 (Results); and Section 3.6 (Conclusion).

3.2 Data and Methodology

3.2.1 Data

For the mobility sample, data from co-resident father-son duos from various NSS rounds (55th in 1999–00, 61st in 2004–05, and 68th in 2011–12) as well as a recent Periodic Labour Force Survey (PLFS 2018–19) were used (NSSO, 2000; NSSO, 2005; NSSO, 2012; PLFS-2019). This data comprises sons who are co-residents with their fathers and part of the workforce aged between the ages of 15 to 45. In this father-son sample, the upper age limit is restricted to 45 years to avoid lifecycle effects (Anti et al., 2012). However, unlike income, broadly defined occupations vary less over the life cycle, making age-related

DOI: 10.4324/9781003361299-3

biases less problematic (Blanden, 2013). For this analysis, female family members were not considered because a sizable proportion of females in the families had left their parental homes following marriage to settle with their husbands (Azam, 2015).

This study works on NSS rather than IHDS data, based on a thorough review of the data in Chapter 2. The NSS is also updated for the most recent time period (PLFS-2018-19), but the IHDS is only updated up to 2011. In addition, there are only two waves of IHDS available (2005 and 2011). Because of the extensive history of NSS data, we can select data prior to 2005. The NSS EUS rounds are typical labor market surveys that are specifically geared to address employment issues. As a result, our findings are comparable to previous research. The IHDS, on the other hand, is a multipurpose survey that intends to collect information on employment, education, income, health, social networks, crime, institutional access and trust, and a range of other areas. For researchers in India, the NSS has garnered the credibility of academics, notably labor economists. Aside from father-son mobility, this work includes information on labor market changes, earnings, employment-unemployment rates, occupational structure and more. As a result, NSS data is an excellent choice for analysis.

Many studies used IHDS-2005 as a representative sample and divided it according to birth cohorts to track changes over time. In the case of NSS, researchers studied general changes from 1983, 1988 or 1993. Such studies include longer time periods, for example, 1983–2011, 1993–2011, etc. For two reasons, we chose 1999–00 as the starting point for our investigation. First, the study's most important social category, "Other Backward Classes", was only included as a discrete social group in the 1999–00 NSS session. Earlier, the same people were part of a bigger Hindu community (other than SCs and STs). To make results comparable with the forwarding rounds, 1999–00 seems to be the best point to start. Second, the 1999–00 data set serves as a baseline for those born between 1954 and 1984 (in the age group of 15–45). The recently completed PLFS-2018–19, on the other hand, comprises people born between 1983 and 2003 (at 15–45 age intervals). As a result, both data sets span two generations and encompass all people born after the country gained independence (see Table 3.1).

In IHDS, fathers' occupational information was asked in a retrospective manner (what was your father's occupation when you were growing up?). Hence, the lifecycle issues are also present in the IHDS data sets. In the current work,

Table 3.1 Survey Rounds and Birth Cohorts

Age Group (15–45)				
Survey Rounds	*1999–00*	*2004–05*	*2011–12*	*2018–19*
Birth Cohort	1954–84	1959–90	1966–96	1983–2003
Father-Son Pairs	34,534	37,374	25,705	19,666

Source: Based on Unit-level data of NSS EUS (2000, 2005, 2012) and PLFS 2019.

we consider NSS as a better option (despite the co-residency) because the IHDS father-son sample comprises a large number of part-time workers.

3.2.2 Co-residency Bias

To determine the level of co-residency in the current sample, the sample is divided into two age groups: sons under 30 years of age and sons over 30 years of age. The gross occupation mobility estimates in both age groups are nearly identical, as seen in Table 3.2. It demonstrates that co-residency is not a major concern in the sample, although, as previously stated, it is found in every sample. It cannot, however, be given greater weight than the critical challenges of part-time and full-time workers, as previously noted.

3.2.3 Lifecycle Issues

Lifecycle concerns are present in NSS, NFHS and IHDS, just as they are in co-residency. The lifecycle issues can be minimized by the fact that occupations, unlike income, vary less over the life cycle. In particular, this work thus favors UPS-based occupational information. As a result, the findings of this study are more reliable than those of other IHDS-based studies. The occupation gets more stable beyond the age of 30. It indicates that post-thirties, fathers' and sons' career choices are steady. Stability facilitates comparability. Nonetheless, our findings indicate that job mobility is comparable between the two age groups i.e., below 30 and above 30 years in age bracket 15 to 45 years (Table 3.2). Consequently, the issue of life cycle is not a big concern in the sample.

3.2.4 Other Data Related Issues

The newly introduced Periodic Labour Force Survey (PLFS) has supplanted the national sample survey employment-unemployment (NSS EUS) rounds. Some information is discontinued, and some new variables are added to the new PLFS. Both surveys use the same sample design, sampling area and recall periods. The NSS and PLFS survey cycles are inextricably linked and comparable (Kannan & Raveendran, 2019; Mehrotra & Parida, 2019; Thomas, 2020). The study of Jajoria and Jatav (2020) is the best document to go to for specifics on revisions, additions, and deletion of variables.

The NSS and PLFS rounds are referred to as 2000, 2005, 2012 and 2019 in this work. The father-son pairs in Table 3.1 serve as the foundation for the rest of this chapter's investigation. More information on the sample characteristics can be found in Appendix A, Table A-3.13.

3.3 Occupational Classification

It is very challenging to have a well-defined set of occupations in any heterogeneous labor market. Based on employment characteristics including pay, skills and

Table 3.2 Gross Mobility Rates for Two Age Groups

	1999–00		*2004–05*		*2011–12*		*2018–19*	
Age group/Year	*Gross Mobility*	*Std. Err.*	*Gross Mobility*	*Std. Err.*	*Gross Mobility*	*Std. Err.*	*Gross Mobility*	*Std. Err.*
Below 30	33.21	0.28	38.57	0.29	41.9	0.36	52.05	0.42
Above 30	32.92	0.55	39.31	0.53	41.41	0.58	52.47	0.68

Source: NSS EUS and PLFS

education, labor economists rank jobs in a hierarchical order. Recent studies in labor economics suggest that a job's precariousness could be a good indicator of employment quality. Precarious work has been defined as employment that is uncertain, unpredictable and risky from the perspective of the worker. The resulting distress, manifested in a variety of ways, serves as a constant reminder of such vulnerability (Kalleberg, 2009). Precarious employment frequently includes no or minimal social security benefits (Standing, 1999; Vosko, 2010, p. 2). The ease with which occupational groups can be identified also serves as a criterion for differentiating between decent and precarious jobs. It is preferable to refer to movement from the working class to the skilled class as "upward mobility" and vice versa.

In India, the post-liberalization era has been marked by an increase in the demand for skilled laborers, an improvement in the skill composition of the labor force, and a rise in the relative remuneration of workers with a higher level of education (Goel, 2017). The skilled and technical occupational categories are therefore analyzed separately from the other occupational categories in this study. The National classification of occupations (NCO, 2004) classifies occupations based on the skills required. As reported in the NSS rounds, the occupational divisions are represented by three-digit numbers. The occupational data for the survey years 2000 and 2005 are now available based on the NCO-1968 scheme.

Occupational data for the survey years 2012 and 2019, in contrast, are based on the NCO-2004 scheme. To ensure consistency across four rounds, occupational data must be converted to either the NCO-1968 or NCO-2004 classification formats. There are two ways to accomplish this: either convert NCO-1968 to NCO-2004 format, or perform the inverse of the first. For this analysis, the first alternative was chosen, and a concordance between NCO-1968 and NCO-2004 was established using the Baruah (2016) approach.

It should be noted that classification alignment between NCO rounds (NCO-1968 and NCO-2004) will never be perfect due to the changing nature and existence of occupations. Since India, unlike the West, has yet to establish a clear work ladder, we did not use a collar-based classification scheme. As a consequence, as illustrated in Table 3.3, we have introduced nine occupational structure divisions.

Employers also provide rigorous training to better equip less-trained and low-skilled employees. Thus, the formal education level is only required at the entry level. We recognize educational credentials only at entry-level jobs, as NSS data do not include this information.

Apart from the established educational requirements, additional information about this nine-division occupational classification has been gathered (Tables 3.4 and 3.5). It includes the actual educational attainment of each occupational group; the monthly per capita consumption expenditure of each occupation holder's family; the monthly wage and earnings; the enterprise type (organized/unorganized); and the share of formal and informal workers for each occupational group. Because self-employed people's monthly earnings are a new feature in PLFS, the newly released PLFS data allow us to map each occupational group's earnings (the same data were unavailable for earlier NSS EUS rounds). Notably,

Table 3.3 Classification of Occupations

NCO (2004) Division	*Title*	*Skill Level*	*Education*
1	Legislators, Senior Officials, and Managers	Skill not Defined	--
2	Professionals	IV	Post-Graduate University Degree More than 15 years of formal education.
3	Associate Professionals	III	First University Degree 14–15 years of formal education.
4	Clerks	II	Secondary Education 11–13 years of formal education.
5	Service Workers and Shop & Market Sales Workers	II	Secondary Education 11–13 years of formal education.
6	Skilled Agricultural and Fishery Workers	II	Secondary Education 11–13 years of formal education.
7	Craft and Related Trades Workers	II	Secondary Education 11–13 years of formal education.
8	Plant and Machine Operators and Assemblers	II	Secondary Education 11–13 years of formal education.
9	Elementary Occupations	I	Primary Education Up to 10 years of formal education and/or informal skills.

Source: National Classification of Occupations (NCO, 2004)

the occupations ranked seventh and eighth in Table 3.4 outperform agriculture and allied in terms of education, monthly per capita consumption expenditure (MPCE), and wage/earnings, respectively. Given the wide heterogeneity among farmers, a more detailed classification of agriculture based on land size might provide more accurate data. However, because such an exercise would result in a massive reduction in the sample size for each of these occupational groups, it is not being attempted.

Furthermore, the second, third, and fourth division occupations are more in the organized sector and have formal workplace arrangements (Table 3.5).[1]

3.4 Methodology

Based on the extensive review on this issue in Chapter 2, this study presents mobility matrices and aggregate measures out of such matrices. As Xie and Killewald (2013) presented, a mobility matrix $M = \begin{bmatrix} P_{11} & P_{12} \\ P_{21} & P_{22} \end{bmatrix}$ is a square matrix

Table 3.4 Occupational Groups and Mean Years of Schooling, MPCE, Monthly Wages/ Earning (PLFS-2019)

NCO (2004) Division	*Mean Years of Schooling*	*Std. Dev.*	*MPCE*	*Std. Dev.*	*Monthly Wages/ Earning*	*Std. Dev.*
1	9.54	4.90	3249.87	2908.81	17053.79	24002.26
2	13.62	3.88	4346.78	3678.38	25294.47	114509.82
3	13.36	3.31	3728.76	2912.98	18614.29	15924.43
4	13.18	3.09	3535.23	2223.45	17979.57	12175.28
5	8.46	4.50	2425.34	1872.11	9942.00	8491.76
6	5.38	4.71	1630.15	941.34	5751.84	6090.80
7	6.8	4.31	2080.41	1289.49	8695.19	6823.01
8	7.87	3.98	2311.85	1417.90	11161.58	7188.14
9	4.4	4.4	1646.63	942.03	6325.71	4292.85
Total	6.97	6.97	2187.49	1869.12	9666.32	26487.85

Source: Estimations are based on unit-level data of PLFS 2019.

Note: Occupations are numbered as Table 3.3. Read Std. Dev. as standard deviation, MPCE as Monthly Per Capita Consumption expenditure.

in which cells contain the marginal distribution of the son's occupations against his father's occupation. The column of the matrix shows the category of father's occupation (origin) and row represents the son's occupation (destination). None of the cells of the matrix exhibit father's occupation and the diagonal cells of the matrix display immobility. Following Xie and Killewald (2013), the absolute mobility rate can be calculated with the following formula

$$\mathrm{M} = 1 - \left(\sum_{i=1}^{N} f_{ii} \right) / f_{++}$$

Table 3.5 Occupational Groups and Enterprise Types (PLFS-2019)

NCO (2004) Division	*Organized (%)*	*Unorganized (%)*	*Formal (%)*	*Informal (%)*
1	17.31	82.69	11.07	88.93
2	60.69	39.31	43.30	56.7
3	74.20	25.8	51.24	48.76
4	81.80	18.2	58.56	41.44
5	22.42	77.58	12.11	87.89
6	0.56	99.44	0.16	99.84
7	23.16	76.84	7.90	92.1
8	31.06	68.94	14.54	85.46
9	16.51	83.49	3.73	96.27
Total	19.79	80.21	10.11	89.89

Source: Estimations are based on unit-level data of PLFS 2019.

where f_{++} shows a total of mobility table and $\sum_{i=1}^{N} f_{ii}$ is the sum of diagonal cells of mobility table. In other words, M represents the fraction of off-diagonal elements, which can also be presented in percentage form. For example, there is a father-son mobility matrix $P = \begin{bmatrix} 12 & 4 \\ 8 & 8 \end{bmatrix}$, in this case, the

$$M = 1 - \frac{(12+8)}{(12+4+8+8)} = 1 - \frac{12}{32} = 0.625$$

In the calculation of intergenerational mobility, the one commonly debated challenge is the difference between "structure mobility" and "association mobility". Altham and Ferrie (2007) proposed addressing the issue by controlling for changes in occupational distribution in the case of traditional matrices. Following the work of Altham and Ferrie (2007), relative mobility rates are calculated in the following way: suppose there is a mobility matrix of 2*2-dimension P (e.g., $P = \begin{bmatrix} 12 & 4 \\ 8 & 8 \end{bmatrix}$) and we want to compare this mobility pattern with another 2*2-dimension matrix Q (e.g., $Q = \begin{bmatrix} 8 & 4 \\ 24 & 4 \end{bmatrix}$), so the Q could be adjusted in a way that it resembles the marginal distribution of matrix P. For that, if the first row of Q is multiplied by a constant, i.e. 2, and divide the first column of the new matrix by ½, so we will get a new matrix Q′ which has the same marginal distribution as matrix P has (e.g., $Q' = \begin{bmatrix} 8 & 8 \\ 12 & 4 \end{bmatrix}$). Such manipulations would be done after imposing the marginal distribution of P on Q. Similarly, Q can be imposed on P, and both can be compared.

3.4.1 Empirical Specification

In the case of discrete occupational categories, a multinomial logit model (MNL) is used. On the left side of the equation are the son's multiple occupational categories, and on the right side is the father's occupation (Constant & Zimmermann, 2003; Doruk et al., 2003; Hout & Guest, 2013; Modalsli, 2017).

For occupational attainment, the probability that a son *i* is employed in the jth occupation depends on his father's occupation.

$$\Pr(\text{Son's Occupation}_i = j \mid X_i) = Pr(\alpha X_i' + \varepsilon_i > 0) \tag{3.1}$$

The relative risk ratios are calculated from the eq. 3.1. Relative risk ratios (the exponentiated form of log odds ratios) account for the relative mobility (net of structural changes), while the predicted probabilities show absolute mobility. The ratio of the two probabilities, for example, the probability of a son entering in occupation

1 (Pr$(y=1)$) compared to enter in occupation 5 (Pr$(y=5)$), could be affected by the changes in occupation 1 compared to other occupations over the period. In this case, the mobility will be absolute (including changes in occupational structure). To measure the relative mobility, it is advised to look for the ratios with two different father's occupational categories (Modalsli, 2017). For example, the probability of a son (father's occupation = 1) to enter in occupation 1 rather than falling to occupation 5 compared to the probability of a son (father's occupation = 5) to enter in category I rather than falling in category V. Here, two father's occupations (2 and 5) are considered. This ratio is relative and is the net of structural changes.

The equation 3.1 can be run with an interaction term to capture variation in the impact of fathers' occupation among different socio-religious communities. It could also be run separately for each of the SRCs. This study chooses the first option; hence, with an SRC interaction with the father's occupation, this model is run separately for each cross-section (2000, 2005, 2012 and 2019).

The interpretations of relative risk ratios in general and of interaction terms in particular are notorious for being difficult to grasp. Estimates on the relative risk ratio scale are often regarded as perplexing. Researchers generally prefer to work with predicted probabilities or marginal effects. However, as mentioned earlier, the predicted probabilities indicate absolute mobility; relative risk ratios or odds ratios are ideal for analyzing relative mobility. Again, the relative risk ratios of interaction terms are difficult to interpret because they involve the referent group from their own category. These multiplicative effects are relative to the baseline odds of their own category. It introduces a number of complications, including the following:

a. A baseline category may have a low probability in a marginalized population, and comparison to that low probability may result in a larger relative risk ratio for that community. In this case, the relative risk ratio is deceptive. The community may not have an advantage in society; the risk ratio looks high because the baseline group is not very good.
b. In addition, this RRR-based MNL model with the father's occupation*SRC interaction includes an SRC base category. This adds to the difficulty of the interpreting process. To address this issue and make the SRC-based mobility study more intelligible, the following steps were taken:

Step 1: First, the average predicted probabilities of interaction (father's occupation*SRC) are estimated. For example, the probability of entering occupational category I is $\Pr(y=1)$, and the probability to enter in occupational category V is $\Pr(y=5)$ for each SRC for different levels of father's occupation.

Step 2: Then, all such probabilities are transformed into relative risks, as relative risk is nothing but the ratio of two probabilities. For example $\frac{\Pr(y=1)}{\Pr(y=5)}$, show the relative risk to enter in category I (comparing group) rather than category V (reference group) for each SRC for different levels of father's occupation.

These probability-based relative risks estimates are a relatively recent development in this field, following Buis' (2010) compelling case for odds ratios, hazard ratios and risk ratios.

Step 3: As the ratio of the two relative risks are nothing but the relative risk ratios; such ratios can be calculated from the relative risks of step 2. For example, $\left\{\frac{\Pr(y=1)}{\Pr(y=5)}\right\}$ father's occupation I / $\left\{\frac{\Pr(y=1)}{\Pr(y=5)}\right\}$ father's occupation V.

Since step 3 again involves the baseline group, that is why the relative risks (from step 2) are presented and discussed in the results section. The relative risk ratios that involve the comparison of two fathers' occupational categories can always be calculated from step 2. Step 3 results in relative mobility since it compares the relative risks of two different occupational categories of the fathers. This issue is further explained in detail in the result section.

In the case of all-India level estimations, the relative risk ratios are presented. In the SRC-wise estimates (father's Occupation*SRC), relative risks are presented.

Fathers' occupations are sub-divided into five occupational categories, namely; category I (Officials and Managers, Professionals, Associate Professionals and Clerks), category II (Service Workers and Shop and Market Sales Workers), category III (Agriculture and allied services), category IV (Craft and Related Trades Workers, Plant and Machine Operators and Assemblers), and category V (Laborers). For fathers' occupational category, the laborers category is treated as a reference point in equation 3.1.

SRCs are categorized into STs, SCs, OBCs, Hindu Others, Muslims and Other Minorities. The mobility rates (M1 and M2) are presented, considering Muslim OBC and Muslim Others as separate groups. Here, both the sub-groups are considered Muslim. Since the data for Muslim OBCs is insufficient, combining the two sub-groups would increase the sample size for regression analysis. Other than that, we observed little difference in the descriptive mobility rates (M1 and M2) of both the sub-groups, despite the fact that STs and SCs differ significantly.

It is important to note that the application of MNL models is subject to the stringent requirement of holding independence of irrelevant alternatives (IIA) assumptions. This assumption states that if a decision-maker chooses option j = 1 over j = 2, then his choice should not be affected by the presence or absence of a third alternative like j = 3. This issue has received considerable attention in the field of discrete choice modeling over the years. To determine whether IIA holds true, the following three tests are popular: Hausman (1978), Small-Hsiao test (Small & Hsiao, 1985), and Hausman-McFadden test (Hausman & McFadden, 1984). Each of these three alternative test procedures has the potential to yield different outcomes. We use the Hausman test (1978) in this analysis to determine the IIA assumption. The Stata output suggests that the test failed to reject the null hypothesis (IIA holds) for equation 3.1. Often, in the research, the issue of negative Chi-values is discussed. In MNL modeling, negative Chi-values are common, and multiple researchers have reported this issue (Vijverberg, 2011). In our case, we also encountered negative Chi-values, despite the fact that negative test results support the IIA hypothesis (Hausman & McFadden, 1984). However, the issue remains largely unresolved, and contemporary scholarship advocates a case-by-case approach. Suppose the researcher is confident that these choice categories are sufficiently distinct and not simple substitutes for one another. In that case, the IIA assumption is not a major concern (Cheng & Long, 2007). Fry and Harris (1996, 1998) and Cheng and Long (2007) demonstrated that both the Hausman-McFadden test and the Small-Hsiao tests perform poorly and are, therefore, unsuitable for applied work. The validity of the IIA test depends majorly on the variables that explain the results and the way the data is set up (Cheng & Long, 2007).

The Multinomial Probit Model (MNP) is a new attempt to move away from the IIA assumption's stringent requirement. Although this pattern is becoming more prevalent in political science, few economists have opted for MNP over MNL. The occupational choices have already been made, most notably in labor market studies (such as this one), and we simply use secondary data to make these selections. The individual has no choice and has already picked up an occupation long ago. It is an ex-post selection, and in such cases, the Probit model may remain unidentified (Keane, 1992). While the MNL model and MNP model estimates may be almost identical, computing MNP may take a longer time. The MNL models are easy to compute and interpret (relative risk ratios are not possible with MNP), and they adhere to accepted practices in the field, making them simple to compare to earlier studies. Kropko (2007) demonstrated that MNL estimates are more reliable than MNP estimates in a computer-based simulation, even though the IIA assumption does not hold. The IIA test results are presented in Appendix A, Table A-3.14.

3.5 Results

3.5.1 Aggregate Occupational Mobility Rates

Table 3.6 shows the absolute (M1) and relative mobility (M2) rates. After holding occupational distribution constant over time, relative mobility is determined. Table 3.6, for example, reveals absolute mobility of 30.54 percent for the year 2000 and 35.94 percent for the year 2005 in column 2. According to the M2 in column 3, 35.11 percent of people were mobile in 2005 (keeping the structure of their jobs the same from 2000 to 2005). Absolute mobility has improved from 30.54 percent in 2000 to 45.14 percent in 2019. When we account for changes in occupational distribution, this increase is reduced, and the pure father-son transmission rate stays at 37.83 percent. Even after 70 years of independence, based on the vast literature on developed countries, it is possible to conclude that Indian society has a low degree of occupational mobility. As per data, parent-child mobility in the United States and the United Kingdom had surpassed 50 percent in the first half of the twentieth century (Long & Ferrie, 2015). Between 1910 and 2011, the mobility rates in Norway were consistently in the range of 45 percent to 50 percent at various points in time (Modalsli, 2017). In 2017, rural Mexico's absolute mobility was estimated to be about 63 percent (Yaschine et al., 2019). It has been observed that the growth of non-farm activities is related to mobility (Emran & Shilpi, 2011; Modalsli, 2017).

Table 3.6 SRC-wise Absolute (M1) And Relative (M2) Mobility Rates

Year	*M1*	*M2*	*M1*	*M2*	*M1*	*M2*	*M1*	*M2*
SRCs	**All**	**All**	**ST**	**ST**	**SC**	**SC**	**OBC**	**OBC**
2000	30.27	31.19	24.72	28.81	31.90	35.10	29.48	31.19
2005	35.84	34.98	32.56	27.19	38.42	34.88	34.94	33.27
2005	35.84	38.06	32.56	37.23	38.42	40.15	34.94	37.62
2012	37.83	35.40	34.53	30.54	39.29	37.27	36.45	33.86
2012	37.83	41.00	34.53	35.87	39.29	43.08	36.45	40.61
2019	45.14	41.19	37.75	37.21	47.31	43.32	45.86	41.30
2000	30.27	37.37	24.72	34.73	31.90	41.55	29.48	38.63
2019	45.14	37.23	37.75	26.39	47.31	36.56	45.86	35.74
SRCs	**Hindu Others**	**Hindu Others**	**Muslim OBC**	**Muslim OBC**	**Muslim Others**	**Muslim Others**	**Other Minorities**	**Other Minorities**
2000	30.86	32.12	36.93	37.20	35.70	36.20	24.49	22.98
2005	36.59	35.66	40.34	40.29	39.67	39.46	30.49	31.76
2005	36.59	37.91	40.34	40.25	39.67	40.77	30.49	36.02
2012	38.26	36.61	38.27	38.12	42.74	41.17	37.45	31.72
2012	38.26	42.25	38.27	39.56	42.74	45.94	37.45	31.72
2019	44.64	39.04	45.59	44.26	50.54	46.16	42.18	36.82
2000	30.86	37.76	36.93	38.20	35.70	42.05	24.49	32.39
2019	44.64	36.14	45.59	43.52	50.54	44.80	42.18	32.94

Source: Estimations are based on unit-level data of NSS EUS Rounds (2000, 2005, 2012) and PLFS-2019.

Note: Other Min refers to Other Minorities; M1=Absolute Mobility, M2=Relative Mobility.

Between 2000 and 2019, India's agriculture sector shrank, causing absolute mobility rates to rise. Other structural shifts in the economy occurred during the reform era when a greater variety of skill-based vocational opportunities became available than in the previous era. Additionally, the expansion of education and institutional changes enabled educated youth to take advantage of such opportunities during the post-reform period. However, it is critical to note that pure father-son occupational mobility (M2) increased by 37.83 percent. Without structural changes, only 37.83 percent of sons would have been able to escape their father's socioeconomic status.

While examining the socio-religious community-wise picture, it appears that the scheduled tribe community is the least mobile in terms of occupation (Table 3.6). After adjusting for occupational distribution, the same community has progressed by less than one percentage point from 2000 to 2019. The same disadvantage is not visible for another constitutionally protected group, i.e., the scheduled castes. Some studies have omitted this difference by combining the two (Azam, 2015; Reddy, 2015; Sinha, 2018). On the other hand, our findings indicate that both groups exhibit varying degrees of IG occupational mobility, with STs having the least. These statistics, however, are aggregate measurements showing how many sons were able to migrate from their father's occupational categories but not the actual migration path. Interestingly, Muslim OBCs and Muslim Forward castes both demonstrated high levels of IG occupational mobility, which could be attributed to their greater involvement in non-farm economic activities, as Muslims have historically been less involved in agriculture (Kulkarni, 2002; Mondal, 2000). Increased engagement with farm activities demonstrates an inverse relationship with IG mobility, particularly when the land area is larger. Nonetheless, Muslims are more mobile than any other community in terms of occupation.

3.5.2 SRC-wise Mobility Rates in Comparison with All-India Occupational Structure

A separate table has been created to compare the two socio-religious communities in India's overall occupational structure, which appears to be a fair comparison of various socio-religious communities. The data set spans two time periods: 2000 and 2019. When we examine the occupational distribution of specific groups at the national level (rows 3 and 5 of Table 3.7), we see that STs are the least mobile.

Additionally, in 2000, SCs and OBCs were disadvantaged, with low occupational mobility across India. However, these communities made rapid progress following that, and the situation in 2019 was dramatically different. Other minorities also had low mobility in 2000 but had not made as much progress as SCs and OBCs by 2019. Our analysis shows that Muslims are still the most mobile group in terms of jobs, and this is something that needs to be looked into more deeply.

Some important observations from occupational mobility include that STs have low occupational mobility, Muslims (both OBCs and others) show the highest occupational mobility, and there is a difference between mobility among Muslim OBCs and forward castes. The high occupational mobility among Muslims could be

Table 3.7 Relative Mobility Rates (M2) for All SRCs Using All-India Occupational Structure

Year	*ST vs All India*	*SC vs All India*	*OBCs vs All India*	*Hindu Others vs All India*	*M OBC vs All India*	*Muslim Others vs All India*	*Other Minorities vs All India*
2000	33.96	34.52	30.92	30.67	31.54	31.54	28.06
2000	22.64	27.53	28.91	30.38	35.40	34.21	26.90
2019	46.37	47.01	45.72	44.96	44.39	45.59	46.80
2019	36.71	45.47	45.33	44.65	46.72	50.06	40.74

Source: Estimations are based on unit-level data of NSS EUS Rounds (2000, 2005, 2012) and PLFS 2019.

explained by the fact that urbanization is the biggest source of social mobility and around 40 percent of Muslims live in urban areas (Chadha & Sahu, 2002; Motiram & Singh, 2012). Urbanization is always high among all the religious minorities in India, except Sikhs. Further, in urban areas, there are no farm-related compulsions. Even in rural areas, Muslims are historically less land-endowed (Alam & Raju, 2007; Kulkarni, 2002; Mondal, 2000). Occupational diversity and caste-based weak occupational ties in urban areas are potential contributing factors to high occupational mobility (Gang et al., 2012; Motiram & Singh, 2012; Reddy, 2015). Further, caste-related ties also appear to be weaker among Muslims. However, the Muslim OBCs' mobility is less than the Muslim others', and it could be a result of caste effect. Still, both Muslim OBCs and others are the most occupationally mobile groups. Scheduled Tribes' low occupational mobility seems to be the result of the fact that they are more concentrated in rural areas and have a dependency on farm-related activities. Further, the largest labor (elementary) supply comes from STs.

While urban locations provide Muslims with various job opportunities, this also fosters segregation, ghettoization (economic and residential), and enclaves (informal economy). As a result, the majority of their employment prospects are limited to job classifications V, IV, and II (semi-skilled and unskilled). However, Breen and Goldthorpe (1997) aptly note that preferences are not homogeneous across social groupings due to variances in openness to mobility. It indicates that those willing to relocate from their current location may have more employment prospects than those not. Thus, unequal access to diverse work opportunities is not always indicative of unequal opportunities.

As discussed in the methodology section, aggregate measures have limitations, and regression-based analysis has some advantages when looking for probable causes. The same analysis is discussed in the following section.

3.5.3 MNL-based Occupational Mobility Analysis

3.5.3.1 Relative Risk Ratios at All-India Level

The relative risk ratios of sons entering various occupations are shown in Table 3.8. With these regression results, we can look at the path from the starting point (the father's job) to the end point (the son's job) in more detail.

Using eq. 3.1, a total of 100 unique relative risk ratios can be calculated using a different set of reference categories for each year for the father and son's occupation. Laborers (class V) are used as the reference category for the father's and son's occupations, with sixteen odds ratios for each cross-section.[2] Relative risk ratios, which are the exponentiated form of log odds ratios, are provided. In 2000, sons of fathers with category I occupations were 310.63 times more likely to work in category I occupations than in category V occupations compared to sons of fathers with category V occupations. This exemplifies the advantage of being born into a family where the father holds a category I position. Additionally, sons of fathers who work in category II occupations have the second-highest probability of entering category I occupations. There is, however, a substantial difference between being the son of a category I and category II parent.

The relative risk ratio is highest in the group where the father is already working, indicating immobility across the occupational categories of fathers. In terms of relative risk ratios, category I has the most immobility, followed by categories II, III and IV. (For the year 2000, see RRRs in Table 3.8.) The intensity of relative risk ratios has weakened over time, indicating that Indian society is becoming more mobile. The RRRs for the farmers' category have fallen from 111.12 in 2000 to 98.71 in 2019. Nonetheless, it has one of the highest rates of persistence of any occupation.

These RRRs with reference group laborers demonstrate the relative advantage other occupational holders have over laborers. The advantages are diminishing over time, but the hierarchy of such advantages remains intact. To be more specific, sons of category I occupation holder fathers continue to have the best chance of joining the category I occupation (though their chances have dwindled), followed by sons of category II occupation holder fathers, category III, and category IV. However, the fact is also that the farmer's son seems to have lost out in the process. He has a lower advantage in 2019 than the son of a father who works in a category IV occupation. When it comes to who enters service, trade, and sales occupations, the majority of the labor supply comes from the sons of fathers who hold the same occupation. The sons of category I occupation fathers have the second-highest labor supply in category II occupations. Sons of fathers in category IV occupations are in third place, followed by sons of farmers. And the condition has remained unchanged over time.

3.5.3.2 Relative Risks for Different SRCs

To capture the variations in being a member of different SRCs at different levels of the father's occupation, the eq. 3.1 is calculated with an interaction term of SRC with the father's occupation. The joint significance test shows that the interaction term (SRC*father's occupation) is significantly different from zero for all survey years[3]. First, the average expected probabilities are determined, and then the relative risks are estimated using these probabilities.[4] As we have included in the all-India level calculation, the reference community for the son's occupation remains category V (laborers). As stated previously, relative risks represent the

Table 3.8 Relative Risk Ratios Based on MNL Eq. 3.1

Father's Occupation	*2000*		*2005*		*2012*		*2019*	
	RRR	*S.E.*	*RRR*	*S.E.*	*RRR*	*S.E.*	*RRR*	*S.E.*
	Son's Occupation: Senior Officials & Managers; Professionals-Associate Professionals, Clerks							
I	310.63	34.99	225.60	24.45	102.80	9.17	37.42	3.29
II	34.68	4.07	21.70	2.35	20.31	2.30	10.53	1.15
III	20.41	1.95	22.69	1.97	17.80	1.46	5.15	0.37
IV	19.47	2.20	10.77	1.13	9.80	0.95	7.93	0.70
Father's Occupation	**Son's Occupation: Service Workers and Shop & Market Sales Workers**							
I	46.54	4.64	27.71	2.70	16.34	1.51	10.15	0.96
II	141.74	11.80	71.40	5.36	74.03	7.25	27.70	2.74
III	7.84	0.58	7.71	0.50	6.58	0.55	3.07	0.23
IV	10.77	0.98	6.63	0.53	7.10	0.67	5.62	0.51
Father's Occupation	**Son's Occupation: Skilled Agricultural and Fishery Workers**							
I	34.38	3.42	49.52	4.86	22.00	2.27	10.85	1.70
II	11.26	1.14	16.52	1.47	17.40	2.15	8.43	1.55
III	111.12	6.84	99.97	6.35	115.86	9.72	98.71	11.28
IV	6.29	0.61	7.75	0.66	9.36	1.00	4.54	0.78
Father's Occupation	**Son's Occupation: Craft and Related Trades Workers; Plant and Machine Operators and Assemblers**							
I	17.61	1.57	11.37	1.03	6.15	0.48	4.86	0.42
II	9.90	0.80	6.68	0.50	7.04	0.67	5.01	0.50
III	4.60	0.25	4.73	0.24	4.51	0.27	2.81	0.17
IV	32.85	2.00	20.61	1.14	19.29	1.23	10.12	0.72

Source: Estimations are based on unit-level data of NSS EUS Rounds (2000, 2005, 2012) and PLFS 2019

Note: Exponentiated coefficients; S.E.: Standard Errors; Category I (Official and Managers, Professionals, Associate Professionals and Clerks), Category II (Service Workers and Shop and Market Sales Workers), Category III (Agriculture and allied services), Category IV (Craft and Related Trades Workers, Plant and Machine Operators and Assemblers) and Category V (laborers);
* $p<0.10$, ** $p<0.05$, *** $p<0.01$

ratio between two probabilities. The first likelihood is that the son will join one of the comparison groups (I, II, III, or IV). Second, the son will fall into the reference group V (laborers). In the sections that follow, these relative risks for different types of fathers' jobs are discussed.

3.5.3.2.1 RELATIVE RISKS OF ENTERING CATEGORY I OCCUPATIONS

In order to avoid ambiguity, instead of presenting all the relative risks, here are the chances of entering category I with the father working in categories I and II are presented. Relative Risks (RRs) indicate that "Hindu Others" with a father employed in category I occupations have a greater chance of entering category I occupations than falling into category V (see I, I/ V, I in column 2 of Table 3.9).

Table 3.9 MNL-Based Estimates (Category I Occupation)

SRCs	*Son's Occupation: Senior Officials & Managers; Professionals-Associate Professionals, Clerks*				
	RRs	*2000*	*2005*	*2012*	*2019*
STs	I,I/V,I	1.2308***	6.6667**	3.8750***	8.2000**
		(0.46)	(2.919)	(0.887)	(3.88)
	I,II/V,II	0.500**	0.263**	0.769**	1.111**
		(0.250)	(0.132)	(0.324)	(0.511)
SCs	I,I/V,I	2.439***	3.784***	3.231***	3.500***
		(0.452)	(0.699)	(0.459)	(0.60)
	I,II/V,II	0.300***	0.420***	1.172***	1.419***
		(0.08)	(0.093)	(0.296)	(0.33)
OBCs	I,I/V,I	7.600***	6.147***	9.785***	8.194***
		(1.205)	(0.765)	(1.156)	(1.10)
	I,II/V,II	0.660***	0.903***	1.737***	2.174***
		(0.108)	(0.129)	(0.289)	(0.387)
H Others	I,I/V,I	20.159***	18.200***	20.700***	12.702***
		(3.114)	(2.956)	(2.997)	(1.92)
	I,II/V,II	2.607***	1.894***	5.042***	3.400***
		(0.39)	(0.288)	(1.127)	(0.65)
Muslims	I,I/V,I	5.256***	10.625***	5.000***	4.348***
		(0.874)	(2.269)	(0.571)	(0.58)
	I,II/V,II	0.493***	0.506***	0.580***	1.724***
		(0.10)	(0.092)	(0.135)	(0.40)
Other Minorities	I,V/V,V	0.029***	0.045***	0.118***	0.178***
		(0.009)	(0.013)	(0.028)	(0.04)
	I,II/V,II	2.111**	1.333***	1.292***	1.111***
		(0.85)	(0.322)	(0.351)	(0.36)

Source: Estimations are based on unit-level data of NSS EUS Rounds (2000, 2005, 2012) and PLFS 2019.

Note: H Others denotes Hindu Others; Categories I (Officials and Managers), II (Service Workers and Shop and Market Sales Workers), III (Agriculture and allied services), IV (Craft and Related Trades Workers, Plant and Machine Operators and Assemblers), and V (Laborers); I, I/V, I denotes that the son of a category I occupation holder will enter the category I occupation rather than the category V occupation.

* $p<0.10$, ** $p<0.05$, *** $p<0.01$

This RR is 20.159, which is statistically significant at the 1 percent level of significance. In this case, the STs have the lowest RR (1.230***), followed by the SCs (2.439***). As we move from 2000 to 2019, the one community that has gained is OBC. Between 2000 and 2019, the majority of labor supply in category I occupations came from the sons of Hindu Others whose fathers worked in trade, service, and sales, followed by Hindu OBCs. Both RRs (5.080 and 2.532) are statistically significant at the 1 percent level of significance. The SCs have the lowest RR at the 1 percent significance level (0.300***) for father's category II. Regarding the Muslim community, their RRs are similar to the STs and SCs. Muslims have also improved their chances of entering category I occupations similar to STs and SCs. In this case, the RRs of SCs improved, but not as much as those of OBCs; STs improved even less than SCs.

The majority of sons born to professional, associate professional, and clerk fathers pursue careers similar to their fathers, demonstrating the benefit of being born into fortunate circumstances. In this case, the father's educational accomplishments, occupation, and social capital, parental expectations of children, children's aspirations, and family environment appear to have had a significant influence on their son's educational prospects and career choices (Erola et al., 2016; Kao & Thompson, 2003; Kim & Kulkarni, 2009). Other occupational groups, such as agriculture and assemblers, craft trades, and operators with a lower level of education who are thus unable to enter so-called decent work, are not eligible for these benefits. Additionally, it significantly reduces their descendants' chances of entering a respectable occupational group. This is true of all communities. Since the 2012 survey, however, there seems to have been a slight rise in the number of sons from occupations other than occupation category I who moved into occupation category I.

3.5.3.2.2 RELATIVE RISKS IN ENTERING CATEGORY II OCCUPATIONS

If the question of interest is who works in the category II occupations, then the answer is that across the socio-religious communities, immobility (the relative risk of staying in the father's category II) is high (Table 3.10). The second category that supplies employment in category II is the category I. The chances of working in category II and having a father also working in category II are the lowest for SCs and STs. The Hindu Others have the highest such relative risks across the years. Muslims and Hindu OBCs are similar; but their relative risks are far away than those of Hindu Others. The low chances of employment of SCs' and STs' sons in category II, even having a father working in the same group, show the disadvantages faced by these two communities. As we have already seen, the sons of category II are not entering category I among marginalized communities; now it is clear they can also not take place in category II. We will see later that this sort of mobility is absorbed into category IV (laborers). Employment in category II (Service Workers and Shop & Market Sales Workers) depends on capital, credit availability, and market linkages. STs and SCs appear to be at a disadvantage regarding such access.

3.5.3.2.3 RELATIVE RISKS IN ENTERING CATEGORY III OCCUPATIONS

The RRs for entering category III occupations rather than category V occupations for sons whose father is employed in category III can be seen to be declining, implying that sons are leaving their father's occupation, i.e., farming (Table 3.11). This decline shows that the sons of farmers are becoming laborers. Researchers have continuously reported that cultivators are becoming farm laborers (Birthal et al., 2014; Gordon & Gupta, 2004). Further, the rise in the supply of construction labor in the post-reform sector mainly came from the agriculture sector. Increasing land segmentation, poor profits from agriculture, increments in production costs, uncertainty in prices, and more frequent weather variations could be reasons for

Table 3.10 MNL-Based Estimates (Category II Occupation)

SRCs	*Son's Occupation: Service Workers and Shop & Market Sales Workers*				
	RRs	*2000*	*2005*	*2012*	*2019*
STs	II,I/V,I	0.385* (0.202)	0.833* (0.505)	0.750*** (0.234)	3.200* (1.64)
STs	II,II/V,II	1.750*** (0.633)	2.421*** (0.660)	3.538*** (1.111)	2.333** (0.93)
STs	II,V/V,V	0.010*** (0.004)	0.052*** (0.011)	0.026*** (0.009)	0.074*** (0.02)
SCs	II,I/V,I	0.902*** (0.205)	2.000*** (0.403)	0.538*** (0.113)	1.273*** (0.26)
SCs	II,II/V,II	1.900*** (0.281)	2.855*** (0.399)	3.931*** (0.818)	3.194*** (0.66)
SCs	II,V/V,V	0.042*** (0.005)	0.059*** (0.007)	0.095*** (0.011)	0.178*** (0.02)
OBCs	II,I/V,I	2.822*** (0.490)	1.467*** (0.220)	1.570*** (0.226)	2.113*** (0.33)
OBCs	II,II/V,II	7.362*** (0.809)	8.670*** (0.902)	9.193*** (1.282)	7.587*** (1.19)
OBCs	II,V/V,V	0.072*** (0.007)	0.137*** (0.011)	0.104*** (0.012)	0.238*** (0.02)
H Others	II,I/V,I	6.568*** (1.063)	5.650*** (0.969)	4.280*** (0.672)	3.702*** (0.61)
H Others	II,II/V,II	19.115*** (2.511)	13.985*** (1.782)	15.958*** (3.358)	7.686*** (1.38)
H Others	II,V/V,V	0.109*** (0.016)	0.190*** (0.026)	0.188*** (0.032)	0.376*** (0.06)
Muslims	II,I/V,I	1.860*** (0.352)	3.250*** (0.759)	1.283*** (0.178)	1.623*** (0.25)
Muslims	II,II/V,II	7.397*** (0.922)	5.865*** (0.673)	6.400*** (0.973)	7.034*** (1.40)
Muslims	II,V/V,V	0.105*** (0.015)	0.115*** (0.015)	0.102*** (0.016)	0.231*** (0.03)
Other Minorities	II,I/V,I	2.174*** (0.548)	4.467*** (1.276)	1.571*** (0.380)	2.133*** (0.67)
Other Minorities	II,II/V,II	20.111*** (6.868)	5.767*** (1.140)	3.042*** (0.716)	2.500*** (0.70)
Other Minorities	II,V/V,V	0.056*** (0.013)	0.098*** (0.019)	0.124*** (0.029)	0.264*** (0.05)

Source: Estimations are based on unit-level data of NSS EUS Rounds (2000, 2005, 2012) and PLFS 2019.

Note: Standard errors are in the bracket; H Others shows Hindu Others; Category I (Official and Managers, Professionals, Associate Professionals and Clerks), Category II (Service Workers and Shop and Market Sales Workers), Category III (Agriculture and allied services), Category IV (Craft and Related Trades Workers, Plant and Machine Operators and Assemblers) and Category V (laborers); I, I/V, I shows the son of category I occupation holder will enter in category I occupation rather than entering in category V occupation.
* $p<0.10$, ** $p<0.05$, *** $p<0.01$

Table 3.11 MNL-Based Estimates (Category III Occupation)

SRCs	*Son's Occupation: Skilled Agricultural and Fishery Workers*				
	RRs	*2000*	*2005*	*2012*	*2019*
STs	III,III/V,III	4.039***	4.451***	5.621***	3.939***
		(0.280)	(0.321)	(0.601)	(0.36)
SCs	III,III/V,III	3.312***	3.472***	3.189***	2.250***
		(0.220)	(0.227)	(0.290)	(0.20)
OBCs	III,III/V,III	8.477***	9.526***	8.895***	5.316***
		(0.406)	(0.469)	(0.574)	(0.34)
H Others	III,III/V,III	13.375***	11.842***	11.303***	6.220***
		(0.895)	(0.830)	(1.068)	(0.64)
Muslims	III,III/V,III	5.137***	5.106***	5.045***	2.691***
		(0.415)	(0.388)	(0.527)	(0.28)
Other Minorities	III,III/V,III	18.455***	24.282***	13.121***	6.621***
		(2.159)	(2.805)	(1.676)	(0.87)

Source: Estimations are based on unit-level data of NSS EUS Rounds (2000, 2005, 2012) and PLFS 2019.

Note: Standard errors are in brackets. H Others indicates Hindu Others, Other Mino indicates Other Minorities; Category I (Officials and Managers), Category II (Service Workers and Shop and Market Sales Workers), Category III (Agriculture and allied services), Category IV (Craft and Related Trades Workers, Plant and Machine Operators and Assemblers), and Category V (Laborers); I, I/V, I indicates that the son of a category I occupation holder will enter category I occupation rather than category V occupation.
* $p<0.10$, ** $p<0.05$, *** $p<0.01$

shrinking cultivation (Bhalla & Singh, 2009; Mishra, 2008). However, Table 3.11 shows the decline in relative risk of a farmer's son becoming a farmer (category III) rather than a laborer (category V) is not so much in the case of ST, SC, and OBCs. On the other hand, the same decline is more profound in the case of Hindu Others and Other Minorities. This could be because both of these communities started at high relative risk. In SCs and STs, the relative risk of joining agriculture (category III) was already low in 2000 compared to Hindu Others and Other Minorities.

3.5.3.2.4 RELATIVE RISKS IN ENTERING CATEGORY IV OCCUPATIONS

For sons whose fathers work in category IV occupations, the RRs for entering category IV occupations rather than category V occupations have remained relatively stable between 2000 and 2019 (Table 3.12). Category IV is one of the occupational categories with the highest RRs for Hindu OBCs and Muslims when it comes to the chance of entering category IV rather than category V, being a son of a category IV occupation holder father. In this case, Muslims have the highest RRs for 2005, 2012 and 2019 (all are significant at a 5 percent level of significance). It is a reference to the Muslim community's historical involvement in crafts and related trades, plant and machine operators, and assemblers.

Table 3.12 MNL-Based Estimates (Category IV Occupation)

SRCs	*Son's Occupation: Craft and Related Trades Workers; Plant and Machine Operators and Assemblers*				
	RRs	*2000*	*2005*	*2012*	*2019*
STs	IV, IV/V, IV	2.348***	2.068***	4.700***	4.471***
		(0.585)	(0.380)	(0.945)	(1.20)
SCs	IV,IV/V,IV	2.632***	3.295***	3.725***	3.539***
		(0.248)	(0.286)	(0.383)	(0.46)
OBCs	IV,IV/V,IV	6.186***	6.102***	6.931***	6.172***
		(0.534)	(0.448)	(0.650)	(0.69)
H Others	IV,IV/V,IV	8.140***	4.789***	5.339***	5.514***
		(1.143)	(0.604)	(0.777)	(0.99)
Muslims	IV,IV/V,IV	6.352***	6.943***	6.020***	4.800***
		(0.667)	(0.721)	(0.650)	(0.59)
Other Minorities	IV,IV/V,IV	5.194***	3.717***	5.933***	2.897***
		(1.019)	(0.575)	(1.171)	(0.54)

Source: Estimations are based on unit-level data of NSS EUS Rounds (2000, 2005, 2012) and PLFS 2019.

Note: Standard errors are in the brackets. H Others indicates Hindu Others, Other Mino indicates Other Minorities; Category I (Officials and Managers), Category II (Service Workers and Shop and Market Sales Workers), Category III (Agriculture and allied services), Category IV (Craft and Related Trades Workers, Plant and Machine Operators and Assemblers), and Category V (Laborers); I, I/V, I indicates that the son of a category I occupation holder may enter category I occupation rather than category V occupation.
* p<0.10, ** p<0.05, *** p<0.01

3.6 Conclusion

The aggregate mobility rates (M1) and (M2) for all India and for different SRCs indicate a progression in occupational mobility. However, it varies by occupational group and socio-religious community. For instance, in the case of occupational category I and a specific socio-religious community, such as STs, occupational mobility is the lowest. It has also been demonstrated that the labor supply in category I occupations is mainly coming from category I (majority) and category II (second highest). The sons of Hindu Others where the father works in occupations like trade, service, and business activities are occupying positions in category I occupations. In terms of entering the category I and category II occupations, the SCs and STs are facing barriers. The Hindu OBCs have improved their relative position and are better off compared to SCs, STs and Muslims.

Notes

1 The organized sector includes government, public-sector, and private corporate entities, as well as non-corporate private establishments with at least ten regular employees. The unorganized sector accounts for the lion's share of the economy. Formal employees are those who work in the organized sector and are compensated by at least one of their employer's social security programmes, such as health care insurance, gra-

tuity, and pension funds. Informal workers make up the rest of the work force (Ghose, 2016; Government of India, 2008).

2 The following Stata command has been used: mlogit Son_occupation ib(last).father_occupation, rrr base(last)

3 The Chi² values for 2000, 2005, 2012 and 2019 are as follows: 235.54, 250.56, 214.74, and 148.67. For all such values the p-value is 0.0000 with 80 degree of freedom. These test statistics are based on Wald type tests. Stata's testparm run these tests to check the effect of the interaction variable against zero.

4 Stata's 'margins' and 'nlcom' facilitates such estimations.

References

Alam, M. S., & Raju, S. (2007). Contextualising inter-, intra-religious and gendered literacy and educational disparities in rural Bihar. *Economic and Political Weekly*, *42*(18), 1613–1622.

Altham, P., & Ferrie, J. (2007). Comparing contingency tables: Tools for analyzing data from two groups cross-classified by two characteristics. *Historical Methods: A Journal of Quantitative and Interdisciplinary History*, *40*(1), 3–16.

Anti, Ø., Vaage, K., Aakvik, A., & Jacobsen, K. (2012). Intergenerational earnings mobility revisited: Estimates based on lifetime earnings. *Scandinavian Journal of Economics*, *114*(1), 1–23.

Azam, M. (2015). Intergenerational occupational mobility among men in India. *Journal of Development Studies*, *51*(10), 1389–1408. https://doi.org/10.1080/00220388.2015.1036040

Baruah, A. (2016). Occupational pattern and workforce participation of women in Indian rural Punjab: A caste perspective. *Millennial Asia*, *7*(2), 153–183. https://doi.org/10.1177/0976399616655029

Bhalla, G. S., & Singh, G. (2009). Economic liberalisation and Indian agriculture: A statewise analysis. *Economic and Political Weekly*, *44*(52), 34–44.

Birthal, P. S., Negi, D. S., Jha, A. K., & Singh, D. (2014). Income sources of farm households in India: Determinants, distributional consequences and policy implications. *Agricultural Economics Research Review*, *27*(1), 37. https://doi.org/10.5958/j.0974-0279.27.1.003

Blanden, J. (2013). Cross-country rankings in intergenerational mobility: A comparison of approaches from economics and sociology. *Journal of Economic Surveys*, *27*(1), 38–73. https://doi.org/10.1111/j.1467-6419.2011.00690.x

Bowles, S., & Gintis, H. (2002). The inheritance of inequality. *Journal of Economic Perspectives*, *16*(3), 3–30. https://doi.org/10.1257/089533002760278686

Breen, R., & Goldthorpe, J. H. (1997). Explaining educational differentials: Towards a formal rational action theory. In *Rationality and society* (Vol. 9, No. 3). https://doi.org/10.1177/104346397009003002

Breen, R., & Jonsson, J. O. (2005). Inequality of opportunity in comparative perspective: Recent research on educational attainment and social mobility. *Annual Review of Sociology*, *31*(1), 223–243. https://doi.org/10.1146/annurev.soc.31.041304.122232

Buis, M. L. (2010). Stata tip 87: Interpretation of interactions in nonlinear models. *STATA Journal*, *10*(2), 305–308.

Chadha, G., & Sahu, P. (2002). Post-reform setbacks in rural employment: Issues that need further scrutiny. *Economic and Political Weekly*, *37*(21), 1998–2026. http://www.jstor.org

Cheng, S., & Long, J. S. (2007). Testing for IIA in the multinomial logit model. *Sociological Methods AMD Research*, *35*(4), 583–600. https://cran.r-project.org/web/packages/mlogit/index.html

Constant, A., & Zimmermann, K. F. (2003). *Occupational choice across generations* (IZA Discussion Papers, No. 975; Institute of Labor Economics, Bonn). https://www.econstor.eu/handle/10419/20211

Corak, M. (2013). Income inequality, equality of opportunity, and intergenerational mobility. *Journal of Economic Perspectives*, *27*(3), 79–102. https://doi.org/10.1257/jep.27.3.79

Doruk, Ö. T., Pastore, F., & Yavuz, H. B. (2003). Intergenerational occupational mobility in Latin American economies: An empirical approach. *IZA Discussion Paper*, *13050*.

Emran, M. S., & Shilpi, F. (2011). Intergenerational occupational mobility in rural economy: Evidence from Nepal and Vietnam. *Journal of Human Resources*, *46*(2), 427–458. https://doi.org/10.1353/jhr.2011.0009

Erola, J., Jalonen, S., & Lehti, H. (2016). Parental education, class and income over early life course and children's achievement. *Research in Social Stratification and Mobility*, *44*, 33–43. https://doi.org/10.1016/j.rssm.2016.01.003

Fry, T. R. L., & Harris, M. N. (1996). A Monte Carlo study of tests for the independence of irrelevant alternatives property. *Transportation Research: Part B, Methodological*, *30*(1), 19–30. https://ageconsearch.umn.edu/record/267413/files/monash-156.pdf

Fry, T. R. L., & Harris, M. N. (1998). Testing for independence of irrelevant alternatives: Some Empirical results. *Sociological Methods and Research*, *26*(3), 401–423.

Gang, I. N., Sen, K., & Yun, M. S. (2012). Is caste destiny? Occupational diversification among dalits in rural India. In *IZA Discussion Papers* (Vol. 6295, No. 2). https://doi.org/10.1057/s41287-016-0011-1

Ghose, A. K. (2016). *India employment report challenges and the imperative of manufacturing-led growth*. Oxford University Press.

Goel, M. (2017). Inequality between and within skill groups: The curious case of India. *World Development*, *93*, 153–176. https://doi.org/10.1016/j.worlddev.2016.12.024

Gordon, J., & Gupta, P. (2004). Understanding India's services revolution. *IMF Working Papers*, *4*(171), 1. https://doi.org/10.5089/9781451858532.001

Government of India (2008). National commission for enterprises in the unorganised sector. http://dcmsme.gov.in/Report_Statistical_Issues_Informal_Economy.pdf

Hausman, J., & McFadden, D. (1984). Specification tests for the multinomial logit model. *Econometrica*, *52*(5), 1219–1240.

Hausman, J. A. (1978). Specification tests in econometrics. *Econometrica*, *46*(6), 1251–1271. http://www.jstor.org/stable/1913827%5Cnhttp://www.jstor.org/%5Cnhttp://www.jstor.org/action/showPublisher?publisherCode=econosoc.%5Cnhttp://www.jstor.org

Hout, M., & Guest, A. M. (2013). Intergenerational occupational mobility in GreatBritain and the United States since 1850: Comment. *American Economic Review*, *103*(5), 2021–2040. https://doi.org/10.1257/aer.103.5.2021

Jajoria, D., & Jatav, M. (2020). Is periodic labour force survey, 2017–18 comparable with employment–unemployment survey, 2011–12? *Economic and Political Weekly*, *55*(3), 12–16.

Kalleberg, A. L. (2009). Precarious work, insecure workers: Employment relations in transition. *American Sociological Review*, *74*(1), 1–22. https://doi.org/10.1177/000312240907400101

Kannan, K. P., & Raveendran, G. (2019). From jobless to job-loss growth: Gainers and losers in India's employment performance during 2012–2018. *Economic and Political Weekly*, *54*(44), 38–44.

Kao, G., & Thompson, J. S. (2003). Racial and ethnic stratification in educational achievement and attainment. *Annual Review of Sociology*, *29*(1), 417–442. https://doi.org/10.1146/annurev.soc.29.010202.100019

Keane, M. P. (1992). A note on identification in the multinomial probit model. *Journal of Business and Economic Statistics*, *10*(2), 193–200. https://doi.org/10.1080/07350015.1992.10509898

Kim, D. Y., & Kulkarni, V. S. (2009). The role of father's occupation on intergenerational educational and occupational mobility: The case of second-generation Chinese Americans in New York. *Sociological Forum*, *24*(1), 104–134.

Kropko, J. (2007). *Choosing between multinomial logit and multinomial probit models for analysis of unordered choice data*. The University of North Carolina at Chapel Hill. https://www.proquest.com/docview/304831227?pq-origsite=gscholar&fromopenview=true

Kulkarni, P. M. (2002). *Inter-state variations in human development differentials among social groups in India* (NCAER Working Paper Series No. 80; National Council of Applied Economic Research, New Delhi, Vol. 80). https://www.ncaer.org/publication_details.php?pID=76

Levine, D. I., & Mazumder, B. (1999). *Choosing the right parents: Changes in the intergenerational transmission of inequality between 1980 and the early 1990s*. (IRLE Working Paper no. 72; Institute for Research on Labor and Employment UC Berkeley). https://doi.org/10.2139/ssrn.323881

Long, J., & Ferrie, J. (2015). Grandfathers Matter (ed): Occupational mobility across three generations in the U. S. and Britain, 1850–1910. *Mimeo*, *1992*, 1–27.

Mehrotra, S., & Parida, J. K. (2019). *India's employment crisis: Rising education levels and falling non-agricultural job growth. October*, 1–22.

Mishra, S. (2008). Risks, farmers' suicides and agrarian crisis in India: Is there a way out? *Indian Journal of Agricultural Economics*, *63*(1), 38–54.

Modalsli, J. (2017). Intergenerational mobility in Norway, 1865–2011. *Scandinavian Journal of Economics*, *119*(1), 34–71. https://doi.org/10.1111/sjoe.12196

Mondal, S. R. (2000). Muslim population in India: Some demographic and socio-economic features India. *International Journal of Anthropology*, *15*(1), 91–107.

Motiram, S., & Singh, A. (2012). How close does the apple fall to the tree? Some evidence from India on intergenerational occupational mobility. *Economic and Political Weekly*, *47*(40), 56–65. http://www.jstor.org/stable/41720217

NCO. (2004). *National classification of occupation*. Ministry of Statistics and Programme Implementation, Government of India. https://labor.gov.in/sites/default/files/CodeStructure.pdf

NSSO. (2000). Employment and unemployment situation in India, fifty Fifth round (July 1990–June 2000). Ministry of Statistics and Programme Implementation, Government of India. http://microdata.gov.in/nada43/index.php/catalog/EUE

NSSO. (2005). Employment and unemployment situation in India, sixty first round (July 2004–June 2005). Ministry of Statistics and Programme Implementation, Government of India. http://microdata.gov.in/nada43/index.php/catalog/EUE.

NSSO. (2012). Employment and unemployment situation in India, sixty eighth round (July 2011–June 2012). Ministry of Statistics and Programme Implementation, Government of India. http://microdata.gov.in/nada43/index.php/catalog/EUE.

PLFS. (2019). Periodic labour force survey (July 2018–June 2019). Ministry of Statistics and Programme Implementation, Government of India. http://microdata.gov.in/nada43/index.php/catalog/EUE.

Reddy, A. B. (2015). Changes in intergenerational occupational mobility in India: Evidence from national sample surveys, 1983–2012. *World Development, 76*, 329–343. https://doi.org/10.1016/j.worlddev.2015.07.012

Sinha, R. (2018). Closer, but no cigar: Intergenerational mobility across caste groups in India. In *Policy research working paper WPS8401, World Bank Group, development research group* (Issue April). https://doi.org/10.1596/1813-9450-8401

Small, K. A., & Hsiao, C. (1985). Multinomial logit specification tests. *International Econometric Review, 26*(3), 619–627.

Standing, G. (1999). Global feminization through flexible labor. *World Development, 27*(3), 583–602. https://doi.org/10.1016/0305-750X(89)90170-8

Thomas, J. J. (2020). Labour Market Changes in India, 2005–18: Missing the Demographic Window of Opportunity? *Economic and Political Weekly, 55*(34), 57–63.

Vijverberg, W. (2011). Testing for IIA with the Hausman-McFadden test. In *IZA Discussion Papers* (IZA Discussion Papers, No. 5826; Institute for the Study of Labor, Bonn, Issue 5826). http://nbn-resolving.de/urn:nbn:de:101:1-201107133399%0AThis

Vosko, L. F. (2010). *Managing the margins: Gender, citizenship, and the international regulation of precarious employment.* Oxford University Press.

Xie, Y., & Killewald, A. (2013). Intergenerational occupational mobility in Great Britain and the United States since 1850: Comment. *American Economic Review, 103*(5), 2003–2020. https://doi.org/10.1257/aer.103.5.2003

Yaschine, I., Vargas, D., Huffman, C., Carreño, H., Hernández, U., & Mendoza, T. (2019). *Long-term study of PROSPERA on intergenerational occupational mobility* (World Bank Policy Research Working Paper 8999; The World Bank, Washington DC, Issue September). http://www.worldbank.org/prwp

Appendix

Table A-3.13 Sample Characteristics

	2000		*2005*		*2012*		*2019*	
Total number of individuals surveyed	5,96,686		6,02,814		4,56,999		4,20,757	
Total number of father-son pair in MNL Analysis (Age 15 to 45)								
All	34,534	%	37,374	%	25,705	%	19,666	%
Hindu ST	2,399	6.95	2,472	6.62	1,790	6.96	1,591	8.09
Hindu SC	4,749	13.75	5,192	13.9	3,505	13.64	3,168	16.11
Hindu OBC	10,795	31.26	12,657	33.88	8,548	33.25	6,406	32.57
Hindu Others	8,998	26.06	7,852	21.02	5,377	20.92	3,643	18.52
Muslims	4,531	13.12	5,205	13.93	4,039	15.71	3,157	16.05
Other Minorities	3,062	8.87	3,981	10.66	2,446	9.52	1,701	8.65

Source: Estimations are based on Unit-level data of NSS 2000, 2005, 2012 and PLFS 2019.

Table A-3.14 Hausman Independence of Irrelevant Alternatives (IIA) Tests For Eq. 3.1

Outcome	*Chi2*	*df*	*p-value*	*Evidence*	*Outcome*	*Chi2*	*df*	*p-value*	*Evidence*
2000					**2005**				
I	-4.50E+03	5	1.00	for Ho	I	-5.50E+03	7	1.00	for Ho
II	-4.50E+03	7	1.00	for Ho	II	-5.50E+03	7	1.00	for Ho
III	-0.001	13	1.00	for Ho	III	-198.332	5	1.00	for Ho
IV	-4.50E+03	7	1.00	for Ho	IV	-5.50E+03	5	1.00	for Ho
V	-4.50E+03	10	1.00	for Ho	V	-5.50E+03	6	1.00	for Ho
2012					**2019**				
I	-2.40E+03	5	1.00	for Ho	I	-695.662	6	1.00	for Ho
II	-2.40E+03	5	1.00	for Ho	II	-695.662	6	1.00	for Ho
III	-530.363	5	1.00	for Ho	III	-695.662	7	1.00	for Ho
IV	-2.40E+03	5	1.00	for Ho	IV	-1.40E+03	5	1.00	for Ho
V	-2.40E+03	6	1.00	for Ho	V	-695.662	6	1.00	for Ho

Source: Estimations are based on Unit-level data of NSS 2000, 2005, 2012 and PLFS 2019.

Note: The Null Hypothesis (H0) that the model holds IIA assumption. Outcome shows the five occupational categories of Sons. df: degrees of freedom.

4 What Drives Occupational Mobility

An Analysis of Parental, Household and Locational Characteristics

4.1 Introduction

In this chapter, we use logit models to explore the distribution of employment and occupational mobility across India's various socio-religious communities. The most intriguing question will be to find out which groups of the socio-religious communities are more likely to work in the category I occupational categories (Officials and Managers, Professionals, Associate Professionals and Clerks) and to what extent parental background, household characteristics and other variables play a role in this.

It is important to note that the Indian economy underwent major structural changes as a result of the 1991 economic reforms. There was a perceptible reduction in agriculture employment due to agricultural stagnation and the availability of jobs in other rapidly expanding industries, as workers began to quit agriculture (Reddy, 2015; Thomas, 2014). For instance, high-tech industries that produce high-paying jobs and GDP growth include telecommunications, software, information technology and computer hardware (Mehrotra et al., 2014; Mukherjee & Majumder, 2011; Ramaswamy & Agrawal, 2012). From 2012 to 2018, the Periodic Labour Force Survey (PLFS) revealed a reduction in manufacturing employment, an increase in education-skilled positions, and an increase in the workforce aged 15 to 59 years (Kannan & Raveendran, 2019; Mehrotra & Parida, 2019; Thomas, 2020).

This chapter is divided into the following sections: Section 4.2 (Theoretical Development); Section 4.3 (Empirics); Section 4.4 (Data and Methodology); Sections 4.5–4.6 (Results and Discussion); and Section 4.7 (Conclusions).

4.2 Theoretical Development

During the 1970s and 1980s, social stratification theories were at the forefront of social mobility research. The theoretical foundations of social mobility research were subsequently supplanted by descriptive statistics and variations in the mobility patterns of black and white, men and women, and majority and minority groups (Kerbo, 2006, p. 12). The growth of social stratification theories has rekindled renewed interest in social mobility research (Bian, 2002; Rytina, 2000). In the

DOI: 10.4324/9781003361299-4

literature on social mobility, the functionalist perspective dominates all notions of social stratification. In this method, occupational categories are used as proxies for social rank (Domanski & Sawinski, 1987). To rank such occupational categories, education, skills, tasks and income are usually employed. Initially, as Marx argued, stratification ideas were linked to society's production system. In response to the groundbreaking work of some outstanding mobility researchers who used a functional approach, Wright developed a Marxian framework of identified classes (Hauser, 1980; Stevens & Featherman, 1981). The functional approach to studying mobility has diverged from Wright's conclusions and interpretation (Western & Wright, 1994). Wright employed a four-class classification system that corresponded to the manufacturing system. The "capitalist class" controls the means of production; the "manager class" oversees the production process; the "workers" are compelled to work for the capitalist class; and the "petty bourgeoisie" administers small production facilities with limited resources. However, the majority of social mobility studies adopt a functional perspective, where a person's employment serves as a surrogate for their social standing.

In the context of India, Agarwala's seminal work (2006) significantly contributes a significant addition to the understanding of classes, production systems and evolving labor dynamics. She proposed a four-tiered class structure, where she identified "informal workers" as a distinct class in response to liberalization and globalization. The dominant classes (capitalists, executives and professionals), the petty bourgeoisie/micro-entrepreneurs or self-employed, the formal proletariat (skilled and unskilled workers with wage contracts), and the informal proletariat (casual workers and regular workers in informal enterprises) are the four tiers of the class structure (2006). Given the scale and diversity of the self-employed (petty bourgeoisie/micro-entrepreneurs) class in India, the functional approach, however, seems more practical. Own-account employees, employers, agricultural producers (marginal, small and large), ferry hawkers, retail vendors and others are included in this class of labor. The NCO-9 division occupational structure is a good example of a well-defined occupational structure that is used by the functional approach to clearly identify the roles of each occupational group.

4.3 Empirics

As discussed in Chapter 1 (Table 1.3), about 33.31 million (10.04 percent) people were employed in category I occupations (officials and managers, professionals, associate professionals and clerks) in year 2000. With a growth of 143.21 percent, the total jobs in these occupations reached 81.04 million in the year 2019. From 2000 to 2005 and from 2012 to 2019, the job increase in these four occupations was modest (6.13 and 16.85 million jobs, respectively), with the most prominent addition occurring between 2005 and 2012 (24.75 million).

Among SRCs, in the year 2019, Hindu Others held 34.51 percent of the jobs of the total available jobs in these four occupations (Chapter 1, Table 1.6). Their share, nevertheless, declined by 13.4 percent in the year 2019 compared with

2000. This decrease in the share of Hindu Others was primarily due to the increase in the share of Hindu OBCs from 22.38 percent in 2000 to 32.43 percent in 2019. Muslim OBCs also saw their proportion of these jobs climb from 2.53 percent in 2000 to 6.68 percent in 2019. Hindu STs, on the other hand, remained the least represented group in these four occupations (3.20 percent), making little progress between 2000 and 2019.

4.4 Data and Methodology

4.4.1 Data

Data for this study were derived from the National Sample Employment-Unemployment Survey (EUS) quinquennial rounds 1999–00 (55th), 2004–05 (61st), 2011–12 (68th), and 2019–19 (PLFS), also known as 2000, 2005, 2012 and 2019. For details, refer to Chapter 3 (section 3.2).

4.4.2 Methodology

The estimation strategy is that we divide the entire mobility sample of the sons into two parts. First, those who have managed to secure employment in the category I occupations (logit = 1). Second, those who are not employed in these occupations (logit=0).

For higher occupational attainment:

$$\Pr\left(Y_i = 1 / X_i\right) = F\left(X_i'\beta\right)$$

$$\begin{aligned} \text{Where} \quad X_i'\beta &= \alpha + \beta_1 \text{age}_i + \beta_2 \text{ Son's Education}_i + \beta_3 \text{ HH Size}_i \\ &+ \beta_4 \left(\text{Rural} - \text{Urban}\right)_i + \beta_5 \text{ SRC}_i + \beta_6 \text{ Father's Occupation}_i \\ &+ \beta_7 \text{ Landholding} + \beta_8 \text{ MPCE Qurtiles} + \beta_9 \text{ Region} \end{aligned} \tag{4.1}$$

Here, Y_i is the nominal dependent variable where 1 represents if the son has moved or stayed in the category I occupations (Officials & Managers, Professionals, Associate Professionals and Clerks), 0 otherwise.

In the above equation, the son's education is classified into five different categories: no formal schooling, primary and middle, up to secondary, senior secondary, and graduate and above. The landholding data have been grouped into the following five categories: No landholding or less than 0.01 hectares is considered as "landless"; greater than 0.01 hectare but less than equal to 1 hectare as "marginal"; greater than 1 hectare but less than equal to 2 hectares as "small"; greater than 2 hectares but less than equal to 4 hectares as "medium"; greater than 4 hectares as "large". This landholding classification is slightly different from that in the Chapter 3 analysis.

The fathers' occupations are sub-divided into five occupational categories, namely; category I (Officials and Managers, Professionals, Associate Professionals, Clerks), category II (Service Workers and Shop and Market Sales Workers), category III (Agriculture and allied services), category IV (Craft and Related Trades Workers, Plant and Machine Operators and Assemblers) and category V (Laborers).

The geographical regions are classified as North, Central, East, Northeast, West and South, with the Central region serving as a reference category. The model has four quartiles of real monthly per capita consumption expenditure (MPCE), with the first quartile serving as the reference group.

For the 2019 survey, the model was run without the "landholding" variable because there were no data on it in the PLFS-2018-19.

4.4.3 Model Selection

To look at the variation in the impact of each explanatory variable on the occupational attainment of sons among socio-religious groups, we have two options. First, regress eq. 4.1 for each socio-religious group separately. Second, insert interaction terms between SRC and each explanatory variable. In the case of the first option, we not only get a reduced sample size but also encounter different impacts of explanatory variables for each SRC. In reality, the impact of each explanatory variable may not differ significantly for different SRCs. It is not just because we are running separate regressions that we are getting different values. In the second option, a full interaction model can be run, where each explanatory variable interacts with SRC. However, there is no need to go for a full interaction model, and we should include only significant interaction terms. We have adopted a strategy in which a no-interaction model has been run. After that, one interaction term has been added to each step. This interaction term's joint impact has been tested; if the term is jointly significant, we keep it in the model; otherwise, it is dropped. The same procedure has been repeated for each explanatory variable.

Estimating different models for each group might result in a loss of statistical power, i.e., it is less likely to reject the null when it is false. Likewise, including too many interaction terms can lead to the same problem. The inclusion of extraneous variables (in this case, extraneous interaction terms) should be avoided if possible.

Following the forward selection criterion, we started from the no-interaction model, and in each step, a new interaction term has been included (Table 4.1). According to the jointly significant test, interaction terms added in steps 2, 4 and 7 are significant; the son's education, the father's occupation and land size interact with SRCs. This means that the impact of a son's education, his father's occupation and land size varies significantly across socio-religious groups in terms of higher occupational attainment.

Table 4.1 Model Selection Steps and Associated Test Results

Step	*Interaction Entered*	*Interaction Removed*	*Number of Interaction*	*chi2*	*P > chi2*	*AIC*
1	SRC*Age		1	6.96	0.2234	13211.828
2	SRC*Son's Education	SRC*Age	1	78.62	0.0000	13208.741
3	SRC*HH Size		2	7.20	0.2065	13171.377
4	SRC*Father's Occupation	SRC*HH Size	2	44.52	0.0013	13164.115
5	SRC*MPCE		3	11.64	0.7059	13182.406
6	SRC*Sector	SRC*MPCE	3	8.25	0.1429	13165.796
7	SRC*Land Size	SRC*Sector	3	41.92	0.0028	13161.694
8	SRC*Region		4	37.58	0.0508	13173.187

Note: These mentioned steps involve data from the year 2000; Chi2 statistic is a result of Wald type test. AIC shows akaike information criteria.

The selected model for the analysis is based on the following specification:

$$\Pr(Y_i = 1 / X_i) = F\left(X'_i \beta\right)$$

Where $X_i'\beta = \alpha + \beta_1 \text{ age}_i + \beta_2 \text{ Son's Education}_i + \beta_3 \; HH \text{ Size}_i$

$$+\beta_4 \left(\text{Rural} - \text{Urban}\right)_i + \beta_5 \text{SRC}_i + \beta_6 \text{ Father's Occupation}_i$$

$$+\beta_7 \text{ Landholding} + \beta_8 \text{ MPCE Qurtiles}$$

$$+\beta_9 \text{ Region} + \beta_{10} \text{ SRC}_i * \text{Son's Education}_i + \beta_{11} \text{SRC}_i * \text{Father's Education}_i$$

$$+\beta_{12} \text{ SRC}_i * \text{Landholding} \qquad (4.2)$$

Given the large number of explanatory factors, it is prudent to avoid risk ratio estimation. The average predicted probabilities, therefore, are estimated using logit eq. 4.2, because the primary concern is the occupational attainment of sons in specific occupations.

4.5 Results

4.5.1 Main Effects

Table 4.2 shows the average estimated probabilities of achieving category I occupations associated with each explanatory variable (main). With each level of age, the average estimated probability of entering category I occupations increases (15, 25, 35, 45). It was lowest at the age of 15 (0.067) and highest at the age of 45 (0.173) in the year 2000. The average predicted probability linked to higher age groups appears to have grown over the study period. The difference between the average predicted probability of being a 25-year-old

Table 4.2 Logit Model-Based Average Predicted Probability of Sons Entering Higher Occupations

Variables	*2000*		*2005*		*2012*		*2019*	
	Aver. Prob.	*S.E.*	*Aver. Prob.*	*S.E.*	*Aver. Prob.*	*S.E.*	*Aver. Prob.*	*S.E.*
Age								
Age=15	0.067	0.002	0.079	0.002	0.153	0.004	0.151	0.005
Age=25	0.094	0.001	0.104	0.001	0.185	0.002	0.191	0.003
Age=35	0.128	0.003	0.134	0.003	0.221	0.004	0.238	0.005
Age=45	0.173	0.007	0.171	0.007	0.261	0.008	0.291	0.010
Household Size								
HH Size=2	0.096	0.003	0.119	0.003	0.183	0.004	0.188	0.007
HH Size=5	0.097	0.002	0.113	0.002	0.189	0.002	0.189	0.007
HH Size=8	0.097	0.001	0.107	0.001	0.194	0.002	0.189	0.006
HH Size=11	0.098	0.002	0.102	0.002	0.200	0.004	0.190	0.006
HH Size=14	0.098	0.003	0.096	0.003	0.205	0.006	0.191	0.006
Sector								
Rural	0.089	0.002	0.102	0.002	0.177	0.003	0.182	0.004
Urban	0.109	0.003	0.123	0.003	0.221	0.004	0.223	0.004
SRCs								
Hindu ST	0.089	0.010	0.131	0.008	0.208	0.010	0.216	0.012
Hindu SC	0.108	0.006	0.119	0.005	0.197	0.007	0.200	0.007
Hindu OBC	0.097	0.003	0.102	0.002	0.193	0.004	0.197	0.004
Hindu Others	0.106	0.003	0.111	0.003	0.208	0.005	0.208	0.006
Muslims	0.110	0.005	0.132	0.005	0.202	0.006	0.217	0.007
Other Minorities	0.087	0.004	0.106	0.004	0.161	0.006	0.190	0.008
Sons' Education								
No formal Education	0.036	0.004	0.034	0.004	0.101	0.010	0.093	0.016
Primary & Middle	0.056	0.002	0.056	0.002	0.124	0.003	0.097	0.004
Up to Secondary	0.097	0.003	0.099	0.004	0.145	0.004	0.134	0.005
Up to Senior Sec.	0.150	0.006	0.188	0.006	0.229	0.006	0.214	0.007

Grad & Above	0.291	0.010	0.326	0.009	0.409	0.009	0.415	0.008
Fathers' Occupation								
Category I	0.265	0.007	0.290	0.007	0.445	0.007	0.390	0.009
Category II	0.047	0.003	0.055	0.003	0.102	0.005	0.143	0.007
Category III	0.078	0.003	0.093	0.002	0.149	0.004	0.157	0.005
Category IV	0.064	0.004	0.069	0.004	0.112	0.005	0.168	0.006
Category V	0.051	0.004	0.059	0.005	0.095	0.006	0.151	0.007
Land Holding								
Landless	0.084	0.004	0.098	0.004	0.193	0.006	-	-
Small	0.088	0.002	0.106	0.002	0.181	0.003	-	-
Marginal	0.072	0.004	0.081	0.003	0.160	0.006	-	-
Medium	0.075	0.004	0.081	0.004	0.166	0.007	-	-
Large	0.062	0.004	0.079	0.003	0.142	0.005	-	-
MPCE Quartiles								
Q1	0.078	0.004	0.086	0.005	0.157	0.005	0.152	0.006
Q2	0.088	0.003	0.092	0.003	0.178	0.004	0.183	0.005
Q3	0.100	0.002	0.108	0.003	0.196	0.004	0.201	0.005
Q4	0.107	0.003	0.120	0.003	0.234	0.005	0.236	0.005
Region								
Central	0.070	0.003	0.087	0.003	0.162	0.005	0.161	0.006
East	0.086	0.003	0.100	0.003	0.222	0.005	0.226	0.007
North	0.104	0.003	0.119	0.003	0.178	0.004	0.192	0.005
North East	0.104	0.006	0.096	0.004	0.188	0.007	0.209	0.009
South	0.111	0.003	0.132	0.004	0.210	0.005	0.216	0.006
West	0.115	0.004	0.112	0.004	0.195	0.005	0.205	0.006
Observations	34510		37359		25705		19665	

Note: Avg. Prob.: Average Predicted Probabilities; S.E.: Standard Errors; All probabilities presented here are significant at 1% level of significance; for 2019, the land data is not available; Category I (Officials and Managers, Professionals, Associate Professionals, Clerks), category II (Service Workers and Shop and Market Sales Workers), category III (Agriculture and allied services), category IV (Craft and Related Trades Workers, Plant and Machine Operators and Assemblers) and category V (Laborers).

Source: Estimations are based on unit-level data of NSS EUS Rounds (2000, 2005, 2012) and PLFS 2019.

worker and a 45-year-old worker has widened significantly. It could be because, as the need for education and skills in the four occupations grows, people of a certain age are able to enter them. The data show that 35 percent of adults in the age group of 20–24 were enrolled in educational institutions in 2019, up from 21.8 percent in 2000 (Chowdhury, 2011). In 2000, 22.90 percent of males between the ages of 15 and 29 were educated, a figure that rose to 37.3 percent in 2019 (Thomas, 2020). These statistics indicate that individuals are spending more time in educational institutions prior to entering the skilled labor sector. Additionally, as shown in Table 4.2, the data suggest that being an urban worker has an advantage when transitioning between the four occupations. The environment in cities is better for these jobs, which is a benefit for city dwellers over their rural counterparts.

The key finding is that, in 2019, the son's education is more relevant in terms of upward career mobility than it was in 2000. From the senior secondary level onwards, there are reasonable prospects of entering category I occupations. Graduates and above have the best chance of entering one of four occupations (0.291 in 2000 and 0.415 in 2019). Higher occupational accomplishments are only available to sons whose fathers are already working in category I occupations. In 2019, the average predicted probability of entering four occupations with a parent in a category I occupation climbed to 0.390 from 0.265 in 2000. The difference between being a son of a father who works in a category I occupation and being a son of a father who works in something other than a category I occupation narrowed in 2019. It demonstrates that the number of sons with access to four occupations is growing among those whose parents do not have a higher occupational background. According to the average predicted probabilities associated with the MPCE quartiles, increasing consumption levels increase the likelihood of entering into higher employment. The gap between the quartiles, on the other hand, is not as wide.

4.5.2 Interaction Effects

The average predicted probabilities estimated for the interaction terms SRC and Son's education are presented in Figure 4.1. In the year 2000, the average predicted probabilities of securing employment in the category I occupations having graduation and above education were equal for SCs, OBCs, Muslims and Other Minorities. The exact probability for the STs was the lowest (0.214). However, in the year 2019, Other Minorities progressed more than SCs, OBCs and Muslims. The average predicted probability of attaining higher occupations with a graduation and above degree increased to 0.51 for Hindu Others, the highest among SRCs. In the period between 2000 and 2019, STs also reported progress in the probability of attaining category I occupations by having higher education.

The average predicted probabilities of attaining a category I occupation with a different level of father's occupation are presented in Figure 4.2. In the year 2000, even after belonging to a category I occupation holder father, an ST son had negligible chances of entering into similar occupations. In the case of other

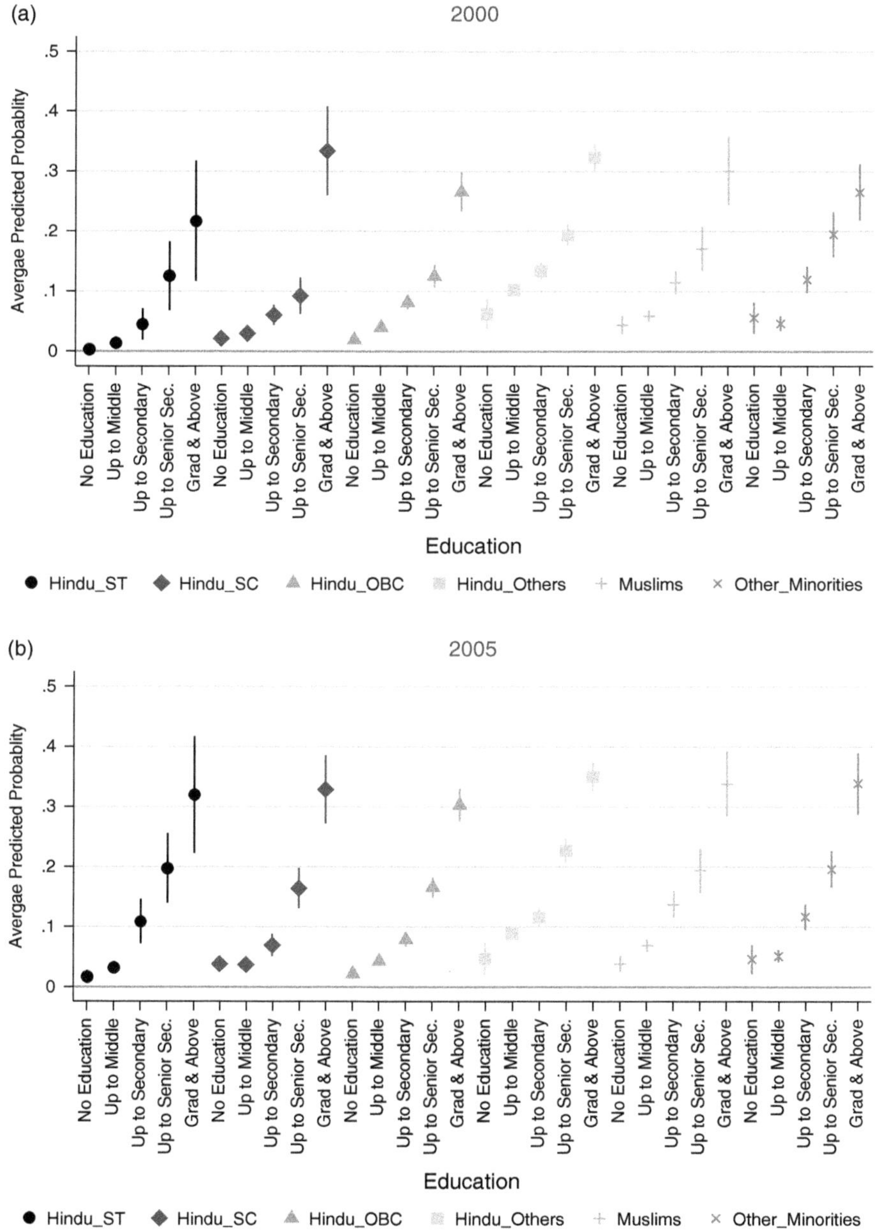

Figure 4.1 Interaction Effect (Son's Education and SRCs) Based on Logit Eq. 4.2. Note: Avg. Pr. Prob.: Average Predicted Probabilities; S.E.: Standard Errors; All probabilities presented here are significant at 1% level of significance; Category I (Officials and Managers, Professionals, Associate Professionals, Clerks). Source: Estimations are based on unit-level data of NSS EUS Rounds (2000, 2005, 2012) and PLFS 2019.

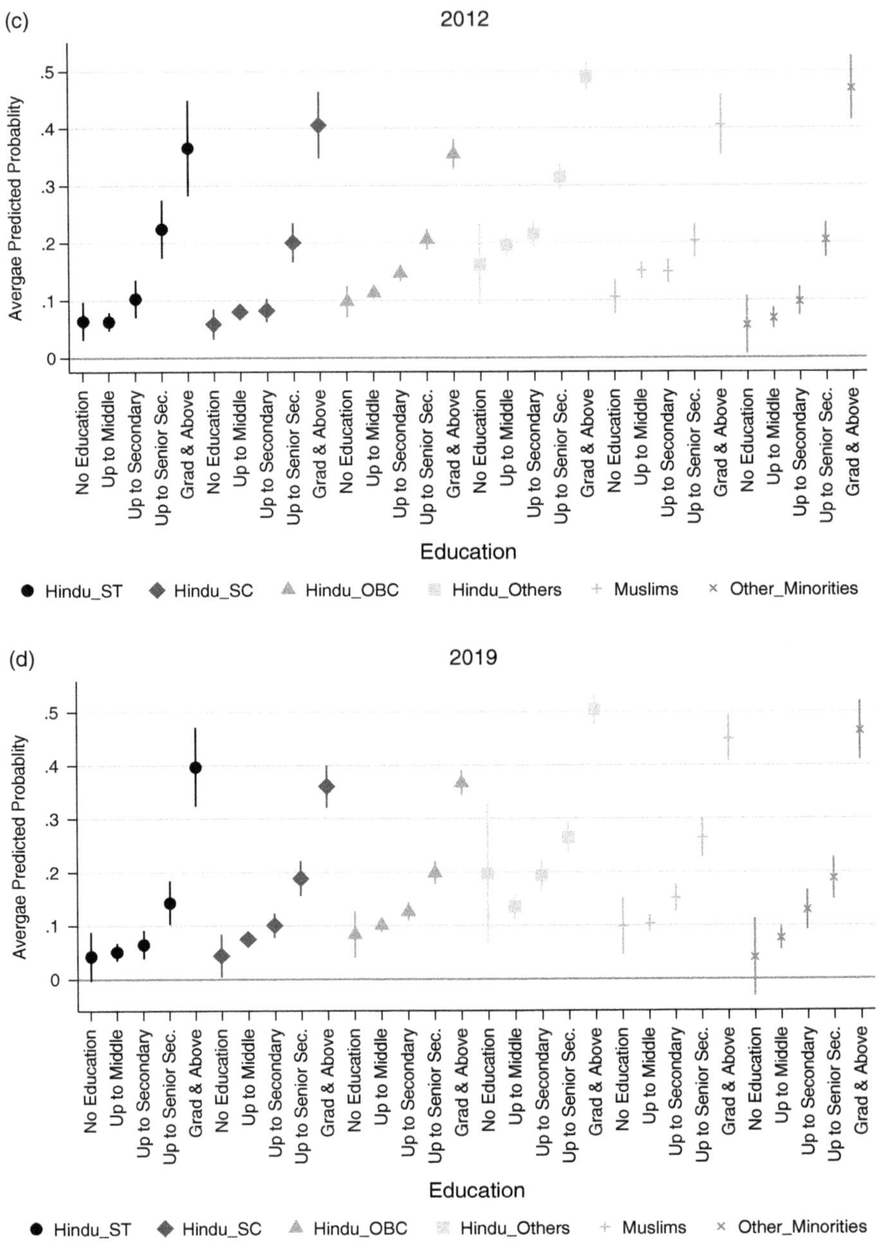

Figure 4.1 (Continued)

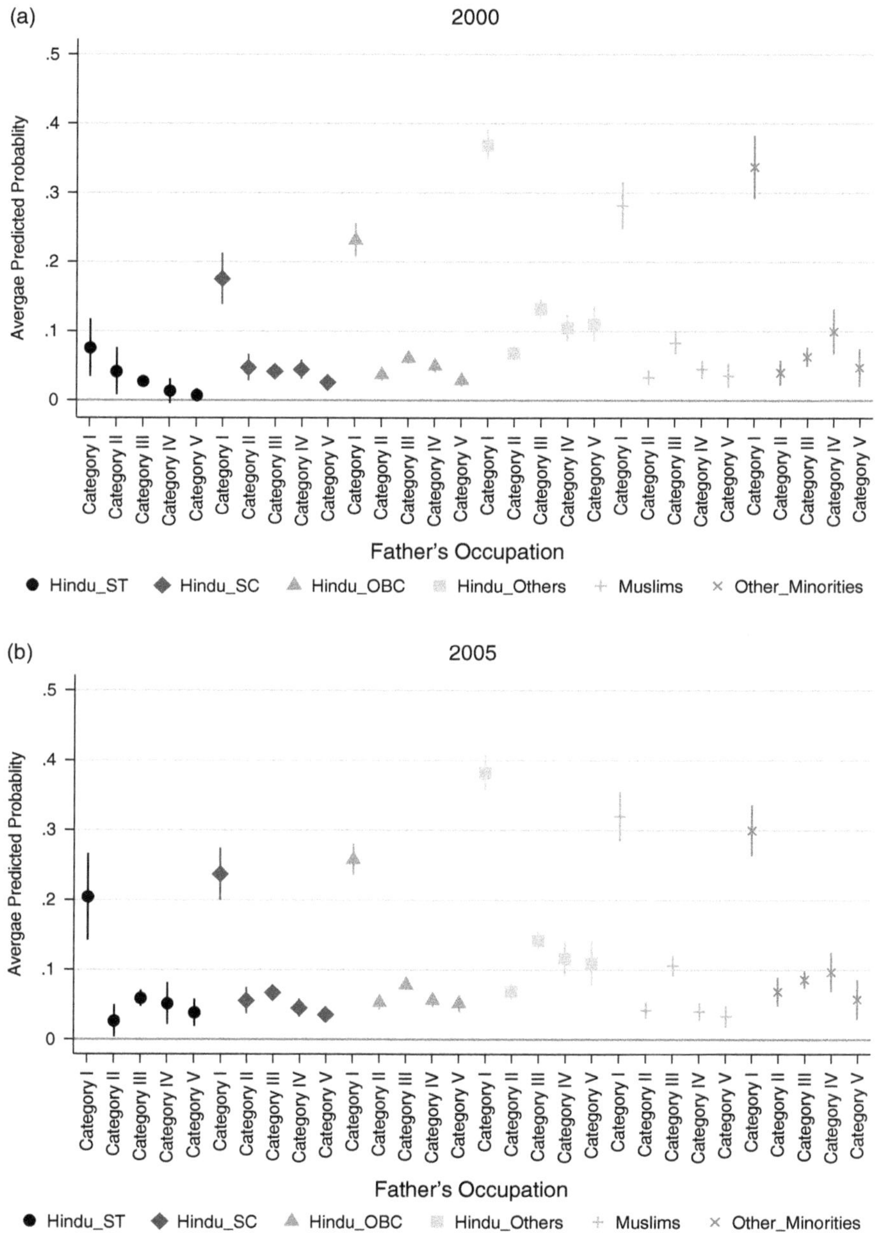

Figure 4.2 Interaction Effect (Father's Occupation and SRCs) Based On Logit Eq. 4.2. Note: Avg. Pr. Prob.: Average Predicted Probabilities; S.E.: Standard Errors; All probabilities presented here are significant at 1% level of significance; for 2019, the land data is not available; Son's and Fathers' occupations: Category I (Officials and Managers, Professionals, Associate Professionals, Clerks), category II (Service Workers and Shop and Market Sales Workers), category III (Agriculture and allied services), category IV (Craft and Related Trades Workers, Plant and Machine Operators and Assemblers) and category V (Laborers). Source: Estimations are based on unit-level data of NSS EUS Rounds (2000, 2005, 2012) and PLFS 2019.

(c) 2012

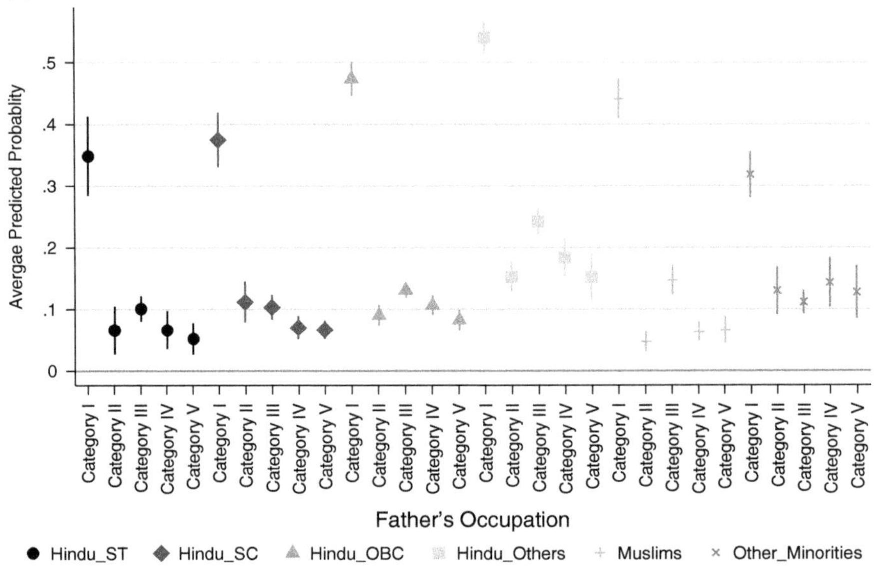

(d) 2019

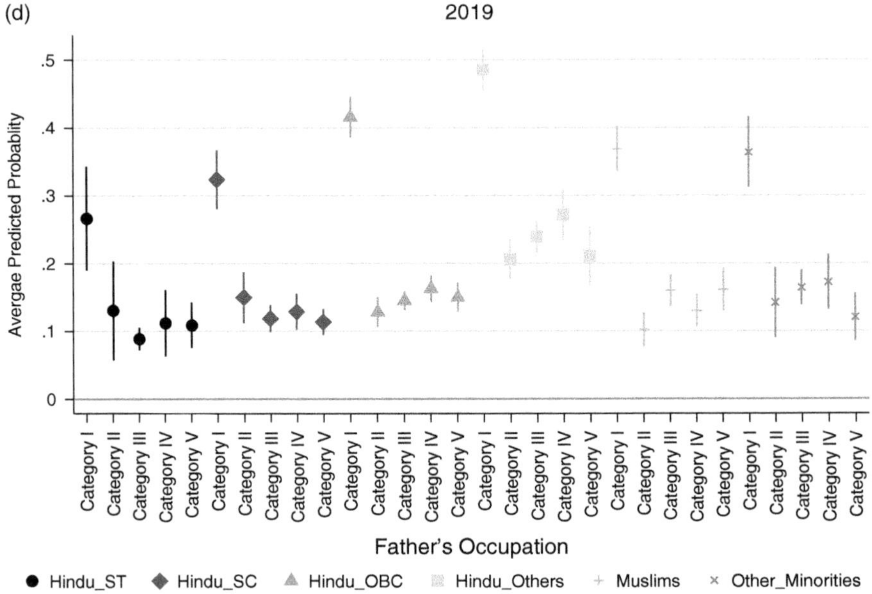

Figure 4.2 (Continued)

communities, particularly for Hindu Others, the same probability was highest (0.384 in the year 2000). However, in the year 2019, STs have increased such chances to 0.281. The fact is also that what STs have achieved in the year 2019, SCs had already achieved in the year 2000. Another noteworthy feature is that Muslims and Other Minorities outperform SCs, STs and OBCs in terms of obtaining employment in the category I occupations if their father works in similar occupations. Another important finding is that across socio-religious groups, the average predicted probabilities of attaining higher occupational employment of having a father working in other than category I occupations are very low. It means employment in the category I occupations is strictly limited to sons who have fathers working in category I occupations. However, in the year 2019, the situation for Hindu OBCs and Hindu Others has improved substantially. For both the mentioned communities, there are fair chances to attain the category I occupations by having a father working in category II, III or IV occupations. It is an important finding that society has become more equitable in 2019, mainly because of the occupational attainment of Hindu Others and OBCs.

The average predicted probabilities of entering the category I occupations having different land sizes are presented in Figure 4.3. In the year 2000, across the SRCs, the higher land size had a negligible impact on higher occupational attainment. This could be because, earlier, if a household had a landholding, the son used to engage in agriculture. Over a period of time, farm-to-non-farm mobility has increased. We have discussed this issue in Chapter 3 at length. Farm-to-non-farm mobility is also visible here; in the year 2012, with different landholding sizes, the probability of attaining the category I occupations has increased. In the year 2012, a clear pattern was visible for SCs, STs, OBCs and Hindu Others that the larger the land size, the lower the chance of attaining higher occupations. This could be simply because higher landholdings restrict mobility outside the farm sector. The same pattern is visible for Muslims and Other Minorities, with a minor difference. Among Other Minorities and Muslims, the landholding size of 2 to 4 acres results in higher average predicted probabilities of attaining the category I occupations. Among Muslims and Other Minorities, only large landholdings restrict mobility; otherwise, the sons of both communities are more mobile than their co-religionists.

4.6 Discussion

The important implication is that the sources of inequalities are the son's education, his father's occupation and landholding. Only these three variables differ significantly among SRCs as far as probabilities of attaining the category I occupations are concerned. That makes the family background more important than geographical factors like region and sector. Within factors related to the family, the father's occupation and landholding are more important than household size and per capita income. Household size and per capita income may have a significant impact on mobility (main effects), but they do not explain inter-socio-religious

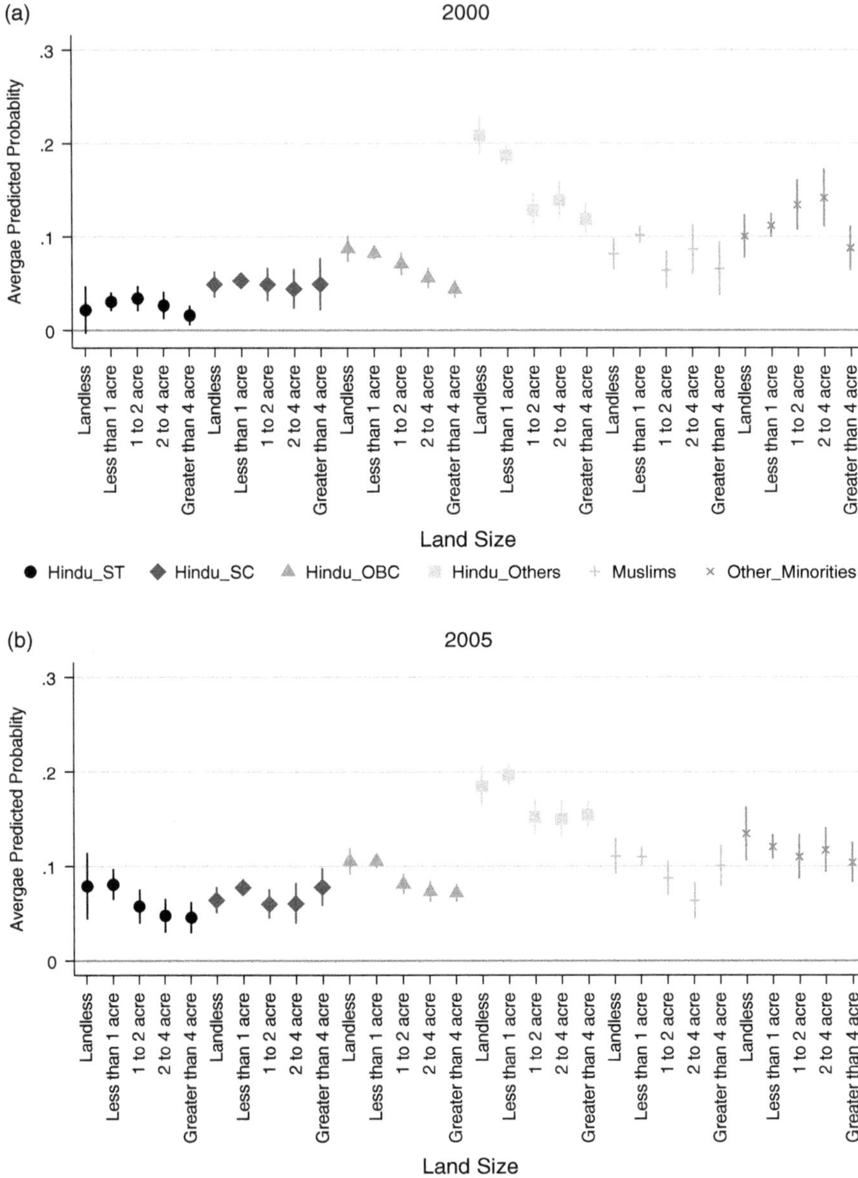

Figure 4.3 Interaction Effect (Land Size and SRCs) Based On Logit Eq. 4.2. Note: Avg. Pr.: Average Predicted Probabilities; S.E.: Standard Errors; All probabilities presented here are significant at 1% level of significance; for 2019, the land data is not available; for 2019, the land data is not available; Son's occupations: Category I Occupations (Officials and Managers, Professionals, Associate Professionals, Clerks). Source: Estimations are based on unit-level data of NSS EUS Rounds (2000, 2005, 2012) and PLFS 2019.

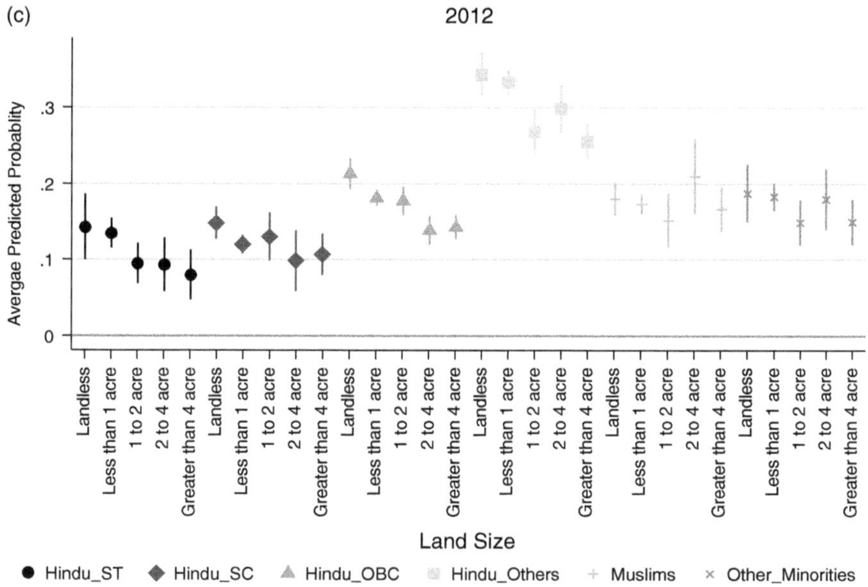

Figure 4.3 (Continued)

differences (interaction effects). The differences in mobility patterns observed in society are the result of differences in human capital (son's education), parental background (father's occupation) and household assets (landholding size). Among all these three variables, landholding size creates differences in the mobility pattern of SRCs because a sizable proportion of people are engaged in agriculture, and there is historical land inequality among different socio-religious groups. Given both these reasons, the differing impact of landholding size is quite understandable. That makes human capital endowment (the son's education) and parental background (the father's occupation) more important.

Research studies have established that better labor market prospects strengthen the stability of families and communities (Bianchi & Milkie, 2010; Orfield, 1999). Conversely, less-educated and low-skilled youths may struggle to find decent jobs in occupational markets (de Grip & Wolbers, 2006). The important implication here is that while better educated and more skilled people may have the advantage of better compensation, the social security system, labor market regulations, relatively faster job growth and productivity progression through continuous learning, their less-educated counterparts may not have access to these benefits.

4.7 Conclusion

The results of logit regression show that having a higher level of education greatly improves chances of getting a job and that educational mobility is very important when choosing a career path to move up. While the study emphasizes the strong influence of the occupational accomplishments of the preceding generation on the next generation across all socio-religious communities, it also brings to the fore the strong impact of the son's education on his occupational choice. This study also notes that three factors, namely the son's education, the father's occupation and landholding, differ significantly among SRCs. Other explanatory variables, such as household size, household expenditure, sector and region, have no discernible effect on the mobility patterns of different SRCs. This study concludes that it is the human capital (son's education), parental background (father's occupations) and household assets (landholding) behind the varying mobility outcomes of different SRCs. This study found that career mobility towards higher occupations is available now for the sons of fathers who are not employed in higher occupations (category I). This statement is more correct for the Hindu Others and Hindu OBCs.

References

Agarwala, R. (2006). From work to welfare. *Critical Asian Studies*, *38*(4), 419–444. https://doi.org/10.1080/14672710601072996

Bian, Y. (2002). Chinese social stratification and social mobility. *Annual Review of Sociology*, *28*(1), 91–116. https://doi.org/10.1146/annurev.soc.28.110601.140823

Bianchi, S. M., & Milkie, M. A. (2010). Work and family research in the first decade of the 21st century. *Journal of Marriage and Family*, *72*(3), 705–725. https://doi.org/10.1111/j.1741-3737.2010.00726.x

Chowdhury, S. (2011). Employment in India: What does the latest data show? *Economic and Political Weekly*, *46*(32), 23–26.

de Grip, A., & Wolbers, M. H. J. (2006). Cross-national differences in job quality among low-skilled young workers in Europe. *International Journal of Manpower*, *27*(5), 420–433. https://doi.org/10.1108/01437720610683930

Domanski, H., & Sawinski, Z. (1987). Dimensions of occupational mobility: The empirical invariance. *European Sociological Review European Sociological Review*, *3*(1), 39–53. http://www.jstor.org/stable/522529

Hauser, R. M. (1980). On "stratification in a dual economy." *American Sociological Review*, *48*(4), 702–712.

Kannan, K. P., & Raveendran, G. (2019). From jobless to job-loss growth: Gainers and losers in India's employment performance during 2012–2018. *Economic and Political Weekly*, *54*(44), 38–44.

Kerbo, H. R. (2006). *Social stratification.* McGraw-Hill. https://doi.org/10.5005/jp/books/10769_7

Mehrotra, S., Parida, J., Sinha, S., & Gandhi, A. (2014). Explaining employment trends in the Indian economy: 1993–94 to 2011–12. *Economic and Political Weekly*, *49*(32), 49–57. https://www.researchgate.net/publication/286723590

Mehrotra, S., & Parida, J. K. (2019). *India's employment crisis: Rising education levels and falling non-agricultural job growth. October*, 1–22.

Mukherjee, D., & Majumder, R. (2011). Occupational pattern, wage rates and earning disparities in India: A decomposition occupational pattern, wage rates and earning disparities in India: A decomposition analysis. *Indian Economic Review*, *46*(1), 131–152. https://doi.org/10.2307/23266420

Orfield, M. (1999). Metropolitics: A regional agenda for community and stability. *Forum for Social Economics*, *28*(2), 33–49. https://doi.org/10.1007/bf02833982

Ramaswamy, K. V., & Agrawal, T. (2012). *Services-led growth, employment and job quality: A study of manufacturing and service-sector in Urban India* (WP-2012-007; Indira Gandhi Institute of Development Research, Mumbai, Issue March). http://www.igidr.ac.in/pdf/publication/WP-2012-007.pdf

Reddy, A. A. (2015). Growth, structural change and wage rates in Rural India. *Economic and Political Weekly*, *50*(2), 56–65.

Rytina, S. (2000). Is occupational mobility declining in the US? *Social Forces*, *78*(4), 1227–1276. https://doi.org/10.1093/sf/78.4.1227

Stevens, G., & Featherman, D. L. (1981). Index of occupational status. *Social Science Research*, *10*(4), 364–395.

Thomas, J. J. (2014). The demographic challenge and employment growth in India. *Economic and Political Weekly*, *49*(6), 15–17. http://www.jstor.org/stable/24479252

Thomas, J. J. (2020). Labour Market Changes in India, 2005–18: Missing the Demographic Window of Opportunity? *Economic and Political Weekly*, *55*(34), 57–63.

Western, M., & Wright, E. O. (1994). The permeability of class boundaries to intergenerational mobility among men in the United States, Canada, Norway and Sweden. *American Sociological Review*, *59*(4), 606–629. https://doi.org/10.2307/2095934

5 Intergenerational Educational Mobility among SRCs, Neighborhood Effects

5.1 Introduction

This chapter analyzes the educational mobility among the various socio-religious communities in India. The chapter's main focus is on whether intergenerational educational persistence and correlation have grown or diminished over time. Also, how do these trends differ between socio-religious groups? For this purpose, this work includes the most recent data and analyses of neighborhood effects. Compared to the work of Emran and Shilpi (2015), we have considered a more refined standing definition of the neighborhood, which lends credibility to this study. One notable departure from the current research is that this study makes an attempt to analyze secondary or more level of educational attainment and the elements that contribute to it.

5.2 Data

Data for this study were derived from the National Sample Employment-Unemployment Survey (EUS) quinquennial rounds 1999–00 (55th), 2004–05 (61st), 2011–12 (68th), and 2018–19 (PLFS), also known as 2000, 2005, 2012 and 2019. For details, kindly refer to Chapter 3 (section 3.2).

It is difficult to gather information at the neighborhood level in India. The Census of India provides this information, albeit it does not include information on religion at the urban level. Emran and Shilpi (2015) conducted their research using NFHS data and primary sample units (PSUs) as neighborhoods. Because PSU refers to a village or an urban unit, we argue that such an approach has limitations. One could argue that a village or urban block is not a neighborhood because it can contain many hamlets that are, in fact, neighborhoods. In NSS, first-stage units (FSUs) are subdivided into hamlets, and big villages are subdivided into multiple hamlets; otherwise, any village-block with a population of less than 1,200 is considered a single hamlet. NSS-PLFS selects two of these hamlets for sampling. As a result, no hamlet exceeds 1,200 residents. This approach is similar to the neighborhood selection of Solon et al. (2000). At least two houses from each neighborhood (hamlet) are included to ensure that the observations (sons) from each neighborhood (hamlet) do not belong to a single home. As a result of these constraints, a smaller sample than the full sample is created, and

DOI: 10.4324/9781003361299-5

this neighborhood sample is referred to in this study as a restricted sample. A minimum of ten observations (son-father pairs) is also specified for each location to ensure adequate observations. The number of observations in the neighborhood impacts varied from 10 to 73, 78, 47 and 60 in 2000, 2005, 2012 and 2019 respectively. For the four specified cross-sections, the average observation in each neighborhood is 26, 22, 16 and 17, respectively.

5.3 Methodology

5.3.1 Educational Mobility

This study employs an OLS regression to assess educational persistence while taking the corpus of literature on intergenerational educational mobility into consideration (Checchi et al., 2008; De Broucker & Underwood, 1998; Hertz et al., 2007). In education equation 5.1, the son's years of schooling are regressed to those of his father.

For educational attainment, the construct given below is followed.

$$\text{Son's Years of Education}_i = \delta_0 + \delta_1 \text{ Father's years of education}_i + \varepsilon_i \qquad (5.1)$$

The coefficient of interest is δ_1 which tells about intergenerational persistence and $(1-\delta_1)$ tells about mobility.

$$\text{The slope coefficient } \widehat{\delta_1 = \frac{\sigma_{\text{sonfather}}}{\sigma^2_{\text{father}}}} = \rho_{\text{sonfather}} \frac{\sigma_{\text{son}}}{\sigma_{\text{father}}}$$

where σ_{son} and σ_{father} are the standard deviations of the sons' and fathers' years of education. $\rho_{\text{sonfather}}$ is correlation coefficient between the son's and father's years of education. The changes in δ_1 over a period of time could be the result of a reduction in $\frac{\sigma_{\text{son}}}{\sigma_{\text{father}}}$. For this reason, if we standardize eq. 5.1 with the standard deviation of father and son, we could get a correlation (ρ) which is free from the evolution in $\frac{\sigma_{\text{son}}}{\sigma_{\text{father}}}$. Both the slope coefficient and the correlation coefficient show persistence in the education between father and son. Slope coefficients are a relative measure of father-son educational transfer, which carries $\frac{\sigma_{\text{son}}}{\sigma_{\text{father}}}$ in it. A correlation coefficient is an absolute measure that shows father-son education correlation, an indicator of educational inequality and absolutely free from children's effort. To follow the standard practice in the literature, we will report both terms.

5.3.2 Secondary Educational Attainment

As aggregate measures δ_1 and ρ do not tell about the direction of the mobility. A separate logit model is estimated to measure chances towards secondary education (ten or more years of schooling). This analysis differs from earlier studies, mostly undertaken in the context and data of developed economies, where educational mobility is high compared to the developing world, where immobility is the norm. For instance, in our sample, while the sons of highly educated parents may continue with higher levels of education, implying immobility, the sons of less educated fathers may remain at their fathers' level of education, implying that upward mobility for such sons may be difficult due to socio-economic-religious and other constraints. This research also deviates from the prevalent trend of examining upward and downward mobility, which may result in information loss.

Keeping this consideration, the following equation is presented:

For educational attainment:

$$Pr(Y_i = 1 / X_i) = F\left(X_i'\delta\right)$$

$$\text{Where} \quad X_i'\delta = \alpha + \delta \text{age}_i + \delta_2 \text{ HH Size}_i + \delta_3 \left(\text{Rural} - \text{Urban}\right)_i$$

$$+\delta_4 \text{SRC}_i + \delta_5 \text{ Father's Education} + \delta_6 \left(\text{Fathers' Education}_i * \text{SRC}_i\right) \quad (5.2)$$

$$+\delta_7 \text{ Landholding} + \delta_8 \text{ MPCE Qurtiles} + \delta_9 \text{ Region}$$

Here, Yi is the nominal dependent variable, where 1 represents if the son has attained secondary or more education, 0 otherwise.

X represents an array of variables such as age, fathers' education of ith individual, household size, socio-religious communities (SRCs), dummies for the rural-urban, landholding size, Monthly Per Capita Expenditure (MPCE) quartiles, and regions.

To account for variance in the effects of fathers' education across various socio-religious groupings, one interaction term has been introduced. There are six categories for a father's educational background: no formal education, up to primary, up to middle, up to secondary, up to senior secondary, and graduate and above. For the fathers' educational category in equation II, the base category is "no formal education". Muslim Others and Muslim OBCs have been combined into a single group called "Muslims", as shown in eq. 3.2 of Chapter 3 of the MNL model.

The geographical regions are classified as North, Central, East, Northeast, West and South, with the Central region serving as a reference category. The states and a few union territories are divided into six regions based on India's administrative division (Kumar et al., 2020). Namely, the northern region includes Chandigarh, Delhi, Haryana, Himachal Pradesh, Jammu and Kashmir, Punjab, Uttarakhand and Rajasthan. The Northeast region includes Assam, Arunachal Pradesh, Manipur, Meghalaya, Mizoram, Nagaland, Tripura and Sikkim. The central region includes Chhattisgarh, Madhya Pradesh and Uttar Pradesh. The eastern region includes Bihar, Jharkhand, Odisha and West Bengal. The western region includes Goa, Gujarat and Maharashtra. The southern region includes Andhra Pradesh, Karnataka, Kerala, Puducherry, Tamil Nadu and Telangana. In the year 2000, the six districts of the Himalayan region of Uttar Pradesh were considered part of Uttarakhand. The other states formed after 2001 are located in the same geographical area as the previous states.

The model includes four quartiles of per capita monthly consumption expenditure (real), the first of which serves as the reference group. The data on household consumption expenditure for each survey year are expressed in nominal terms. To convert nominal consumption data to real terms, the year 2018 is used.

The landholding data is presented in hectares in the NSS EUS round. The landholding data have been grouped into the following six categories: No landholding or less than 0.01 hectares is considered as "landless"; greater than 0.01 hectare but less than equal to 1 hectare as "Marginal"; greater than 1 hectare but less than equal to 2 hectares as "Small"; greater than 2 hectares but less than equal to 4 hectares as "Medium", greater than 4 hectares but less than equal to 10 hectares as "large"; greater than 10 as' very large'. After carefully reviewing some well-documented studies on the subject (Birthal et al., 2014; Chakravorty et al., 2019; Kumar, 2016; Rawal, 2008) and government publications, the authors of this study modified this land classification scheme (Agricultural Statistics at Glance, Ministry of Agriculture & Farmers Welfare, 2018).

Here, we are primarily concerned with the secondary or more level educational attainment of sons from various SRCs. Hence, for this, average predicted probabilities are calculated. In the case of logit eq. 5.2, the forward selection criterion of model building, is used.

The influence of a father's education on his son's educational attainment has been extensively researched. This study attempts to answer a novel question: what role does a father's occupation play in the educational success of his sons? The father's occupation cannot be included in the base model eq. 5.2 since many fathers do not work and their occupational information is missing. We will lose a considerable amount of the educational mobility sample if we include the father's occupation in equation 5.2. To address this issue, we devised a new equation 5.3 that incorporates the father's occupation as an explanatory variable and its interaction with the SRC. In the results section, this method employs a lower number of observations.

$$Pr(Y_i = 1 / X_i) = F\left(X_i'\delta\right)$$

$$\text{Where} \quad X_i'\beta = \alpha + \delta_1 \text{age}_i + \delta_2 \text{ HH Size}_i + \delta_3 \left(\text{Rural} - \text{Urban}\right)_i + \delta_4 \text{SRC}_i$$

$$+\delta_5 \text{ Father's Education} + \delta_6 \text{ Father's Occupation} + \delta_7 \left(\text{Fathers' Occupation}_i * \text{SRC}_i\right)$$

$$+\delta_8 \text{ Landholding} + \delta_9 \text{ MPCE Qurtiles} + \delta_{10} \text{ Region} \tag{5.3}$$

The new addition is the father's occupation, which is subdivided into five occupational categories, namely; category I (Officials and Managers, Professionals, Associate Professionals and Clerks), category II (Service Workers and Shop and Market Sales Workers), category III (Agriculture and allied services), category IV (Craft and Related Trades Workers, Plant and Machine Operators and Assemblers), and category V (laborers). All other explanatory variables remain as presented in eq. 5.2.

The forward selection criterion of model building is being applied in the case of logit eq. 5.3.

5.3.3 Neighborhood Effects

In cross-sectional data, fixed effects are entered as dummy variables. Each cross-section contains thousands of neighborhoods. Stata will not perform a cross-section regression on a data set with a large number of dummies. For this, there is a regress command that can be run with absorb (neighborhood id). The eq. 5.1 was run twice for each cross-section and community, first without and then with neighborhood fixed effects. This neighborhood exercise was conducted on a restricted sample.

5.4 Results

5.4.1 Full Sample-based IGRC and IGC Estimates

The intergenerational regression coefficients (IGRC) and intergenerational correlation (IGC) coefficients are presented in Table 5.1. As discussed in the methodology section, while the slope coefficient contains the ratio of standard deviations of father-son schooling ($\frac{\sigma_{\text{son}}}{\sigma_{\text{father}}}$), on the other hand, the standardized coefficient (correlation) is free of such standard deviations. The standardized regression coefficients are more robust for alternative educational classifications and less volatile over a period of time (Hertz et al., 2007). However, the interpretation of both varies, and in line with standard practice, both are presented here. The slope coefficients are referred to as grad persistence and standardized coefficients as standardized persistence (Hertz et al., 2007). As the OLS equation is run separately for each SRC and cross-section, multiple regression results are obtained.

Between 2000 and 2019, grade persistence declined in all populations. However, the decline was not so sharp until 2012. The STs had the highest level of persistence in 2000. This level of tenacity was significantly higher than the national average (0.566) and the Hindu Others (0.463). Other communities, such as SCs, OBCs and Muslims, exhibited nearly the same level of intergenerational persistence. However, until 2012, Muslims did not demonstrate the same decline in IG persistence as the other three communities. Hertz et al. (2007) present intergenerational education inertia figures for Nepal in 2003 (0.96) and for Sri Lanka in 2000 (0.51) (see table 2 of Hertz et al. (2007), p. 7, for more such comparisons). For the Indian setting, Azam and Bhatt (2015) estimated intergenerational education inertia at 0.63 using IHDS-2005.

The faster decline in grade persistence shows that the sons of poorly educated parents are receiving an education (Hertz et al., 2007). It is worth noting that between 2012 and 2019, the "Hindu Others" did not experience as steep a decline in grade persistence as other groups. This could be because they began with a lower level of persistence or because sons of more educated parents are more likely to follow in their parent's footsteps.

There was little progress in terms of standardized coefficients until 2012, but these coefficients were lowered in 2012. The reduction in the standardized coefficients was higher for STs than for SCs and OBCs. The significant drop in grade persistence and standard coefficients could be interpreted as a positive sign,

Table 5.1 IG Educational Mobility: Beta Coefficient (δ_1) and Correlation (ρ)

Year	*2000*	*2005*	*2012*	*2019*	*2005*	*2000*	*2012*	*2019*
SRCs	δ_1	δ_1	δ_1	δ_1	ρ	ρ	ρ	ρ
All	0.566 (0.004)	0.527 (0.004)	0.468 (0.004)	0.356 (0.004)	0.529 (0.004)	0.543 (0.004)	0.522 (0.004)	0.400 (0.004)
Hindu ST	0.701 (0.021)	0.599 (0.020)	0.499 (0.020)	0.330 (0.017)	0.476 (0.016)	0.505 (0.015)	0.467 (0.018)	0.308 (0.016)
Hindu SC	0.505 (0.013)	0.467 (0.012)	0.431 (0.013)	0.301 (0.011)	0.420 (0.010)	0.411 (0.011)	0.424 (0.013)	0.297 (0.010)
Hindu OBC	0.531 (0.008)	0.479 (0.007)	0.426 (0.007)	0.329 (0.007)	0.471 (0.007)	0.467 (0.007)	0.477 (0.008)	0.365 (0.008)
Hindu Others	0.463 (0.006)	0.470 (0.007)	0.393 (0.007)	0.351 (0.007)	0.546 (0.008)	0.531 (0.007)	0.512 (0.009)	0.457 (0.009)
Muslims	0.539 (0.011)	0.507 (0.011)	0.495 (0.011)	0.348 (0.010)	0.476 (0.010)	0.501 (0.010)	0.499 (0.011)	0.362 (0.011)
Other Minorities	0.526 (0.012)	0.493 (0.011)	0.426 (0.012)	0.356 (0.011)	0.520 (0.011)	0.531 (0.012)	0.503 (0.014)	0.421 (0.013)

Source: Estimations are based on unit-level data of NSS EUS Rounds (2000-2012) and PLFS 2019.

Note: Standard Errors are in the bracket; All β coefficients in this table are significant at 1% level.

indicating that more sons are obtaining education and, as a result, reducing their reliance on their fathers' educational status. This phenomenon also happened in the Nordic countries (Hertz et al., 2007).

As rightly pointed out by Emran and Shilpi (2019), studies on intergenerational mobility overlook intercept coefficients. The intercept coefficient can yield interesting results in developing countries where a large proportion of parents have little or no formal education. The intercept coefficient is critical because it provides information about the educational attainment of those whose parents did not receive a formal education.

Table 5.2 displays the intercept coefficients of schooling OLS equations for India as a whole and for various SRCs. Intercept coefficients indicate that in the year 2000, an ST son had the lowest level of schooling if his father had no formal education. Between 2012 and 2019, the situation improved, and a son with an illiterate father will now receive some schooling. In both 2000 and 2019, the intercept coefficient for Hindu Others was at its peak (6.463 to 9.063). It demonstrates the Hindu Others' advantage over other communities. Between 2000 and 2019, Hindu OBCs, SCs and STs have recorded a substantial improvement. Even though Muslims were in a better position than STs in 2000, their intercept terms were the lowest in 2012 and 2019.

The intercept term illustrates the importance of expanding educational opportunities for the lowest social strata (sons of the least educated parents). Typically, members of this category have low occupational and income levels. Even the poorest communities are obtaining some knowledge as education develops, but several challenges remain critical:

1) There is a threshold for the lowest group of people to cross. They can only get eight or nine years of education without crossing the line.
2) Furthermore, a son born to illiterate Muslim parents has the lowest level of education.

Table 5.2 IG Education Mobility: Intercept Coefficient (δ_0)

SRCs	*2000*	*2005*	*2012*	*2019*
All	4.843 (0.023)	5.306 (0.023)	6.546 (0.028)	8.388 (0.024)
Hindu ST	3.108 (0.077)	4.116 (0.081)	5.700 (0.101)	7.798 (0.079)
Hindu SC	4.271 (0.057)	4.861 (0.055)	6.102 (0.071)	8.267 (0.058)
Hindu OBC	4.913 (0.042)	5.634 (0.040)	6.972 (0.048)	8.703 (0.042)
Hindu Others	6.463 (0.006)	6.558 (0.052)	7.852 (0.064)	9.063 (0.056)
Muslims	4.174 (0.060)	4.457 (0.058)	5.472 (0.067)	7.790 (0.062)
Other Minorities	5.373 (0.076)	5.694 (0.068)	7.172 (0.088)	8.290 (0.075)

Source: Estimations are based on unit-level data of NSS EUS Rounds (2000, 2005, 2012) and PLFS 2019.

Note: Standard Errors are in the bracket; All intercept coefficients in this table are significant at 1% level.

3) The improvement in the educational attainments of STs, SCs and OBCs could be attributed to affirmative actions, as some studies have documented. However, we believe that the benefits for STs (and, to a lesser extent, SCs) are only visible in terms of education. The STs, in particular, have not demonstrated occupational mobility (M1 and M2) or mobility to category I occupations (MNL equation). In the discussion portion, we delve deeper into this subject.

5.4.2 Logit Analysis and Secondary-level Educational Attainment

The results of the OLS regression raise two significant issues. First, the persistence of the "Hindu Others" could be attributed to sons following in their fathers' educational footsteps. Second, when compared to other marginalized sections of society, Muslims' poor performance, particularly low educational attainment among low-educated families, may also be prevalent among better-educated Muslim families. Additionally, it is worth noting that estimates of grade, standardized and intercept coefficients do not reveal the mobility's trajectory. To address these questions, a logit-based analysis has been conducted in which the mobility towards secondary or more education (10 or more years of schooling) has been conducted.

5.4.2.1 Father's Education and Son's Educational Attainment

Before presenting average probabilities, it is important to look into the significance test results of fathers' education in logit eq. 5.3. Table 5.3 carries such results. The first column shows the educational categories, and it should be read as a statement of the null hypothesis. For example, in the first column, the first row shows that the difference between the marginal predictions of primary level education and no formal education (of fathers) on their sons' secondary-level educational attainment is equal to zero. The second column shows the degree of freedom (df), the third shows the test statistic (chi2), and the fourth column shows the p-value associated with the test statistic. These tests are repeated for each cross-section and are well depicted in Table 5.3. The "joint" shows the joint impact of the father's education on the son's secondary-level educational attainment. All the hypotheses are against the null. Hence, marginal predictions produced by each level of the father's education significantly differ in terms of the impact of the son's educational attainment. Also, the joint impact of the father's education (H0=Father's Education=0) is significantly different from zero. Both the above statements are valid for all the cross-sections, as can be seen in Table 5.3.

The effect of the interaction term (SRC*father's education) is also tested against zero (H0), and the results from Table 5.3 suggest that the interaction term is significantly different from zero. It shows that the marginal predictions for the son's secondary or more level education level based on the father's education significantly differ across the SRCs.

Figure 5.1 depicts the logit-based average predicted probabilities of sons' educational attainment in relation to their fathers' educational attainment. The findings indicate that the persistence of Hindu Others is due to the fact that they

Table 5.3 Significance Test Results for Father's Education in Logit Eq. 5.2

Null Hypothesis	*2000*			*2005*		
Col. (1)	*Col. (2)*	*Col. (3)*	*Col. (4)*	*Col. (5)*	*Col. (6)*	*Col. (7)*
Levels of father's Education	df	Chi^2	p-value	df	Chi^2	p-value
(Primary vs No Formal Education)	1	188.59	0.0000	1	255.19	0.0000
(Middle vs No Formal Education)	1	452.36	0.0000	1	804.00	0.0000
(Secondary vs No Formal Education)	1	1210.24	0.0000	1	1440.50	0.0000
(Senior Sec. Vs No Formal Education)	1	813.01	0.0000	1	1309.48	0.0000
(Grad & Above No Formal Education)	1	1011.17	0.0000	1	1715.76	0.0000
(Middle vs Primary)	1	138.66	0.0000	1	276.01	0.0000
(Secondary vs Primary)	1	746.35	0.0000	1	841.99	0.0000
(Senior Sec. vs Primary)	1	591.91	0.0000	1	910.62	0.0000
(Grad. and Above vs Primary)	1	799.24	0.0000	1	1309.37	0.0000
(Secondary vs Middle)	1	249.04	0.0000	1	211.38	0.0000
(Senior Sec. vs Middle)	1	331.48	0.0000	1	406.37	0.0000
(Grad & Above vs Middle)	1	528.65	0.0000	1	741.83	0.0000
(Senior Sec. vs Secondary)	1	66.73	0.0000	1	78.19	0.0000
(Grad & Above vs Secondary)	1	199.92	0.0000	1	282.43	0.0000
(Grad & Above vs Senior Secondary)	1	32.92	0.0003	1	58.67	0.0000
Joint	5	2567.22	0.0000	5	3843.82	0.0000
SRC*Father's Education	25	53.01	0.0009	25	50.78	0.0017
No. of Observations	52,001			53,391		
Null Hypothesis	**2012**			**2019**		
	df	Chi^2	p-value	df	Chi^2	p-value
(Primary vs No Formal Education)	1	159.19	0.0000	1	81.64	0.0000
(Middle vs No Formal Education)	1	569.16	0.0000	1	423.79	0.0000
(Secondary vs No Formal Education)	1	1359.07	0.0000	1	784.96	0.0000
(Senior Sec. Vs No Formal Education)	1	1559.71	0.0000	1	906.15	0.0000
(Grad & Above No Formal Education)	1	2033.28	0.0000	1	1427.54	0.0000
(Middle vs Primary)	1	195.07	0.0000	1	148.33	0.0000

(*Continued*)

Table 5.3 Continued

Null Hypothesis	*2000*			*2005*		
Col. (1)	*Col. (2)*	*Col. (3)*	*Col. (4)*	*Col. (5)*	*Col. (6)*	*Col. (7)*
(Secondary vs Primary)	1	790.70	0.0000	1	470.31	0.0000
(Senior Sec. vs Primary)	1	1110.04	0.0000	1	648.35	0.0000
(Grad. and Above vs Primary)	1	1541.73	0.0000	1	1106.73	0.0000
(Secondary vs Middle)	1	197.80	0.0000	1	139.76	0.0000
(Senior Sec. vs Middle)	1	527.55	0.0000	1	326.29	0.0000
(Grad & Above vs Middle)	1	854.90	0.0000	1	665.17	0.0000
(Senior Sec. vs Secondary)	1	137.99	0.0000	1	68.52	0.0000
(Grad & Above vs Secondary)	1	337.18	0.0000	1	239.39	0.0000
(Grad & Above vs Senior Secondary)	1	37.54	0.0000	1	38.85	0.0000
Joint	5	3864.62	0.0000	5	2434.68	0.0000
SRC*Father's Education	25	28.03	0.3066	25	83.16	0.0000
No. of Observations	37,676			38,052		

Note: The null hypothesis is tested with Anova-style Wald tests after calculating marginal predictions. Here the test statistics are applied to see the difference between marginal predictions. Stata's Contrast syntax is meant for such categorical variables and their interaction effect testing. DF refers to degrees of freedom.

Source: Estimations are based on unit-level data from NSS (2000, 2005, 2012) and PLFS 2019.

have the highest average predicted probability of attaining secondary or more education, particularly among sons of well-educated fathers. For Hindu Others, the average predicted probability increased in 2019, and their slope coefficient for 2019 also suggested persistence among them. While it comes to the Muslims they are not doing better compared to Hindu Others and Hindu OBCs, however they have similar probability as STs and SCs.

Some additional margins have been estimated for rural-urban regions, land ownership, income, and household size. Medium-sized landholdings, as well as the smallest and largest landholdings, appear to be associated with lower educational attainment. Rural people have fewer probabilities of obtaining secondary or more as the urban environment is more conducive to it in terms of opportunities. Also, when a household's consumption level rises, indicating higher wages, so does the likelihood of receiving higher education. There is no discernible trend in the region-wise average expected probabilities over time. Instead of regional dummies, as in some other studies, putting state-fixed effects is also not a sound idea. States in India are divided into regions, each with its own distinct physical characteristics and stage of development. Western Uttar Pradesh, for example, differs greatly from Bundelkhand and Eastern UP in terms of industries, education and agriculture. Likewise, the Western MP is distinct from the Gwalior-Chambal or Baghelakhand regions. Another drawback of state-level analysis is the limited number of observations.

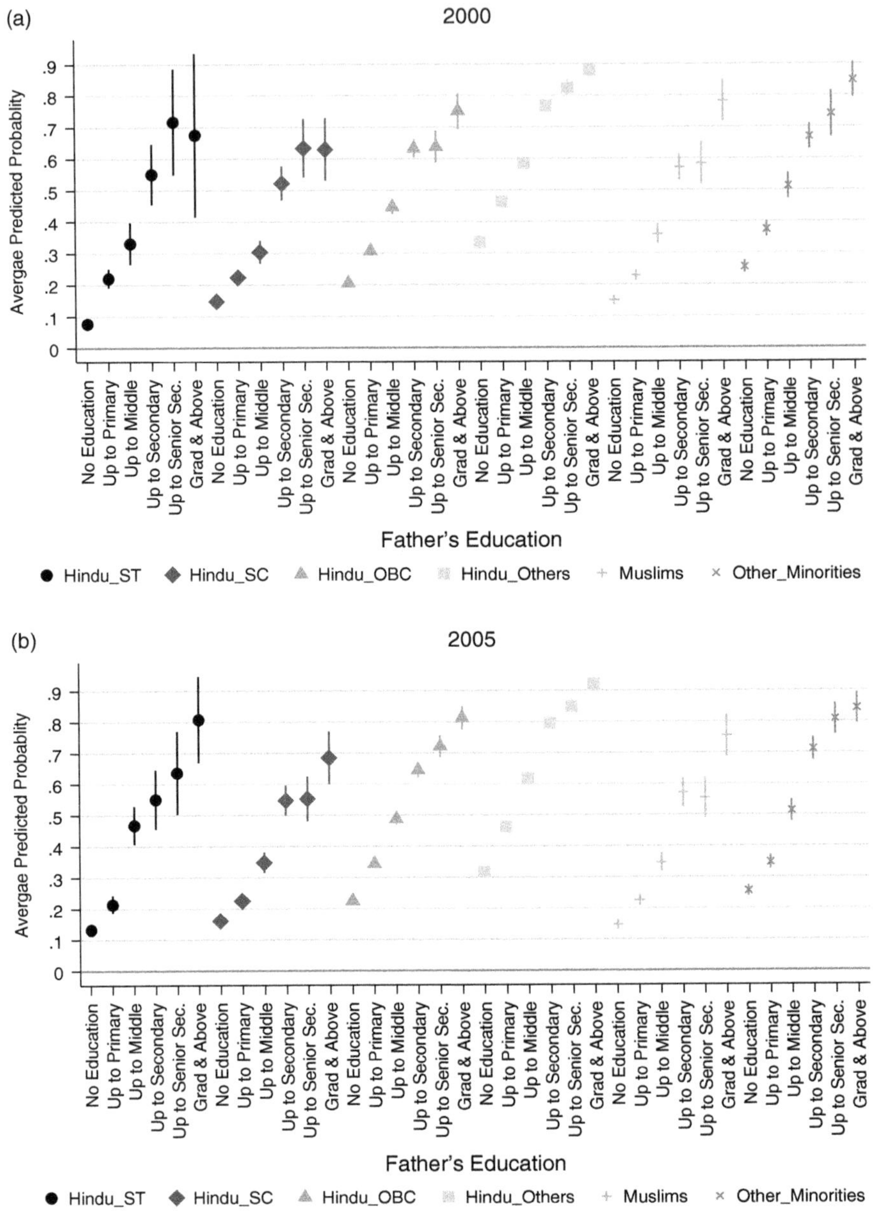

Figure 5.1 Logit Equation 5.2 Estimates (Father's Educational Level). Note: Category I (Official and Managers, Professionals, Associate Professionals and Clerks); Read No Education as No formal education, Primary as Up to Primary, Middle as Up to Middle, High School as Up to High School, Senior Sec. as Up to Senior Secondary, Grad & Above as Graduation and Above; Y-axis of each graph is same; The bars represent the 95% confidence intervals (CIs). Source: Estimations are based on unit-level data from NSS 2000–2012 and PLFS 2019.

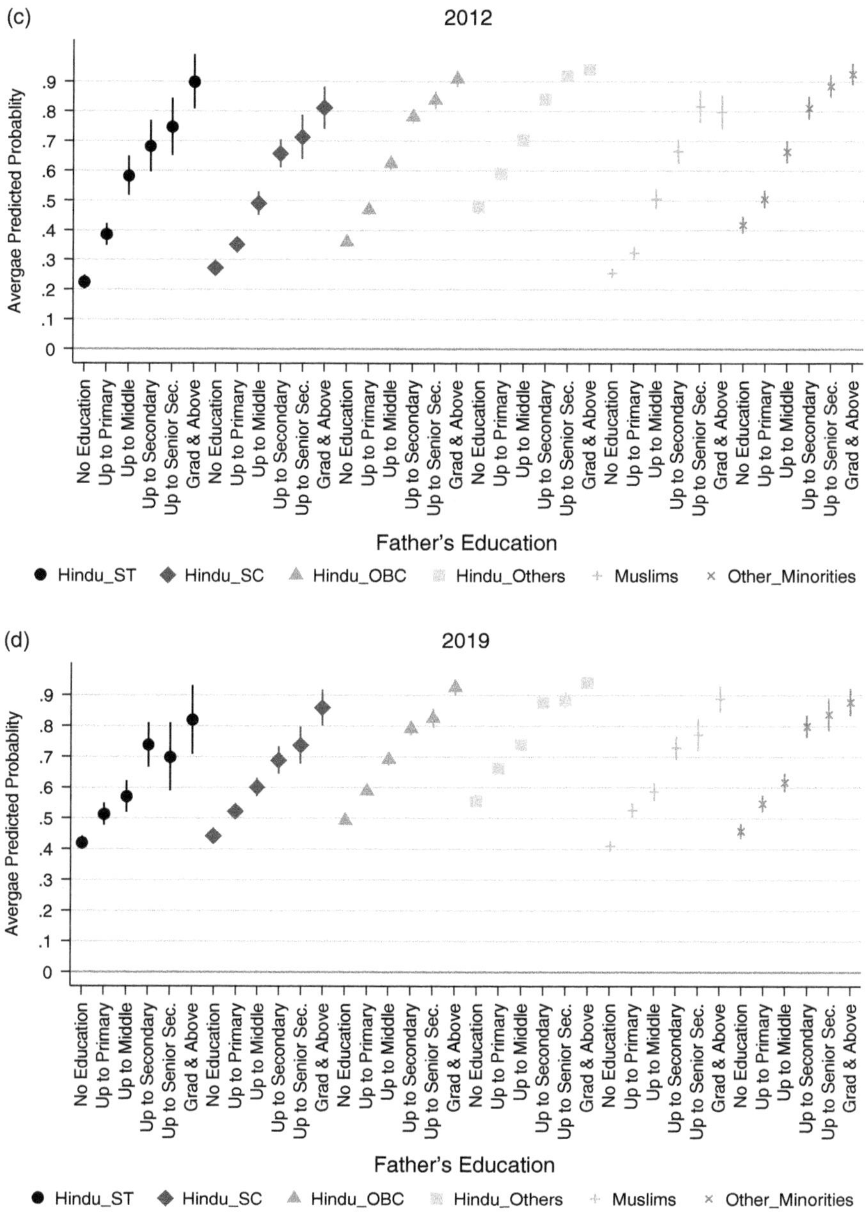

Figure 5.1 (Continued)

5.4.2.2 Father's Occupation and Son's Secondary or More Educational Attainment

Table 5.4 presents the test results on the impact of the father's occupation. The first column of Table 5.4 shows the null hypothesis, and the other columns show the different attributes of the test results. In Col. (1), the third row shows that the difference between an agriculture father (III) and a category I (I) father is equal to zero. The test results suggest that this is not true, and that both the levels of the father's occupation differ when it comes to their impact on the son's secondary or more educational attainment. The majority of such group comparisons are significant. Also, the combined effect of a father's job and his son's secondary or more education level is significantly different from zero in all survey years.

By plotting SRC-wise average expected probabilities of completing 10 or more years of schooling at various levels of fathers' occupation, we investigate the effect of fathers' occupation on the educational attainment of their sons. Figure 5.2

Table 5.4 Significance Test Results for Father's Occupation in Logit Eq. 5.3

Col. (1)	*2000*			*2005*		
	Col. (2)	*Col. (3)*	*Col. (4)*	*Col. (5)*	*Col. (6)*	*Col. (7)*
Father's Occupation	*df*	*Chi2*	*p-value*	*df*	*Chi2*	*p-value*
(II vs I)	1	3.35	0.0672	1	7.42	0.0064
(III vs I)	1	18.68	0.0001	1	21.39	0.0001
(IV vs I)	1	29.84	0.0000	1	46.64	0.0000
(V vs I)	1	98.44	0.0000	1	90.58	0.0000
(III vs II)	1	5.61	0.0179	1	2.51	0.1129
(IV vs II)	1	13.60	0.0000	1	18.43	0.0000
(V vs II)	1	71.99	0.0000	1	56.27	0.0000
(IV vs III)	1	2.33	0.1272	1	11.22	0.0008
(V vs III)	1	56.68	0.0000	1	53.30	0.0000
(V vs IV)	1	27.78	0.0000	1	14.34	0.0002
Joint	4	43.01	0.0020	4	109.44	0.0000
No. of Observations		40, 145			42,545	
		2012			**2019**	
(II vs I)	1	3.64	0.0565	1	12.54	0.0004
(III vs I)	1	4.18	0.0410	1	7.97	0.0048
(IV vs I)	1	52.28	0.0000	1	30.40	0.0000
(V vs I)	1	82.14	0.0000	1	77.06	0.0000
(III vs II)	1	0.05	0.8281	1	1.48	0.2235
(IV vs II)	1	21.97	0.0000	1	2.06	0.1512
(V vs II)	1	45.59	0.0000	1	20.95	0.0011
(IV vs III)	1	34.98	0.0000	1	10.13	0.0015
(V vs III)	1	70.38	0.0000	1	61.63	0.0000
(V vs IV)	1	7.28	0.0028	1	13.67	0.0002
Joint	4	121.96	0.0000	4	100.56	0.0000
No. of Observations		29,482			28,032	

Source: Estimations are based on unit-level data from NSS (2000, 2005, 2012) and PLFS 2019.

Note: The null hypothesis(s) is tested with Anova-style Wald tests after calculating marginal predictions. Here the test statistics are applied to see the difference between marginal predictions. Stata's Contrast syntax is meant for such categorical variables and their interaction effect(s) testing. DF refers to degrees of freedom.

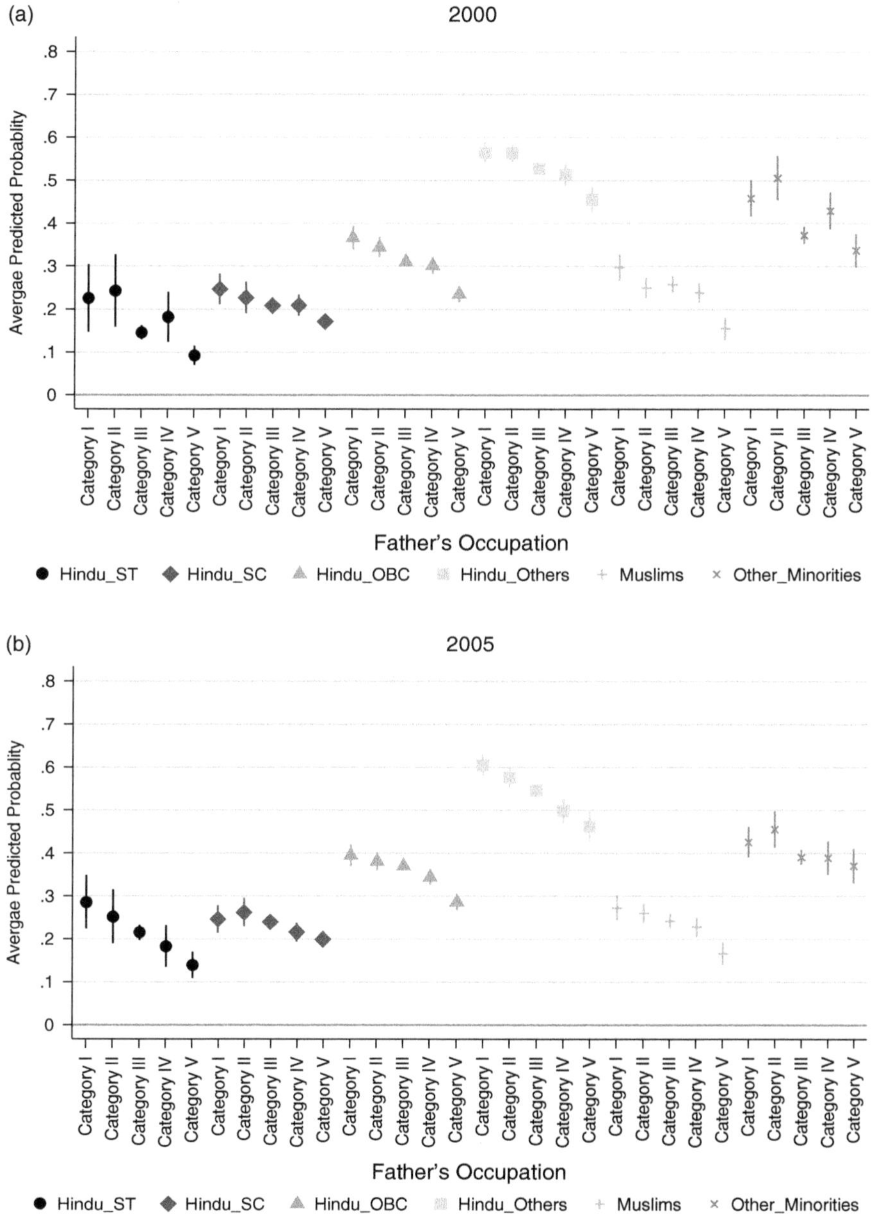

Figure 5.2 Logit Equation 5.3 Estimates (Father's Occupation Level). Note: Category I (Officials and Managers, Professionals, Associate Professionals and Clerks); Read No Education as No formal education, Primary as Up to Primary, Middle as Up to Middle, High School as Up to High School, Senior Sec. as Up to Senior Secondary, Grad & Above as Graduation and Above; The Y-axis of each graph is the same; The bars represent the 95% confidence intervals (CIs); Source: Estimations are based on unit-level data from NSS 2000-2012 and PLFS 2019.

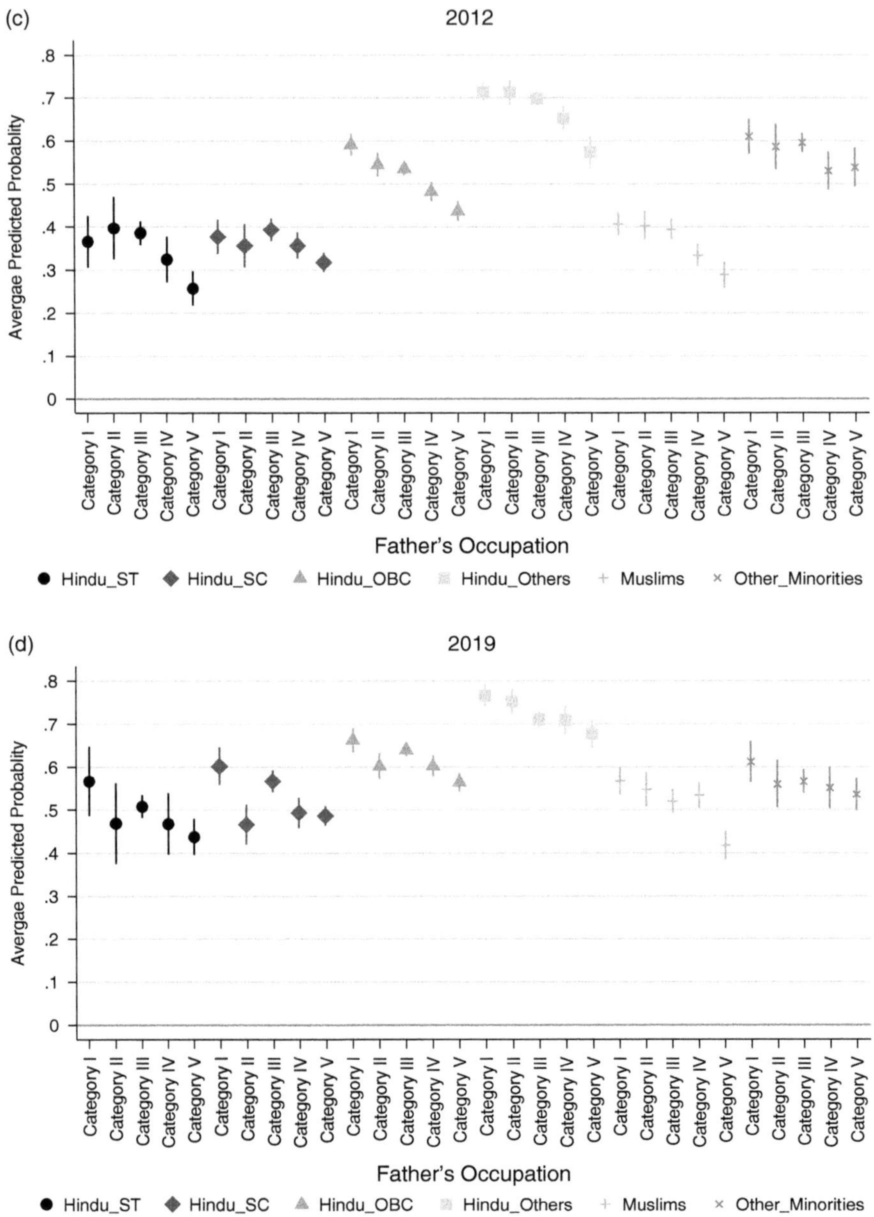

Figure 5.2 (Continued)

depicts this information. With varying levels of a father's occupation, the average predicted probability of their sons attaining secondary or more education rarely exceeds 0.4 for STs, SCs, OBCs and Muslims in years 2000 and 2005. More specifically, it did not exceed 0.3 between 2000 and 2005 for STs, SCs and Muslims. The father's occupation is associated with a low predicted probability of the son's educational attainment compared to the father's education we observed in the last section. This finding have important implications: a father's occupation is not a substitute for his education, and the predicted probability of the son receiving secondary or more education is more influenced by the father's education. It is important to keep in mind that fathers who work in category I jobs may have a strong desire for their sons to go to college.

Another important finding is that even in higher-income families, particularly those with parents employed in category I occupations, the average predicted probability of a Muslim son achieving a secondary or more of education is lower when compared to a son born in another SRC in the year 2019. It seems to be validated by the fact that Muslims do not show any notable educational improvement in either low or highly educated families, as shown by OLS intercepts and Figure 5.2 probabilities, respectively.

5.5 Intergenerational Educational Mobility and Neighborhood Effects

The first panel of Table 5.5 shows that the son-father OLS equations are run without the neighborhood effects, and IG regression coefficients (IGRCs) and IG correlation coefficients (IGCs) are measured. Without taking into account neighborhood influences, the IG correlation coefficient at all-India levels in 2000 was 0.541. When the neighborhood effects were taken into consideration, the value was reduced to 0.416. This reduction is consistent across all cross-sections. However, it should be emphasized that the reduction in IGC in 2019 is small (0.402 vs 0.378). The fact that neighborhood impacts result in lower IGC coefficients demonstrates the importance of neighborhood. However, a modest proportion of educational immobility in the years 2000, 2005, and 2012 was attributed to neighborhood effects (as IGC reduction was about 0.10 points for all three cross-sections). These findings highlight that a high level of educational immobility is linked to a family's background and its surroundings. The coefficients of the IGRC decrease in lockstep with the coefficients of the IGC.

As for each SRC and cross-section, the OLS equation 5.1 is run separately (with and without neighborhood effects) multiple regression results are obtained.

The current findings are consistent with Emran and Shilpi's (2015) IGC estimations based on NFHS for 1993 and 2006. (Table 5.6). After controlling for neighborhood effects, these metrics show a 0.10-point drop in IGC coefficients. In developed countries, the importance of neighborhood effects continues to play a minor role in determining educational attainment (Björklund & Salvanes, 2011; Solon, 1999).

Table 5.5 IGRC (Beta), IGC (Rho) And Neighborhood Effects (Restricted Sample)

SRCs\Years	*2000*		*2005*		*2012*		*2019*	
	δ_1	ρ	δ_1	ρ	δ_1	ρ	δ_1	ρ
All	0.564 (0.004)	0.541 (0.004)	0.527 (0.004)	0.529 (0.004)	0.477 (0.005)	0.530 (0.005)	0.366 (0.004)	0.408 (0.005)
Hindu ST	0.700 (0.022)	0.501 (0.016)	0.596 (0.020)	0.478 (0.016)	0.489 (0.022)	0.463 (0.021)	0.358 (0.020)	0.330 (0.018)
Hindu SC	0.500 (0.014)	0.408 (0.011)	0.467 (0.012)	0.420 (0.011)	0.437 (0.015)	0.432 (0.015)	0.318 (0.013)	0.320 (0.013)
Hindu OBC	0.529 (0.009)	0.465 (0.008)	0.479 (0.007)	0.471 (0.007)	0.443 (0.009)	0.494 (0.009)	0.339 (0.008)	0.374 (0.009)
Hindu Others	0.462 (0.006)	0.529 (0.007)	0.472 (0.007)	0.548 (0.008)	0.390 (0.008)	0.510 (0.011)	0.356 (0.008)	0.460 (0.010)
Muslims	0.535 (0.011)	0.498 (0.011)	0.503 (0.011)	0.471 (0.011)	0.492 (0.012)	0.495 (0.012)	0.346 (0.012)	0.361 (0.012)
Other Minorities	0.523 (0.013)	0.527 (0.013)	0.490 (0.011)	0.515 (0.012)	0.420 (0.013)	0.500 (0.016)	0.371 (0.013)	0.436 (0.015)
SRCs\Years	**2000**		**2005**		**2012**		**2019**	
	δ_1	ρ	δ_1	ρ	δ_1	ρ	δ_1	ρ
All	0.433 (0.005)	0.416 (0.005)	0.432 (0.005)	0.433 (0.005)	0.396 (0.006)	0.441 (0.007)	0.340 (0.005)	0.380 (0.006)
Hindu ST	0.485 (0.033)	0.347 (0.024)	0.384 (0.034)	0.308 (0.027)	0.283 (0.041)	0.268 (0.039)	0.301 (0.032)	0.277 (0.030)
Hindu SC	0.404 (0.022)	0.330 (0.018)	0.346 (0.020)	0.311 (0.018)	0.349 (0.026)	0.345 (0.026)	0.271 (0.021)	0.273 (0.021)
Hindu OBC	0.370 (0.013)	0.325 (0.011)	0.358 (0.011)	0.352 (0.011)	0.363 (0.014)	0.405 (0.016)	0.309 (0.012)	0.340 (0.014)
Hindu Others	0.314 (0.010)	0.360 (0.011)	0.359 (0.012)	0.417 (0.013)	0.312 (0.015)	0.409 (0.019)	0.328 (0.014)	0.424 (0.018)
Muslims	0.405 (0.016)	0.377 (0.015)	0.406 (0.016)	0.380 (0.015)	0.421 (0.017)	0.423 (0.017)	0.335 (0.016)	0.349 (0.017)
Other Minorities	0.305 (0.020)	0.307 (0.020)	0.336 (0.017)	0.352 (0.018)	0.270 (0.020)	0.322 (0.024)	0.304 (0.020)	0.357 (0.023)

Source: Estimations are based on unit-level data of NSS EUS Rounds (2000, 2005, 2012) and PLFS 2019.

Note: Standard Errors are in the bracket; All intercept coefficients in this table are significant at 1% level.

Table 5.6 IGC Estimates and Neighborhood Effects by Emran and Shilpi (2015)

IGC coefficients	*1993*	*2006*
Without Neighborhood Effects	0.574 (107.42)	0.540 (105.48)
With Neighborhood Effects	0.479 (97.66)	0.443 (95.66)
Observations	**34,585**	**39,562**

Source: Data is based on the work of Emran and Shilpi (2015)

Another intriguing observation is that, after controlling for neighborhood influences, the drop in IGC coefficients varies among SRCs and across India. The Other Minorities (0.537 to 0.307) and Hindu Others (0.529 to 0.360) had the biggest drop in IGC coefficient owing to neighborhood impacts in the year 2000, followed by the STs (0.501 to 0.347). Contrary to popular belief, the two progressive communities of Hindu Others and Other Minorities (predominantly Jains, Christians, Sikhs, Buddhists, and Parsis) have the most powerful neighborhood effect. In simple terms, neighborhood effects, rather than familial factors, account for a sizable portion of the educational immobility in these places. According to the findings, those from advanced educational families face more disadvantages if they reside in an impoverished neighborhood than those with less educated parents (Mcdool, 2017). It simply indicates that intra-group inequality is high among "Other Minorities" and "Hindu Others". Members of these two communities that are educated may reside in underserved areas, restricting their access to and quality of education. Still, rather than being solely familial, the root of immobility is the neighborhood. Residential mobility may ease the immobility associated with the neighborhood.

Borjas's (1992) finding that children are more likely to interact with people from their own ethnic group in the same neighborhood may explain why there isn't a 'neighborhood effect' in disadvantaged castes and religious groups. Peers of the same ethnicity will have a greater influence in this situation than the other neighbor. Additionally, individuals from the same ethnic group who don't reside in the same neighborhood but who are family or friends to the child might serve as role models and have an impact, which would mitigate the neighborhood's negative consequences. Nevertheless, as poor-income families generally live in poor neighborhoods (Logan et al., 2002; Owens et al., 2016), neighborhood and family effects converge. Low-income families live in impoverished neighborhoods, and IG educational correlation is primarily attributed to family rather than neighborhood effects.

In 2019, all SRCs were trending in the same direction as the national average, with only slight reductions in IGC coefficients. It's unclear why neighborhood impacts have such a small impact on IG educational mobility. However, similar kinds of findings are reported by researchers in developed nations and in India.

5.6 Conclusion

Educational mobility metrics (dell and rho) for all-India levels and for various SRCs indicate that educational mobility is increasing but varies by socio-religious community. It is, for example, the lowest for STs. The results demonstrate how the formal educational and professional achievements of the preceding generation have had a major impact on the current generation across all socio-religious divisions. The study also notes an improvement in the academic performance of sons of illiterate parents during the course of the investigation. There is a limit, though, and they can only finish eight years of education. In this category, Muslims fare poorly.

References

Agricultural Statistics at Glance, Ministry of Agriculture & Farmers Welfare. (2018). Ministry of agriculture & farmers welfare. Government of India. Retrieved October 2021, from https://agricoop.nic.in/en/divisiontype/oilseeds/statistics.

Azam, M., & Bhatt, V. (2015). Like father, like son? Intergenerational educational mobility in India. *Demography*, *52*(6), 1929–1959. https://doi.org/10.1007/s13524-015-0428-8

Birthal, P. S., Negi, D. S., Jha, A. K., & Singh, D. (2014). Income sources of farm households in India: Determinants, distributional consequences and policy implications. *Agricultural Economics Research Review*, *27*(1), 37. https://doi.org/10.5958/j.0974-0279.27.1.003

Björklund, A., & Salvanes, K. G. (2011). Education and family background: Mechanisms and policies. *Handbook of the Economics of Education*, *3*, 201–247. https://doi.org/10.1016/B978-0-444-53429-3.00003-X

Borjas, G. J. (1992). Ethnic capital and intergenerational capital. *Quarterly Journal of Economics*, *107*(1), 123–150. http://www.nber.org.ezproxy.uwc.ac.za/papers/w3788.pdf

Chakravorty, S., Chandrasekhar, S., & Naraparaju, K. (2019). Land distribution, income generation and inequality in India's agricultural sector. *Review of Income and Wealth*, *65*(S1), S182–S203. https://doi.org/10.1111/roiw.12434

Checchi, D., Fiorio, C. V., & Leonardi, M. (2008). Intergenerational persistence of educational attainment in Italy. *IZA Discussion Papers*, *3622*. https://doi.org/10.1016/j.econlet.2012.10.033

De Broucker, P., & Underwood, K. (1998). Intergenerational education mobility in Africa. *Education Quarterly Review*, *5*(2), 30–51.

Emran, M. S., & Shilpi, F. (2015). Gender, geography, and generations: Intergenerational educational mobility in post-reform India. *World Development*, *72*, 362–380.

Emran, M. S., & Shilpi, F. J. (2019). *Economic approach to intergenerational mobility: Measures, methods, and challenges in developing countries* (No. 2019/98). WIDER Working Paper.

Hertz, T., Jayasundera, T., Piraino, P., Selcuk, S., Smith, N., & Verashchagina, A. (2007). The inheritance of educational inequality: International comparisons and fifty-year trends. *BE Journal of Economic Analysis and Policy*, *7*(2), 1–46.

Kumar, D. (2016). Discrepancies in data on landholdings in rural India: Aggregate and distributional implications. *Review of Agrarian Studies*, *6*(1), 39–62. http://ras.org.in/0d79fb7ec609764cc65809eecd96f6a0

Kumar, K. R., Sivakumar, I., Saravanakumar, N., & Sathishkumar, R. (2020). Regional Disparities and Indian States: A Macro Level Study. *Journal of Critical Reviews*, *7*(13), 89–92.

Logan, J. R., Alba, R. D., & Zhang, W. (2002). Immigrant enclaves and ethnic communities in New York and Los Angeles. *American Sociological Review*, *67*(2), 299–322.

Mcdool, E. (2017). Neighbourhood effects on educational attainment: Does family background influence the relationship? *Sheffield economic research paper series, 2017002*, 35.

Owens, A., Reardon, S. F., & Jencks, C. (2016). Income segregation between schools and school districts. *American Educational Research Journal*, *53*(4), 1159–1197. https://doi.org/10.3102/0002831216652722

Rawal, V. (2008). Ownership holdings of land in rural India: Putting the record straight. *Economic and Political Weekly*, *43*(10), 43–47.

Solon, G. (1999). Intergenerational mobility in the labor market. In *Handbook of Labor Economics* (Vol. 3, pp. 1761–1800). Elsevier. https://doi.org/10.2307/587229

Solon, G., Page, M. E., & Duncan, G. J. (2000). Correlations between neighboring children in their subsequent educational attainment. *Review of Economics and Statistics*, *82*(3), 383–392.

6 Survey Design and Profile of Surveyed Districts

6.1 Introduction

Several empirical studies have been conducted on the heterogeneities in the Indian labor market (Duraisamy & Duraisamy, 2016; Madheswaran & Attewell, 2007; Mukherjee & Majumder, 2011; Sengupta & Das, 2014). It is also worth noting that over 80 percent of employed people in India work in the informal sector (ILO, 2018). Additionally, the growing demand for skilled workers, coupled with the shrinking nature of some traditional occupations, places a significant strain on the available labor force, which has most likely not been upgraded to meet the requirements of new jobs that require appropriate skills, a minimum educational level, training, industry affiliations and other factors. The situation varies significantly across various social and religious groups, to the disadvantage of marginalized communities that lack the necessary skills and do not meet the dynamic requirements of knowledge-based businesses, service industries and technology, to name a few. When such a heterogeneous population is analyzed using nationally representative data, a community may be depicted as a homogeneous group. On the other hand, data collection for such a heterogeneous and vast population is a mammoth task and beyond the capacity of any single researcher. Although the NSS data surveys are rich sources, secondary data sources will always have some limitations. In fact, without field experience, a researcher cannot develop a comprehensive perspective and appreciate ground realities. A focused study of a specific region may yield an alternative perspective and provide insights into ground veracity. The purpose of this study is to collect data on Muslims' socio-economic and educational status in West Uttar Pradesh. It should be obvious that the goal of data collection is not simply to build a quantitative profile of Muslims based on their employment status, but also to get insight into the underlying causes of Muslim backwardness. However, it should be noted that the primary data from this study is not intended to be a substitute for NSS data sets but rather to supplement them.

6.2 Study Area

With all of the constraints of an individual researcher, including time and money, deciding which state/district/city/village to conduct the primary survey is critical.

DOI: 10.4324/9781003361299-6

Table 6.1 Eleven States with a High Muslim Population Concentration (in Millions)

State	*Total Population*	*Muslim Population*	*Muslim Population In Percentage*	*Percentage of the Urban Population to the Total Population*	*Percentage of Muslim Population in Urban Areas*
Gujarat	60.44	5.85	9.67	42.6	64.95
Rajasthan	68.55	6.22	9.07	24.87	49.13
Karnataka	61.1	7.89	12.92	38.67	63.46
Andhra Pradesh	84.58	8.08	9.56	33.36	64.87
J & K	12.54	8.57	68.31	27.38	25.81
Kerala	33.41	8.87	26.56	47.7	52.08
Assam	31.21	10.68	34.22	14.1	7.51
Maharashtra	112.37	12.97	11.54	45.22	73.04
Bihar	104.1	17.56	16.87	11.29	13.45
West Bengal	91.28	24.65	27.01	31.87	22.34
Uttar Pradesh	199.81	38.48	19.26	22.27	37.23

Note: J & K refers to Jammu and Kashmir.

Sources: Census 2011.

To arrive at any representative sample region, all of India's states having a Muslim population of at least 10 percent are accounted for (Table 6.1). Following that, each of these districts was classified into one of four categories (i) Districts with a minimum of one million Muslim population (ii) Districts with a Muslim population between 0.5 and 1 million; (iii) Districts with a Muslim population between 0.25 and 0.5 million; and (iv) Districts with a Muslim population between 0.1 and 0.25 million (Table 6.2).

The districts with more than a million Muslims were then identified. It was discovered that both Uttar Pradesh and West Bengal have nine districts, each with a Muslim population of above one million people. In addition, Uttar Pradesh has 19 districts with Muslim populations ranging from 0.5 million to one million people. Uttar Pradesh has the largest Muslim population of any state, which is why

Table 6.2 Muslim Population Density by State in Terms of Size

Category/States	*All-India*	*RJ*	*UP*	*BH*	*AS*	*WB*	*GJ*	*MH*	*AP*	*KA*	*KL*
Above 1 million population	30	0	9	2	4	9	0	2	1	1	2
0.5 to 1 million	51	2	19	3	4	5	2	5	3	3	5
0.25 to 0.5 million	79	6	21	8	2	3	8	12	9	8	2
0.1 to 0.25 million	84	11	18	12	4	2	7	9	5	13	3
Total	244	19	67	25	14	19	17	28	18	25	12

Note: RJ refers to Rajasthan, UP to Uttar Pradesh, AS to Assam, WB to West Bengal, GJ to Gujrat, MH to Maharashtra, AP to Andhra Pradesh, KA to Karnataka, KL to Kerala.

Sources: Census 2011.

Table 6.3 Muslim Population Concentration in Western Uttar Pradesh

Muslim Population	*District*	*Rural*	*Urban*	*Total*	*Percentage of Total Population of Districts*
Above 1 million population	**Moradabad**	1.39	0.86	2.25	47.12
	Muzaffarnagar	1.13	0.58	1.71	41.3
	Bijnor	0.96	0.62	1.59	43.04
	Saharanpur	0.91	0.55	1.45	41.95
	Ghaziabad	0.5	0.69	1.19	25.35
	Meerut	0.52	0.66	1.19	34.43
	Rampur	0.77	0.41	1.18	50.57
0.5 to 1 million population	Jyotiba Phule Nagar	0.45	0.3	0.75	40.78
0.25 to 0.5 million	**Baghpat**	0.27	0.1	0.36	27.98
0.1 to 0.25 million	Gautam Budh Nagar	0.09	0.13	0.22	13.08
Total		6.98	4.9	11.88	68.71

Sources: Census 2011.

it was picked as the representative state. The observations discussed are listed in Table 6.2.

Four population size categories and different districts of Uttar Pradesh were cross-tabulated, using Uttar Pradesh as a model state for drawing the sample of the Muslim population. This experiment revealed that seven of the nine Muslim-populated districts with populations of over one million people are located in Western Uttar Pradesh. This region of Uttar Pradesh is home to 32 percent of the state's total Muslim population of 11.9 million people (Table 6.3).

Given that the primary objective of this study is to analyze intergenerational mobility among Muslims, the first step is to identify the districts with a high Muslim population concentration in order to collect primary data to supplement the secondary data. The Ministry of Minority Affairs, India has identified some regions/districts with a high concentration of Muslim populations,[1] but they are trailing behind in terms of socio-economic and educational development (see also, Reddy, 2008). The majority of these districts are in developing states, such as Uttar Pradesh (West UP), Bihar (Simanchal), West Bengal (Murshidabad-Malda-North Dinajpur), and Assam (districts of the Brahmaputra and Barak valleys). It is also worth noting that Uttar Pradesh has nine districts with a Muslim population of more than one million people, seven of which are located in Western Uttar Pradesh. It was thus decided to concentrate on West UP because drawing an all-India sample would be beyond the capabilities of a single researcher, and also because there is some overlap in terms of occupational and educational backwardness among these districts with a high concentration of Muslim population. This region of Western Uttar Pradesh is divided into three administrative divisions: Saharanpur, Moradabad and Meerut. Due to the significant concentration of Muslims in the Upper Doab (Districts of Saharanpur, Muzaffarnagar and Meerut) and Northern Rohilkhand

(Districts of Bijnor, Moradabad, and Rampur), the requisite sample was drawn from these areas. These districts in Western Uttar Pradesh are also a hub for micro and small industrial activities such as brassware (Moradabad), wooden handicrafts (Saharanpur), sports equipment (Meerut), the sugar industry, paper mills, and steel rolling mills (Muzaffarnagar), the Mentha oil industry, wooden handicrafts, transportation, and bone processing mills (Sambhal), and fabric-embroidery work (Rampur). As a result, West UP serves as an excellent case study for assessing occupational outcomes. The districts are subdivided further into two fundamental strata: the rural stratum (r) and the urban stratum (u). The rural stratum encompasses the district's entire rural territory, whereas the urban stratum contains the district's entire urban area. Baghpat's agricultural operations are predominantly sugarcane-based, with few associated industries, whereas the latter two districts (Saharanpur and Moradabad) have industrial clusters focused on exports.

6.3 Sample Size

In each selected district, a list of all villages was compiled using Census 2011 data, and finally, three villages from each district were selected. Furthermore, three wards from each district headquarters were selected for the survey. In this case, we have a total of nine villages and nine urban wards in three districts. We have taken a 15-time sample of selected survey frames (villages and wards). This procedure results in a sample size of 270 (18×15 = 270). To distribute the sample equally among all three districts, we have added 30 more sample households. A summary of it is given below.

Sample size	300
State	Uttar Pradesh and Districts
Region	West UP
Districts	(Moradabad, Saharanpur and Baghpat)
Wards	3 x 3 = 9 (Each district: three wards)
Villages	3 x 3= 9 (Each district three villages)
Households (Muslim)	300

More detailed information is provided in Table 6.4.

6.4 Sample Profile of Selected Districts

The survey of 300 randomly selected households yields data on 2,240 individuals, referred to here as an "individual sample". Each district received a random sample of hundreds. The allotted sample is divided into rural and urban areas in each district in proportion to the district's rural-urban population. According to the census of India, Baghpat district is home to 69 percent of rural residents, whereas Moradabad and Saharanpur have roughly 60 percent of the population living in rural areas (Census, 2011). In accordance with this rural-urban share, the sample is divided among rural-urban areas (Table 6.5). The total sample size

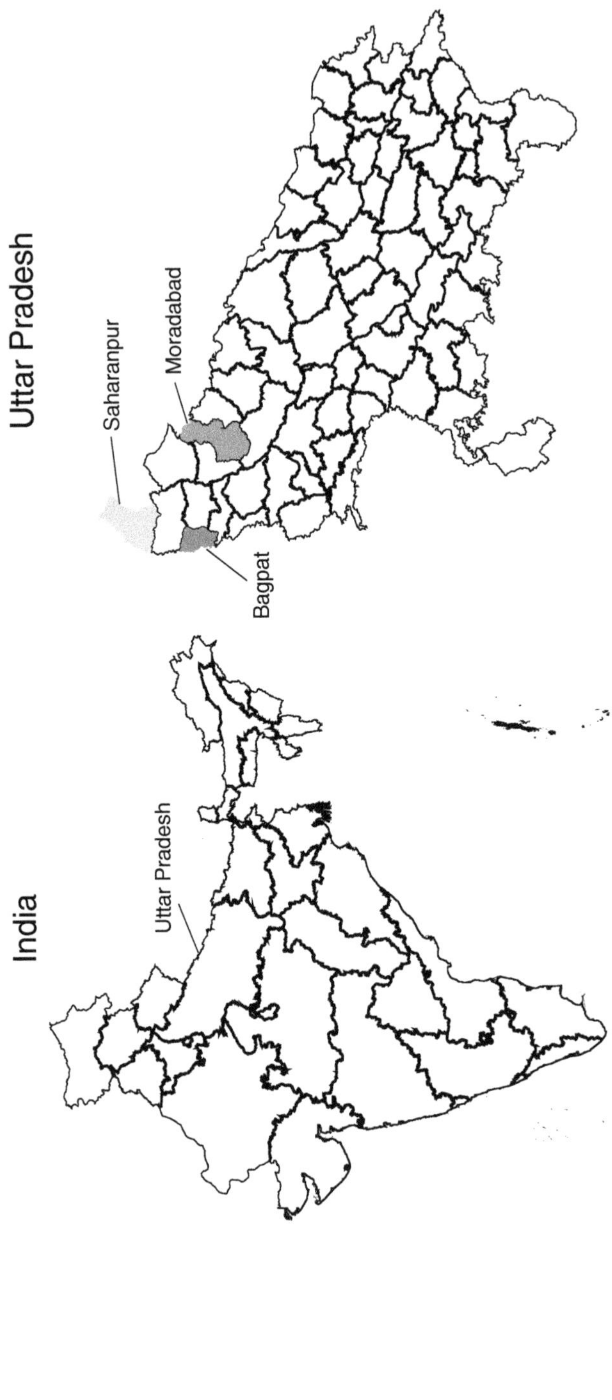

Figure 6.1 Location Map of Study Area. Source: Authors.

Table 6.4 Selected Towns and Villages

Region	*Districts*	*Sector*	*Villages*	*Sample Size*
West UP	Moradabad	Rural	Massompoor	20
			Sarai Kharju	20
			Mahlakpur Mafi	20
		Urban	Moradabad (M.Corp)	40
	Saharanpur	Rural	Chakwali	20
			Harora	20
			Khujnawar	20
		Urban	Saharanpur (M.Corp)	40
	Baghpat	Rural	Niwara	25
			Oshika	22
			Aminagar Sarai	22
		Urban	Baghpat (NPP)	31
Total				300

Source: Prepared by author.

Table 6.5 Distribution of Sample Households

Indicator	*Baghpat*	*Moradabad*	*Saharanpur*	*Total*
Sector				
Rural	69	60	60	189 (63)
Urban	31	40	40	111 (37)
Total	100	100	100	300 (100)
Caste				
Muslim Others	33	59	34	126 (42)
Muslims OBCs	67	41	66	174 (58)
Total	100	100	100	300
Land Sizes				
Less than 2 acres	28.00 (90.32)	30 (71.43)	13 (46.43)	71 (70.30)
2.1 to 3 acres	3.00 (9.68)	9 (21.43)	6 (21.43)	18 (17.82)
Greater than 3 acres	0.00 (0.00)	3 (7.14)	9 (32.14)	12 (11.88)
Total	31 (100.00)	42 (100.00)	28 (100.00)	101 (100.00)

Note: Figures in parenthesis are in percentage terms.

Source: Primary survey-based calculation by author.

of 300 was divided into 189 (63 percent) rural respondents and 111 (37 percent) urban respondents.

Table 6.5 also shows the social group-wise distribution of the sample households. The bulk of the households are from the other backward classes (58 percent). More than 65 percent of sample households in Baghpat and Saharanpur have identified themselves as other backward classes (OBCs). West UP has a multi-layered caste system. The Muslim forward caste comprises Sayyad, Shiekh, Mughal, Pathan and Muslim Rajputs (Hindu Forward Caste converted to Islam and are currently referred to as Muslim forward castes). The Muslim backward class group includes Gurjar, Ansari, Teli, Pinjara, Abbasi, Lohar, Rayeen, etc. (Hindu lower castes, working population converted to Islam), Faqir, Bhishti, Mehtar, etc. (they have even lower status than other castes in the backward class group). Dhobis (Occupation: washing clothes), Mochis (Occupation: shoe-making and repairing), Mehtars (Occupation: manual scavenging), and Faqirs (Occupation: begging, digging graves, and burying dead bodies) are scheduled castes, but they are not constitutionally protected in the same way as other scheduled castes among Hindus, Sikhs and neo-Buddhists. In this study, Muslims have been subdivided into Muslim OBCs and Muslim Others. The Muslim SCs are very small in number and, therefore, are clubbed with the Muslim OBCs.

It is interesting to see the landholding patterns among the sample households of the West UP (Table 6.5). West UP is one of India's most fertile regions, located on the Upper Ganges plain. The majority of the sample households have less than two acres of land. Only a few households have more than three acres of land. In district Baghpat, none of the sample households reported owning more than three acres of land. In the category of less than two-acre landholding, there are 70.30 percent of households. According to NSS 2011–12, a similar percentage was around 90 percent at the national level (NSSO, 2012). The high number of landholdings in the district of Moradabad is because of the presence of a sizable population of Shiekhzade (Muslim upper caste) in rural Moradabad.

If we examine the distribution of individuals across the sectors, we find that out of 2,240 individuals, 1,501 (67 percent) reside in rural areas. The same percentage for Baghpat is 69.85 (Table 6.6). Out of 2,240 individuals, 1,019 (45.49 percent) are females. All three districts, more or less, have the same female representation in the surveyed population.

Around 64.42 percent of respondents in this sample are in the age group of 15 to 65 years. Only 2.81 percent of the total individual sample is over the age of 65 (Table 6.7). Baghpat has the highest proportion of children in the age group of 0–4 years (14.07 percent). By implication, the dependency ratio (ratio of people younger than 15 or older than 65 to the working population—15–65 age group) is

Table 6.6 Location and Gender-Wise Distribution of the Sample Population

Indicator	*Baghpat*	*Moradabad*	*Saharanpur*	*Total*
Sector				
Rural	556 (69.85)	456 (65.14)	489 (65.73)	1,501 (67.01)
Urban	240 (30.15)	244 (34.86)	255 (34.27)	739 (32.99)
Total	796 (100)	700 (100)	744 (100)	2,240 (100)
Sex				
Male	431 (54.15)	394 (56.29)	396 (53.23)	1,221 (54.51)
Female	365 (45.85)	306 (43.71)	348 (46.77)	1,019 (45.49)
Total	796 (100)	700 (100)	744 (100)	2,240 (100)

Note: Figures in parenthesis are in percentage terms.

Source: Primary survey-based calculation by author.

Table 6.7 Age-Wise Distribution of the Sample Population

Age Groups (in Years)	*Baghpat*	*Moradabad*	*Saharanpur*	*Total*
0–4	112 (14.07)	47 (6.71)	56 (7.53)	215 (9.60)
5–14	197 (24.75)	149 (21.29)	173 (23.25)	519 (23.17)
15–19	88 (11.06)	114 (16.29)	96 (12.90)	298 (13.30)
20–25	113 (14.2)	94 (13.43)	115 (15.46)	322 (14.37)
26–35	122 (15.33)	100 (14.29)	115 (15.46)	337 (15.04)
36–45	50 (6.28)	75 (10.71)	76 (10.22)	201 (8.97)
46–55	53 (6.66)	62 (8.86)	59 (7.93)	174 (7.77)
56–65	38 (4.77)	37 (5.29)	36 (4.84)	111 (4.96)
66 and Above	23 (2.89)	22 (3.14)	18 (2.42)	63 (2.81)
Total	796 (100.00)	700 (100.00)	744 (100.00)	2,240 (100.00)

Note: Figures in parenthesis are in percentage terms.

Source: Primary survey-based calculation by author.

53 percent. According to World Bank estimates (WDI, 2019), in 2019, India had a dependency ratio of 49.24 percent, Bangladesh had a dependency ratio of 48 percent, Pakistan had a dependency ratio of 65 percent, Nepal had a dependency ratio of 55 percent, Bhutan had a dependency ratio of 46 percent, and Afghanistan had a dependency ratio of 82 percent. The high dependency ratio suggests that fewer people are participating in the workforce.

There are 1,507 (67.28 percent) individuals in the age group of 15 years and above (Table 6.8). Their education profile suggests that Saharanpur has the highest mean years of schooling (7.08 years) among the three selected districts (Moradabad, 6.47 years, and Baghpat, 5.08 years). The mean years of schooling of all individuals (15 years and above) is 6.23 years. The mean years of schooling are associated with a high standard deviation, implying that significant educational inequality exists within the sample population.

Of the 2,240 individual samples, only 656 people are in the workforce (Table 6.9). This 29.29 percent work population rate (WPR) is far lower than any national or international standard. The low WPR among sample households is because few Muslim women reported themselves as working. The methodological debate in

Table 6.8 The Mean Years of Schooling of the Sample Population (15 Years and Above)

District	*Mean*	*Std. Dev.*	*Freq.*
Baghpat	5.08	4.89	487
Moradabad	6.47	5.57	504
Saharanpur	7.08	5.42	516
Total	6.23	5.37	1,507

Source: Primary survey-based calculation by author.

Table 6.9 Work Participation Rate in the Sample Population

WPR	*Baghpat*	*Moradabad*	*Saharanpur*	*Total*
Person				
Not in workforce	590 (74.12)	465 (66.43)	529 (71.10)	1,584 (70.71)
In workforce	206 (25.88)	235 (33.57)	215 (28.90)	656 (29.29)
Total	796 (100)	700 (100)	744 (100)	2,240 (100)
Male				
Not in workforce	240 (55.68)	182 (46.19)	196 (49.49)	618 (50.61)
In workforce	191 (44.32)	212 (53.81)	200 (50.51)	603 (49.39)
Total	431 (100)	394 (100)	396 (100)	1,221 (100)
Female				
Not in workforce	350 (95.89)	283 (92.48)	333 (95.69)	966) (94.80
In workforce	15 (4.11)	23 (7.52)	15 (4.31)	53 (5.20)
Total	365 (100)	306 (100)	348 (100)	1,019 (100)

Note: Figures in parenthesis are in percentage terms.

Source: Primary survey-based calculation by author.

the recent past has been an issue about how to assess women's work participation (Desai & Joshi, 2019). It has been observed that many women are working on their own farms or tending livestock but do not identify themselves as working. Even though they disclose the working hours for all activities, they do not count them as working activities. Nonetheless, female labor force participation in the sample households is extremely low.

There are 519 children in the age group of 5–14 years (Table 6.10). Only a small proportion of this age group are employed (2.50 percent). However, 15.22 percent of children in this age group are not in school. Similarly, around 21.14 percent of people aged 15 to 19 work. This is a sizable proportion, which includes school dropouts. As discussed in Chapter 1, new entrants to the labor market are disproportionately dropouts among Muslims, and the same is true among the sample households. It is also important to mention that 8.86 and 26.24 percent of total children in the age group of 5 to 14 years are enrolled in Madrasas and Maktabs, respectively.[2]

The working people's activity status is depicted in Table 6.11. A total of 356 people (54.26 percent) declared themselves to be self-employed. Of these self-employed people, 84 work from home or from a structure linked to their home (self-employment-2). 41.46 percent of the population is self-employed, either working for someone else's business, owning a store, or operating as a vendor (self-employment-1). Casual laborers account for 27.67 percent of employment in the Baghpat district. Baghpat district has a higher proportion of casual laborers than other districts due to the presence of numerous brick-making businesses

Table 6.12 provides an overview of the workers' broader occupational groups based on the work descriptions provided by respondents. Agriculture is the most common economic activity in sample households, employing 14.63 percent of the population in a variety of roles, such as cultivator, agricultural laborer and animal caretaker. Cultivators, agricultural laborers, and animal care workers account for

Table 6.10 Work Participation and Enrollment Rate in the Age Groups of 5–14 And 15–19 Years

Enrollment Rate								
Enrollment	*Age (5–14 Years)*				*Age (15–19 Years)*			
	Baghpat	*Moradabad*	*Saharanpur*	*Total*	*Baghpat*	*Moradabad*	*Saharanpur*	*Total*
Not in education	39 (19.80)	25 (16.78)	15 (8.67)	79 (15.22)	50 (56.82)	60 (52.63)	40 (41.67)	150 (50.34)
In education	158 (80.20)	124 (83.22)	158 (91.33)	440 (84.78)	38 (43.18)	54 (47.37)	56 (58.33)	148 (49.66)
Total	197 (100)	149 (100)	173 (100)	519 (100)	88 (100)	114 (100)	96 (100)	298 (100)
Work Participation Rate								
WPR	**Age (5–14 Years)**				**Age (15–19 Years)**			
	Baghpat	**Moradabad**	**Saharanpur**	**Total**	**Baghpat**	**Moradabad**	**Saharanpur**	**Total**
Not in workforce	193 (97.97)	142 (95.30)	171 (98.84)	506 (97.50)	69 (78.41)	83 (72.81)	83 (86.46)	235 (78.86)
In workforce	4 (2.03)	7 (4.70)	2 (1.16)	13 (2.50)	19 (21.59)	31 (27.19)	13 (13.54)	63 (21.14)
Total	197 (100)	150 (100)	173 (100)	520 (100)	88 (100)	114 (100)	96 (100)	298 (100)

Note: Figures in parenthesis are in percentage terms.

Source: Primary survey-based calculation by author.

Table 6.11 Activity Status of Sample Working Population

Srl. No.	*Activity Status*	*Baghpat*	*Moradabad*	*Saharanpur*	*Total*
1	Self-employed-1	90 (43.69)	90 (38.30)	92 (42.79)	272 (41.46)
2	Self-employed-2	22 (10.68)	42 (17.87)	20 (9.30)	84 (12.80)
3	Self-employed 1+2	112 (54.37)	132 (56.17)	112 (52.09)	356 (54.26)
4	Regular Wage Salaried	37 (17.96)	54 (22.98)	63 (29.30)	154 (23.48)
5	Casual Labour	57 (27.67)	49 (20.85)	40 (18.60)	146 (22.26)
6	Total (3+4+5)	206 (100.00)	235 (100.00)	215 (100.00)	656 (100.00)

Note: Figures in parenthesis are in percentage terms.

Source: Primary survey-based calculation by author.

10.98, 2.13, and 1.52 percent of the workforce, respectively. Another industry is construction, which employs a large number of people in various capacities, including construction labor (4.27 percent), other construction workers (1.83 percent), and masons (1.68 percent). Another construction-related business is brick manufacturing, which employs 3.20 percent of the workforce. Furthermore, 1.83

Table 6.12 Broader Occupational Activities Among the Sample Working Population

Work Activity	*Frequency*	*Percentage*
Cultivators	72	10.98
Agriculture labor	14	2.13
Animal care	10	1.52
Barber	4	0.61
Brass handicraft	30	4.57
Brick-making labor	21	3.20
Cattle trading/Chicken-Meat selling	10	1.52
Construction labor	28	4.27
Construction Workers (other than labor)	12	1.83
Mason (construction)	11	1.68
Painters (building)	12	1.83
Fabrication/Aluminum/Iron related work	21	3.20
Ferry (cloth, fruits, spices, eatables etc.)	18	2.74
Petty Kirana	16	2.44
Loading-unloading labor	9	1.37
Mechanic	14	2.13
Petty hotel/eatery	8	1.22
Tailor	26	3.96
Teacher	24	3.66
Vegetables/fruit sellers	9	1.37
Welder	22	3.35
Wooden handicraft	32	4.88
Other	233	35.52
Total	**656**	**100.00**

Source: Primary survey-based calculation by author.

percent of the population works in the construction industry as a building painter. Fabricators and iron and aluminum workers make up 3.20 percent of the workforce. Their skills are different from those of welders, who make up 3.35 percent of the sample. In brass handicraft production plants, 4.57 percent work as modulators, sheet cutters and other artistically talented employees. This job is located in the district of Moradabad, which has a long history of brass-related handicraft businesses. Similarly, Saharanpur has a high number of small-medium and large wooden handicraft units. The wooden handicrafts segment employs 4.88 percent of the labor force. Tailoring (3.96 percent), teaching (3.66 percent), and mechanics (2.13 percent) are some of the other occupations found in the various sample districts. Other occupations mentioned by workers include petty grocery stores, small restaurants, vegetable selling, and peddling (clothes, eatables, etc.).

The information on the economic status of the sample households was gathered using three methods. To begin with, the respondents were extensively questioned about their consumption spending. Second, data on weekly household expenditures was gathered. Third, respondents were asked about their self-reported income. In all three districts, the monthly income corresponds to the self-reported income (Table 6.13: col. 2). It reveals that participants recorded their income and expenses accurately. However, monthly consumption expenditure is only marginally higher than self-reported income (col. 3). It demonstrates that respondents overstated their consumption expenditures while understating their income. However, it remains a wild guess because the difference between income and consumption (which also includes saving) in underdeveloped nations is so modest (The Canberra City Group, 2011).

Respondents were also asked to report their total weekly consumption, which was subsequently converted to monthly figures (col. 4). This expenditure is below the monthly expenditure calculated from the listed items (col. 3). It is because, in listed items, two types of information were collected. First, data on expenditure on durable goods, education, health care, tourism, assets, recreation and weddings were gathered for a 365-day period. Second, spending on food, cooking and eatables was recorded during the 30-day recall period. This method covers both short-term and long-term consumption expenditures.

While responding to questions about weekly consumption (col. 4), it appears respondents did not include their long-run expenditures, even after clearly stating they should do so. Still, multiple ways of information collection helped to determine the quality of substitutable indicators.

6.5 Structure and Content of the Schedule/Questionnaire

A structured interview schedule was devised to collect both qualitative and quantitative data. A semi-structured interview format was used. The main goal was to create a parent-offspring profile based on occupation and education. "What was your parents' occupation when you were growing up?" was one of the questions posed to the household head (Hout, 1984). Similarly, the another question was posted "What are/were your parents' educational levels?" If the household head

Table 6.13 Monthly Income and Monthly Consumption Among Sample Households

Col. (1)	*Col. (2)*		*Col. (3)*		*Col. (4)*		*Col. (5)*
Districts	*Self-reported income*		*Monthly consumption expenditure (from the listed items)*		*Monthly consumption expenditure (self-reported as total)*		*Total observations*
	Mean	*Std. Dev.*	*Mean*	*Std. Dev.*	*Mean*	*Std. Dev.*	
Baghpat	4770.988	6898.6014	4523.785	9725.7297	2671.663	2833.0356	100
Moradabad	5866.694	10960.515	3922.969	4149.5714	2969.122	3475.4359	100
Saharanpur	4222.524	3143.0652	4065.889	4222.8129	3827.135	6954.7815	100
Total	4953.402	7698.9331	4170.881	6556.7123	3155.973	4786.7194	300

Note: Figures are in Indian rupees.

Source: Primary survey-based calculation by author.

is not working, then the same questions were posed to the principal breadwinner of the household. Out of a total of 300 households, there were 242 responses from the household head himself and 58 responses from the main breadwinners. Data on all household members is collected to acquire information on the offspring's educational and occupational attainment. Another piece of information, called "relation to the head", was gathered in order to connect offspring with their parents. Respondents were given a list of consumption products in order to elicit information about consumption spending. Additionally, the total weekly consumption expenditure was elicited. After answering both the consumption-related questions, respondents were asked to state their total monthly family income. A job history profile of the primary breadwinner was created to gather information on intra-generational movements. A direct open-ended question was posed about intergenerational expectations: "What do you expect of your children or the future generation in terms of education, employment, and social status?" Additionally, information on caste-related issues is gathered.

6.6 Definition of Major Terms Used in the Schedule/Book

6.6.1 Locational Information (District, Tehsil, Village, Mohalla (Locality), Gram Panchayat, Ward)

According to the 2011 census, India is a vast federal republic with 28 states and eight union territories. These states and territories are subdivided further into districts. Currently, there are 718 districts. Each district is subdivided further into tehsils in India. The lowest primary administrative entities are villages in rural areas and towns in urban areas. At the time of the 2001 census, the country had approximately 6.49 lakh villages, with approximately 5.94 lakh of them inhabited. The Gram Panchayat (Village Council) is a popularly elected body that governs a village or group of villages and was founded following the 73rd amendment to the Indian constitution. Similarly, the term "ward" refers to the municipal body wards established under the Indian constitution's 74th amendment.[3]

6.6.2 Household and Household Head

A household is composed of a group of people (1) living in the same dwelling space, (2) taking food from a common kitchen, and (3) who acknowledge the authority of a man or woman. Such a person is referred to as the head of the household (Beaman & Dillon, 2011).

6.6.3 Caste

The caste system is a Hindu classification system in which people are divided into four hierarchically ranked castes known as varnas (Deshpande, 2010). Here for study purposes, the Hindu caste system is divided into four broader groups: Scheduled Caste, Scheduled Tribes, Other Backward Classes, and Others (the forward caste). Here, Muslims are divided into two groups: OBCs (other backward classes) and Others (forward castes). For reference, those who have ancestry from outside the sub-continent were regarded as Ashraf (includes Arab, Persian, Turk, Afghan), while the local Muslims were regarded as Ajlaf (includes local backward class people and high-class people). The Sayyad, Sheikh, Mughal and Pathan four constitute the Ashraf category and Teli, Mochi, Bhishti, Julaha, Qureshi etc. are in the Ajlaf category. The Ashraf and Ajlaf dichotomy have both birthplace and ethnicity (Momin, 2016; Zainuddin, 2003). However, ground realities differ, and the "Ashraf-Ajlaf" classification appears academic only. On the ground, the backward caste and forward caste terminologies are familiar among people. Among Muslims, the nature, origin and current dynamics of the caste system are debatable and these issues are separate matters of research. The importance of caste remains significant in terms of occupation, marriage and social status. The degree to which hierarchy plays its role varies from region to region and it is not in any way homogeneous.

6.6.4 Activity Status

A person's activity status indicates their active participation in both economic and non-economic activities during a specific reference period. Furthermore, economic activity demonstrates the production of commodities and services that add value to the national output. Non-market activities include the production of commodities for self-consumption and the construction of fixed assets for one's own account [Annual Report, Periodic Labour Force Survey, 2017–2018 (Ministry of Statistics & Programme Implementation, Government of India, 2018)].

6.6.5 Maktab and Madrasa

Maktab (day school for religious teachings) and Madrasa (boarding school for religious teachings) (Sachar Committee Report, 2006).

6.6.6 Description of Work

Detailed description of economic activity

6.6.7 Occupation

A job or activity in which a person decides to engage in economic activity. Here, the NCO-2004 classification has been used (Safri, 2009).

6.6.8 Industry

National industrial classification-2008 (NIC–2008) based industrial classification of economic activities.

6.6.9 Subsidiary Activity

A second economic activity which a person is engaged in for monetary gain other than the principal activity.

6.6.10 Intra-Generational Mobility

A person's occupational movement over time (Burkhauser & Couch, 2009, p. 254).

6.6.11 Consumption Expenditure

The sum of the monetary values of all the goods and services consumed by the household during the reference period (NSSO Sixty Eighth Round Report, 2012, p. 59).

6.6.12 Affirmative Actions

Affirmative actions (AAs) are a set of positive measures aimed at increasing the participation of disadvantaged socio-economic groups in previously under-represented areas, such as employment, education and elected forums.[4]

6.7 Conclusion

The description of the data selection strategy and study area in this chapter serves as the foundation for the next chapter, which discusses the sample population's mobility in more detail. This chapter concludes that West UP has a Muslim population that cuts across multiple layers of caste. Also, a high dependency ratio, a greater share of self-employment and early dropouts are some characteristics of the sample population. It is also found that district Baghpat has the highest casual laborers, lowest female workforce, lowest average years of schooling, and highest number of farmers with less than two acres compared to the other two sampled districts.

Notes

1 https://www.icssr.org/sites/default/files/imp-link/Overview-Report.pdf.
2 There is difference between the Maktab (day school for religious teachings) and Madrasa (boarding like school for religious teachings) (Sachar Committee Report, 2006).
3 https://www.india.gov.in/my-government/constitution-india/amendments/constitution-india-seventy-third-amendment-act-1992;
https://www.india.gov.in/my-government/constitution-india/amendments/constitution-india-seventy-fourth-amendment-act-1992
4 https://plato.stanford.edu/entries/affirmative-action/

References

Beaman, L., & Dillon, A. (2011). Do household definitions matter in survey design? Results from a randomized survey experiment in Mali. *Journal of Development Economics*, *98*(1), 124–145.

Burkhauser, R. V., & Couch, K. A. (2009). *Intragenerational inequality and intertemporal mobility* (B. Nolan, W. Salverda, & T. M. Smeeding, Eds.) (Vol. 996, No. 522–546, pp. 1–60). Oxford University Press.

Census. (2011). *Census*. Registrar General of India, Ministry of Home Affairs, Government of India. https://censusindia.gov.in/Census_and_You/religion.aspx

Desai, S., & Joshi, O. (2019). The paradox of declining female work participation in an era of economic growth. *Indian Journal of Labour Economics*, *62*(1), 55–71. https://doi.org/10.1007/s41027-019-00162-z

Deshpande, M. S. (2010). History of the Indian caste system and its impact on India Today [California Polythechnic State University, San Luis Obispo]. In *Social Sciences Department College of Liberal Arts California Polythechnic State University, San Luis Obispo: Vol. Fall* (Issue SOCS 461, 462 Senior). https://doi.org/10.1126/scisignal.632000pe2

Duraisamy, M., & Duraisamy, P. (2016). Gender wage gap across the wage distribution in different segments of the Indian labour market, 1983–2012: Exploring the glass ceiling or sticky floor phenomenon. *Applied Economics*, *48*(43), 4098–4111. https://doi.org/10.1080/00036846.2016.1150955

Hout, M. (1984). Occupational mobility of Black men: 1962 to 1973. *American Sociological Review*, *49*(3), 308–322.

ILO. (2018). *World employment social outlook*. International Labour Organization. https://doi.org/10.18356/cfa20042-en

Madheswaran, S., & Attewell, P. (2007). Caste discrimination in the Indian urban labour market: Evidence from the national sample survey. *Economic and Political Weekly*, *42*(41), 4146–4153.

Momin, R. A. R. (2016). Review: Muslim caste: Theory and practice. *Economic and Political Weekly*, *10*(14), 580–582.

Mukherjee, D., & Majumder, R. (2011). Occupational pattern, wage rates and earning disparities in India: A decomposition occupational pattern, wage rates and earning disparities in India: A decomposition analysis. *Indian Economic Review*, *46*(1), 131–152. https://doi.org/10.2307/23266420

National Industrial Classification. (2008). *National industrial classification*. Central Statistical Organisation, Ministry of Statistics and Programme Implementation, Government of India, New Delhi., available at: https://www.ncs.gov.in/Documents/NIC_Sector.pdf

NSSO Sixty Eighth Round Report. (2012), *Employment and unemployment situation in India, (July 2011–June 2012)*. http://microdata.gov.in/nada43/index.php/catalog/EUE.

PLFS. (2018). Periodic labour force survey (July 2017–June 2018). *Ministry of statistics and programme implementation*. Government of India.

Reddy, D. N. (2008). Baseline survey of minority concentration districts: An overview of the findings. Indian Council of Social Science Research, New Delhi. https://citeseerx.ist.psu.edu/document?repid=rep1&type=pdf&doi=702f12bc70e77d4bbcc2bf0dfe11d5232b6aa572

Sachar Committee Report (2006). Social, economic and educational status of the Muslim community of India. In *A Report, Government of India*. http://minorityaffairs.gov.in/reports/sachar-committee-report

Safri, M. (2009). The economics of occupation. *Economists' Voice*, *9*(3), 19–21. https://doi.org/10.1515/1553-3832.1900

Sengupta, A., & Das, P. (2014). Gender wage discrimination across social and religious groups in India: Estimates with unit level data. *Economic and Political Weekly*, *XLIX*(21), 71–76.

The Canberra City Group. (2011). *Handbook on household income statistics* (B. McColl, J. Billing, B. Kindermann, & H. Burgess, Eds.). Canberra Group.

WDI. (2019). *World development indicators*. The World Bank Group. https://databank.worldbank.org/source/world-development-indicators

Zainuddin, S. (2003). Islam, social stratification and empowerment of Muslim OBCs. *Economic and Political Weekly*, *38*(46), 4898–4901. http://www.jstor.org/stable/10.2307/4414285

7 Primary Survey-Based Evidence on Muslim Occupational and Educational Mobility

7.1 Introduction

In India, there has been a simmering debate on the causes of Muslim backwardness. There is a growing trend to examine the enduring inequity and underachievement of marginalized groups from an intergenerational perspective (Bhattacharya & Mazumder, 2011; Chetty et al., 2014; Torche, 2018). Significant attempts have been made in India to investigate the intergenerational mobility of various socio-economic strata. These works, however, do not address the Muslim perspective (Iversen et al., 2017; Majumder, 2010; Reddy & Swaminathan, 2014; Reddy, 2015).

The current work is an attempt to investigate intergenerational occupational and educational mobility among Muslims in India based on primary data collected from Muslim households in Western Uttar Pradesh, a region of India with a high concentration of Muslims. Utilizing mobility matrices, intergenerational occupational and educational mobility as well as aggregate mobility steps are analyzed.

The research on intergenerational mobility in India generally focuses on aggregate mobility patterns, with little attention paid to the variables that affect these trends. This study used linear regression (for educational mobility) and a multinomial logit model to examine the factors that may impact sample households' educational and occupational choices (for occupational mobility).

The chapter is structured into different sections. Section 7.2: data, occupational classification and measurement. Sections 7.3/7.4 present mobility matrices on intergenerational occupational and educational mobility. From Section 7.5 onwards, various issues have been discussed with the help of micro-details.

7.2 The Data, Occupational Classification and Measurement

For this study, 300 Muslim households in the Saharanpur, Moradabad and Baghpat districts of Western Uttar Pradesh were randomly chosen and interviewed. The survey design and sample collection method described in Chapter 6 in detail serve as the foundation for the primary data. In addition to these 300 father-son pairs, an additional 290 pairs, including brothers and sons in the same household, were identified. Thus, 590 father-son pairs were identified in total. The sample consists of individuals who have had some form of employment between the ages of 15 and 65. The examination

DOI: 10.4324/9781003361299-7

of mobility is restricted to male members exclusively since female labor force participation is exceptionally low among the sample households, and the reasons outlined in Chapter 3 reveal that women leave their parental household after marriage.

The collected data is a cross-section, and the father's information was asked in a retrospective manner. Unlike the NSS data used in the earlier chapters, here, the sample includes both co-resident and non-co-resident father-son pairs (see Table 7.1 for sample characteristics).

Table 7.1 Sample Characteristics of the Sample Households

Total surveyed households (HHs)		300	
Individuals in the household (HH)		2,241	
Total Male		1,221 (54.49 percent)	
Total Female		1,020 (45.51 percent)	
Total number of people employed		688	
Total number of males employed		626	
Total number of females employed		62	
Total number of Father-Son pairs with Occupational Information in the age group 15 to 65 years		590	
Variable		**Mean**	**Std. Dev.**
HH size		8.56	3.77
Son's years of Schooling		6.88	5.20
Father's years of Schooling		3.43	4.50
Landholding (acres)		0.63	1.55
Variables		**Observations**	**Percentage**
Social Group	Forward Caste	260	44.07
	OBC	330	55.93
Sector	Rural	362	61.36
	Urban	228	38.64
Son's Occupation	I	60	10.17
	II	76	12.88
	III	70	11.86
	IV	269	45.59
	V	115	19.49
Father's Occupation	I	42	7.12
	II	46	7.8
	III	169	28.64
	IV	193	32.71
	V	140	23.73
Age Cohort	1954–70	122	20.68
	1971–90	204	34.58
	1991–04	264	44.75
Income Quartiles	Q1	127	21.53
	Q2	145	24.58
	Q3	178	30.17
	Q4	140	23.73

Source: Based on Primary Data collected [by the authors]; I = Legislators, Senior Officials, and Managers, Professionals, Associate Professionals, and Clerks, II = Service Workers and Shop and Market Sales Workers, III= Skilled Agricultural and Fishery Workers, IV= Craft and Related Trades Workers, and Plant and Machine Operators and Assemblers, V = Elementary Occupations.

7.3 Intergenerational Occupational Mobility

The father-son mobility matrix (Table 7.2) demonstrates that a sizable fraction of the sons stick to their fathers' respective occupational categories, indicating many possibilities. The factors that contribute to a high level of social inequality and, consequently, unequal opportunities include individual preferences, reluctance to switch professions, slow job growth in a particular occupational group, widening opportunity gaps across social groups, and skill-biased technological advancement (Corak, 2013; Krueger, 2012). Motiram and Singh (2012) have also observed that many offspring of low-skilled and low-paid employees stay in the same profession as their parents. These results are backed by Reddy and Swaminathan (2014). When specifics are analyzed, it is found that almost half of the sons were disconnected from their fathers' occupational category (specifically non-routine jobs). They also observed that their fathers have shifted from occupation I (specific non-routine jobs) to occupational categories IV and V. In occupational category II, a roughly identical pattern is evident. But compared to the sons in occupational group I, the sons in this group seemed to have done better, since none of them went down to the rank of jobs that didn't require a specific skill, such as construction work or something similar.

In comparison to categories I, IV and V occupational individuals, category III individuals comprising skilled agricultural and fishing employees appeared to be more versatile, as shown in Table 7.2. Some of them were able to move beyond their parents' occupational categories. It reflects a shift in agricultural labor force to other sectors, with over 63 percent of farmer fathers' sons moving to other sectors (Mehrotra et al., 2014; Thomas, 2014). On the other hand, agricultural households performed poorly in migrating to category I occupations compared to migrating to some other occupational categories. Because of the relative scarcity of work in this occupational group, moving to category IV seems to be a realistic option. Two of the three districts, namely Moradabad (brass and metalware) and Saharanpur (woodcraft and furniture), are the hubs for handicraft production. There is always a

Table 7.2 Mobility Matrix for Intergenerational Occupational Mobility

Son's Occupation	*Father's Occupation*					
	I	*II*	*III*	*IV*	*V*	*Total*
I	**45.24**	8.70	5.92	10.88	4.29	10.17
II	16.67	**45.65**	7.69	9.33	12.14	12.88
III	7.14	0.00	**35.50**	3.11	0.71	11.86
IV	19.05	34.78	39.64	**62.69**	40.71	45.59
V	11.90	10.87	11.24	13.99	**42.14**	19.49
Total	100	100	100	100	100	100

Note: The diagonal cells show immobility. Source: Based on Primary Data collected by the authors; I = Legislators, Senior Officials, Managers, Professionals, Associate Professionals, and Clerks, II = Service Workers and Shop and Market Sales Workers, III= Skilled Agricultural and Fishery Workers, IV= Craft and Related Trades Workers, and Plant and Machine Operators and Assemblers, V = Elementary Occupations

need for craft and related trades workers, plant and machine operators, and assemblers in these two districts. The sons of the fathers belonging to occupational category IV appeared to have performed better than categories III and V, as over 20 percent could move to the I and II occupational categories. The higher occupational mobility of the sons of the fathers of occupational category IV in both districts can be attributed to the evolving nature of industries. For instance, in the 1980s and 1990s, even though 90 percent of the brassware industry employees were Muslims, the industry experienced significant changes as a result of child labor and environmental issues in importing countries, especially western countries, resulting in high automation and a decrease in the demand for manual labor. As a result, the next generation of laborers had to pursue jobs in other sectors. In Saharanpur's industrial cluster, similar conditions prevailed (Ahmed & Nauriyal, 2021).

Nearly half of the overall sample sons were willing to step away from their father's career, as per the $M_{3(occupation)}$=50.8 summary measure. This measure is in the context of what Azam (2015) proposed for separate cohorts (ranging from 47.4 to 54.4) using the IHDS 2011–12. Although Reddy (2015) offers mobility metrics based on NSS data (which stays in the 24.9–28.9 range), it implies insufficient mobility. When we contrast the national and SRC-level estimates with the mobility estimate derived from primary data, we find that sample households have higher mobility (Table 7.3). Additionally, the sample household's absolute mobility in 2018 is comparable to that of the Muslim Others (forward caste).

7.4 Intergenerational Educational Mobility

The educational mobility matrix, based on the primary data acquired, includes individuals from the intergenerational mobility sample (Table 7.4). The data shown in Table 7.4 corroborate the general notion that children of highly educated parents are more likely to pursue higher education, and vice versa. One reason for this trend is that parents with higher education levels typically place more emphasis on their children's academic performance. They recognize that education paves the way for improved career prospects, higher wages and job stability (Chevalier et al., 2013). Parents who joined the workforce with little to no education and who

Table 7.3 NSS-Based Estimates On Total Mobility

SRCs	*Total Mobility (2019)*
All	45.14
Hindu STs	37.75
Hindu SCs	47.31
Hindu OBC	45.86
Hindu Others	44.64
Muslim OBCs	45.59
Muslim Others	50.54
Other Minorities	42.18

Source: Data is taken from table 3.6, chapter 3

Table 7.4 Mobility Matrix for Intergenerational Educational Mobility

Son's Education	*Father's Education*						
	No Formal Education	*Up to Primary*	*Up to Middle*	*Up to Secondary*	*Up to Senior Secondary*	*Graduation and Above*	*Total*
No Formal Education	**33.64**	15.22	3.70	7.84	11.11	0.00	22.54
Up to Primary	22.94	**20.65**	9.88	11.76	5.56	0.00	18.47
Up to Middle	21.41	20.65	**37.04**	25.49	11.11	0.00	22.71
Up to Secondary	11.31	20.65	18.52	**21.57**	33.33	0.00	14.92
Up to Senior Secondary	3.98	10.87	12.35	13.73	**11.11**	19.05	7.80
Graduation and Above	6.73	11.96	18.52	19.61	27.78	**80.95**	13.56
Total	100	100	100	100	100	100	100

Source: Based on Primary Data collected by the authors.

have not finished a higher education level are more prone to believe that higher education is not worth the expense. The total education mobility M3(education) = 67.9 indicates that 67.9 percent of sons could switch away from their father's educational category. The fraction of off-diagonal values below the diagonal cells represents upward education mobility at 57.2 percent. The fraction of off-diagonal values above diagonal cells is 10.2 percent, indicating downward movement. Choudhary and Singh (2017) find comparable figures for young girls (ages 15 to 24) from six different Indian states in 2006–07. This study reports that the overall intergenerational educational mobility among young women in India is almost 69 percent. The upward component of intergenerational educational mobility accounts for 55 percent of the total (Ahmed & Nauriyal, 2021).

Furthermore, in this context, education cannot be considered a homogeneous good because the quality of education provided in publicly funded and privately run institutions varies significantly. Government-run schools, which either provide free education or charge a modest fee, are often chosen by parents who are illiterate, undereducated or have limited resources. On the other hand, better-off parents are more likely to enroll their children in private schools, which are believed to offer greater support, facilities and academic outcomes. Consequently, children attending various schools could have varied levels of intellectual capital. In addition, the parents' lack of education, combined with poor neighborhood, family, and school settings, has a regressive effect on their children's chances of moving up the educational ladder (Dubow et al., 2009; Khan, 2016).

7.5 Occupational Selection: A Micro-Detail

Previous research indicates that out-migration of the workforce from agriculture is a complex process due to the involvement of a generational shift. The success of the first generation will determine who (in the second generation) will be absorbed into which profession. For instance, when farming families grow in size, they may pursue alternative occupations because the land may not be able to support them all. Regardless of their efforts to manage resources by partaking in related pursuits such as dairying and animal husbandry, at least half of the members will probably ultimately transition to other forms of employment. Basu, K. and Tzannatos (2003) found that the workforce is primarily motivated by job opportunities and the potential cost of not working. Depending on their level of education, individuals may transition to other occupations. They may become a normal, paid employee if they complete their studies. If not, they may raise funds to assume the roles of milk producers, truck owners, brick-making site owners, etc. A person's decision to seek an education is influenced by a variety of factors, including the financial stability of their home, their social networks and agents of change. Similar to this, the capacity to establish a business depends on one's existing financial resources and the availability of financing. Obtaining semi-skilled work training is the third option if neither wealth nor education are accessible. In this case, the third option is to obtain training in fields such as welding, tailoring, electrical work, building painting, tile finishing, etc., and launch their own businesses. Success is impacted by a number of factors, including location, social network, credit availability, income and the general attitude that children are economic assets ready to contribute to the family coffers from an early age. If they are unable to execute either of the aforementioned tasks, they may become unskilled laborers (Hedman et al., 2015; Oreopoulos, 2003; Ranjan, 2001).

It should be mentioned that many landless people in a typical Muslim-majority hamlet are divided into castes such as Qureshi, Lohars, Abbasis, Dhobis, Telis, Salmanis, etc. The Telis, Lohars and Ansaris stand out for their proclivity to educate their offspring, indicating a higher appreciation of the benefits of education. The rest of the castes appear to be largely indifferent[1]. Many of them are not exposed to modern schooling, based on the perception that there are few employment opportunities for young Muslim men. In hindsight, this could be because children are viewed as vital economic assets who begin contributing to family resources as early as childhood.

The political economy of West UP is rooted in land ownership. This is especially relevant in light of land reform's modest success and the Green Revolution's greater success (Yadav, 2000; Kothari, 1990; Jaffrelot, 2003; Jeffrey, 2001). Some intermediate caste groups such as the Jats and Gurjars in West UP were able to ascend the socio-economic and political ladder thanks to the assertion of peasant movements in the 1970s and 1980s (Verniers, 2016). The mobility debate is inextricably linked to land ownership in every village economy. As discussed in micro-detail in the last two paragraphs, occupational selection is dependent on the landholding and size. To understand more about the consequences of land ownership and size, we utilized a multinomial logit model with the son's jobs and numerous explanatory factors on the right hand side, including land size.[2] The findings imply that land ownership has a considerable impact on the occupational choices of the next generation[3] (Figure 7.1). A larger landholding size will

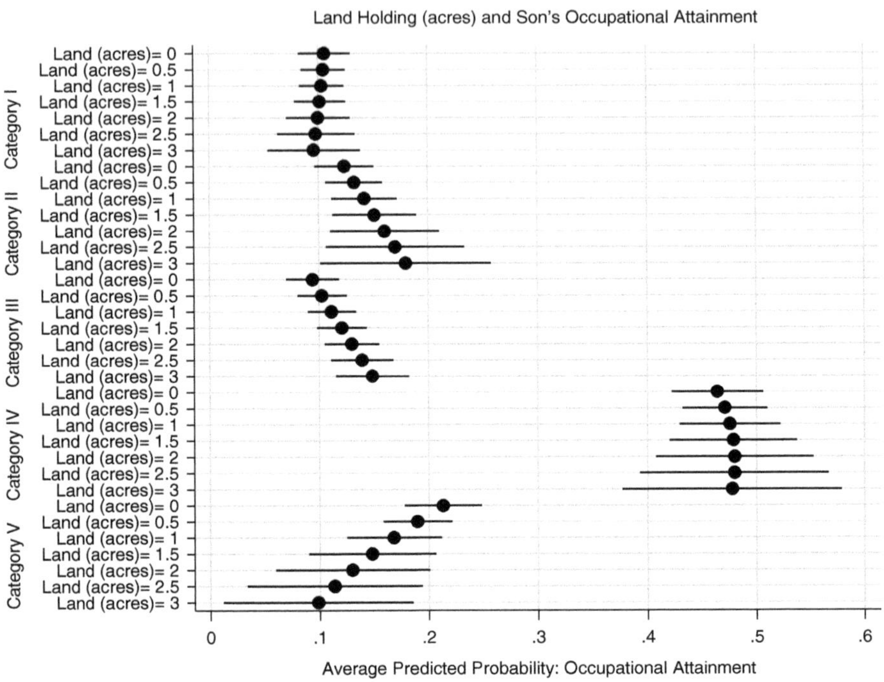

Figure 7.1 Average Predicted Probabilities Based on 590 Father-Son Pairs (as per Size of Landholding). Note: The Son's Occupation at the y-axis is categorized into five distinct groups, as mentioned in the mobility matrix. Source: Primary Survey-Based Estimates.

restrict occupational mobility, as there is no compulsion to relocate to search for a living (Birthal et al., 2014). The average predicted probability of a son pursuing a career in agriculture rises in direct proportion to agricultural land holding area (see Figure 7.1). However, a smaller landholding might not be sufficient to fully support the family, necessitating the search for alternative sources of income (Chakravorty et al., 2019; Ranganathan et al., 2015).

7.6 Intra-Generational Mobility

It was observed from the respondents' work histories, which were compiled from a survey of 300 working people, out of whom only 292 responded to this questionnaire, that only 32.53 percent of them remained engaged in their first profession. The remaining 68 percent eventually changed their line of work (Table 7.5).

It should be noted here that people primarily change jobs when they consider that their current employer does not offer enough compensation and prospects for advancement. If they find greener pastures elsewhere, they are highly inclined to relocate. Another incentive to avoid parents' occupations, which may be many

Table 7.5 Intra-Generational Mobility

The serial number of occupations in the life cycle at the time of reporting the data	*Frequency*	*Percentage*
1	95	32.53
2	108	36.99
3	57	19.52
4	20	6.85
5	7	2.40
6	5	1.71
Total	**292**	**100**

Source: Based on Primary Data collected by the authors.

people's first jobs, is that alternative realms provide many more career options than the father's occupation. However, further research is needed to discover more about the significance of changing occupations if they are not the same as the father's. Individuals are working as apprentices or assisting their fathers, for example, as the home attempts to make greater use of family labor, particularly child labor (Basu & Tzannatos, 2003; Edmonds & Turk, 2002). The child could also work as a helper in someone else's business for a different reason, such as eventually graduating and launching their own self-employed enterprise in the same field. Therefore, the transition is not in the profession but in the progression from becoming a helper to owning a new business in the same economic activity line. It may be a barbershop, an auto mechanic shop, a small grocery store, a meat store, a welding shop, an auto repair shop or a tailoring shop. Approximately 70 percent of respondents have suggested a change in career as a result of this (Table 7.6). Only the remaining 30 percent of respondents may have had a genuine change in profession, such as going from farmer to manual worker, etc. In order to comprehend each respondent's priorities when entering the workforce for the first time, related information was requested from the respondents (Ahmed & Nauriyal, 2021). The information gathered is compiled in Table 7.6.

7.7 Intergenerational Expectations

During the field trip, it was discovered that many villagers continue to deny their children an education by not enrolling them in schools. There are frequent delays in admissions. It displays a lack of awareness or interest in the benefits of contemporary education. It was also discovered that the behavior of the urban poor and working class did not differ significantly from that of their rural counterparts. For example, in the urban regions of Galshaheed and Pakka Bag in Moradabad and Mughal Pura in Baghpat, parental and child education levels were exceedingly low. It raises concern regarding the absorption of such a workforce for employment. In comparably rich Muslim neighborhoods in Moradabad, such as Lajpat Nagar, the situation appeared to be virtually the same. Each of these households appears to create a socio-cultural-economic milieu that has the capacity to impact

Table 7.6 Key Preferences of Individuals at the Time of their First Entry into the Labor Market

Srl. No.	*First Work Activity*	*Frequency (Percentage)*	*Comment(s)*
1.	HH agriculture	40 (13.70)	Only 20 remain in agriculture. Remaining 20 may shift to another economic activity
2.	Labor: loading/unloading/brick making /agricultural labor/ Construction labor	42 (14.38)	No Change
3.	Apprentice for skilled works like welding, tailoring, wooden, brass artwork, driving etc.	36 (12.33)	All would end up having independent business ventures
4.	HH self-employment viz., grocery shop, flour mill, tea stall etc.	18 (6.16)	The majority end up in the same occupation as their enterprises
5.	HH skilled self-employment viz., brass-work, wooden work, fabrication works, electric repair shop	16 (5.48)	The majority end up in the same occupation as their enterprises
6.	Unskilled Helper at other's enterprises like tea stalls, grocery shops, cleaners, etc.	12 (4.11)	No Change
7.	Teacher	9 (3.08)	No Change
8.	Street Vendor	8 (2.74)	No Change
9.	Construction labor as a secondary activity	8 (2.74)	The primary economic activity is mostly agriculture
10.	HH helper (unskilled) at family's enterprise such as grocery shop scrap etc.	4 (1.37)	No Change
11.	Agriculture as a secondary activity	4 (1.37)	The primary economic activity is mainly construction labor
12.	Automobile Driver	4 (1.37)	No Change
13.	Miscellaneous work activities	91 (31.17)	
14.	**Total**	**292 (100)**	

Source: Based on Primary Data collected by the authors.

the personal and professional decisions of future generations, whether consciously or subconsciously (Mortimer et al., 2017). Interestingly, existing literature also supports the hypothesis of "family capital" (Swartz, 2008). It assumes that parents are capable agents who assist and enable future generations to advance up the social ladder through educational attainment and occupational choices (Conger & Dogan, 2007; Crosnoe et al., 2002; Mortimer et al., 2017; Taylor et al., 2004). Multiple studies have found a high correlation between parents' socio-economic status, educational attainment, aspirations and goals for their children, and their children's educational attainment, occupational aspirations and outcomes (Andrew & Hauser, 2011; Bozick et al., 2010; Gregg & Washbrook, 2011; Hitlin, 2006; Reynolds & Johnson, 2011). Several studies have reported a strong correlation between parental educational goals, parenting effectiveness, cognitive ability and academic interests (Crosnoe et al., 2002; Fergusson et al., 2008). During the interactions, parents acknowledged that high parental expectations and a reasonable investment in education contribute to their children's academic success (Davis-Kean, 2005). Conversely, lower parental expectations can be discouraging, if not downright detrimental, to children's academic development. This issue was found to be compounded further by the low levels of education among Muslim parents and children. A direct inquiry with a brief context explanation was posed to the heads of a sample of Muslim households with school-aged children in order to get the necessary information. Out of 300 families, 40 did not respond since the questions were unrelated or the sample households did not provide any input. The remaining 260 responses are organized into groups based on the similarity of their responses and are shown in Table 7.7.

As can be seen from the last column of Table 7.7, approximately 65 percent of parents desire their children to attend school, while the remaining 35 percent prefer that they start working at a very early age. The field investigations indicated that "everyone now sends their children to kindergarten" or "everyone goes to school", but that is still not the case. Despite what appears to be a totally different reality on the ground, the data on literacy, the expansion of educational infrastructure, and school enrollment provide the appearance that advancements are occurring, albeit at a slower rate. However, the issue is not whether parents have exhibited a lack of interest in their children's education or a desire for early work for them; rather, a major factor in why children may drop out of school is that their parents are unsure of what they want to do with their lives (Ahmed & Nauriyal, 2021).

It would be crucial to look at the connection between household's educational successes and the household's aspirations. The data in Table 7.8 show that there is strong public support for children's continued education and prospective future occupations as their educational levels grow. Compared to parents with less education, parents with more than 12 years of education seem to be less apprehensive about their children's prospects. Furthermore, Table 7.8 reveals that these parents do not view their financial condition as a major concern, indicating that they are better educated and more financially stable than other groups.

Table 7.8 appears to indicate that parents with lower academic attainment want their children to begin working early. This is most likely owing to their desperate need to supplement the family's income, their confusion about the potential advantages of schooling, and the time lag involved. Consequently, the opportunity cost of schooling is significantly raised (Fields, 2019). Notably, the emphasis is likely to be more on survival than education for parents with low-income levels. In some measures, parents of all educational levels favor religious instruction for their children. About 4 percent of parents have indicated their preference for religious education for their children. It is important to note that 8 percent of children

Table 7.7 Average Years of Education of the HH and Aspirations for the Future Generation

Srl. No.	*Preferences*	*Average Years of Education of the HH*					*Distribution of HHs*
		Up to 5 yrs	*Up to 8 yrs*	*Up to 10 yrs*	*Up to 12 yrs*	*Greater than 12 yrs*	
1.	Willing to support children's education	38.02	45.71	45.24	21.05	50.00	40.38
2.	Want their children to come up as professionals such as a doctor, engineers, advocates, central and state civil services or other reputed government jobs	6.61	15.71	21.43	26.32	25.00	13.46
3.	Willing to support only religious education to the children and see them as Hafiz, Maulana etc.	8.26	0.00	0.00	0.00	12.50	4.23
4.	Willing to support the education of children but not much sure of real support because of acute financial crunch	7.44	5.71	4.76	15.79	0.00	6.92
5.	Not thought about the probable careers of their children/ Are largely indifferent	23.14	11.43	2.38	5.26	12.50	15.00
6.	Want their children to go for self-employment or some business	10.74	12.86	9.52	5.26	0.00	10.38
7.	Diverse kinds of responses which cannot be clubbed with any other category	5.79	8.57	16.67	26.32	0.00	9.62
8.	Aggregate	100	100	100	100	100	100

Note: Read yrs as years; All figures are in percentage. Source: Based on Primary Data collected by the authors.

aged 5 to 14 are enrolled in madrasas, which is far higher than the 4 percent statistic for all of India reported by the Sachar Committee Report (2006).

Parents begin planning for their children's education in the early years based on their own education, interactions with the outside world, social network, neighborhood experiences and influences, and available resources. Prior research indicates that low-income families with low levels of education, limited exposure, poor social networks and unfavorable neighborhood effects do not prioritize their children's education. This is further supported by the data presented in Table 7.8, which demonstrates that households in the first income quartile place less value

Table 7.8 Per Capita Income Quintiles and Aspirations for the Future Generation

S. No.	*Preferences*	*4 Quintiles of Per Capita Household Monthly Income*				*Distribution of HHs*
		1	*2*	*3*	*4*	
1	Willing to support children's education	35.94	39.71	42.65	43.33	40.38
2	Want their children to come up as professionals such as doctor, engineer, advocate, IAS, PCS or other reputed government jobs	10.94	10.29	14.71	18.33	13.46
3	Willing to support only religious education to the children and want to see them as Hafiz, Maulana etc.	1.56	7.35	2.94	5	4.23
4	Willing to support the education of children but not much sure of real support because of acute financial crunch	14.06	7.35	4.41	1.67	6.92
5	Not thought about the probable careers of their children/ Are largely indifferent	28.13	5.88	11.76	15	15
6	Want their children to go for self-employment or some business	4.69	16.18	11.76	8.33	10.38
7	Diverse kinds of responses which cannot be clubbed with aforementioned categories	4.69	13.24	11.76	8.33	9.62
8	Aggregate	100	100	100	100	100

Note: All figures are percentage. Source: Based on Primary Data collected by the author(s)

on education and appear unconcerned with their children's career prospects, making it uncertain whether they will be willing to muster sufficient resources to support their children's education. If parents have no employment aspirations for their children's future, it may seem reasonable not to take resources into account. Furthermore, though parents in higher-income households value their children's improved job opportunities, a significant proportion of them have not given the subject any thought. This appears to be a disturbing trend that should be investigated further to understand the roots of such apathy. One probable explanation is that almost one-fourth of parents continue to view self-employment as a viable career path (Ahmed & Nauriyal, 2021).

Estimates of educational mobility from one generation to the next confirm that low-income, low-education households have little optimism for the career and education prospects of the next generation. When son's years of education were run on the father's years of education,[4] it was found that intergenerational educational inertia is γ_1 =.54 (0.0419)[5]. Going the other way round, the intergenerational educational mobility among sample households is $(1-\gamma_1) = 0.46$. The low educational attainment among poor-income and low-educated families is further visible in the intercept coefficient. The $\gamma_0 = 5.08$ (0.2387) suggests that a son with

Table 7.9 NSS-Based Estimates on Educational Mobility

SRCs/ Year	*2019*	
	Intercept	*IG Grad persistence*
All	8.388 (0.024)	0.356 (0.004)
Hindu ST	7.798 (0.079)	0.330 (0.017)
Hindu SC	8.267 (0.058)	0.301 (0.011)
Hindu OBC	8.703 (0.042)	0.329 (0.007)
Hindu Others	9.063 (0.056)	0.351 (0.007)
Muslims	7.790 (0.062)	0.348 (0.010)
Other Minorities	8.290 (0.075)	0.356 (0.011)

Source: Data are taken from the tables 5.1 and 5.2, chapter 5

an uneducated father receives five years of schooling. The intercept term emphasizes the significance of giving the most disadvantaged people in society access to education, i.e., the sons of the least educated parents. Typically, such a group is associated with low occupational and income groups.

It is interesting to compare primary data-based estimates with Chapter 5's secondary data-based estimates. Educational mobility indicators at the national and SRC levels are presented in Table 7.9. Table 7.9 indicates that grad persistence in India in 2019 was lower than the estimate for the sample population (0.35 vs 0.46). This suggests that there is significant schooling inertia among the sample households. In comparison to estimates at the national and SRC levels, the OLS estimation using primary data yields a relatively moderate intercept term (5.08). Simply put, it suggests that, on a national level, a son of illiterate parents is likely to finish at least eight years of schooling. However, in the sample households, this number is just five years. Still, the intercept coefficients of sample households are lower (5.08) than those of Muslim households as a whole (7.79).

7.8 The Struggle for Labor

In the three visited districts, an overwhelming percentage of people work as semi-skilled or unskilled workers or as casual laborers. The wooden work of Saharanpur, the brass-work of Moradabad, and the brick-making sites at Baghpat are sectors where such workers are employed in large numbers. However, in Baghpat, many people nowadays have started working as E-rickshaw service providers. Interaction with such families speaks volumes about the causes of educational backwardness. For instance, almost all the households spoke of the worsening quality of government schools as the prime reason for households' unwillingness to send their children to government schools. Different researchers have also reported rising dropouts from government schools due to the deteriorating quality of education owing to the indifference and absence of the teachers (Alam & Raju, 2007; Jeffrey et al., 2004; Razzack, 2019). In such a scenario, households having access to more resources choose to send their children to private schools. Thus, at this crucial stage, some of the children are denied a perceived quality education due to the poor resource access of their parents. In one of the villages of Baghpat, upon asking questions about why there is an absence of a good education profile for the village (Oshika, Baghpat), despite the government schools' being good in the past, the remote location of the schools and the rise in cost thereof due to transportation expenses was also reported as a demotivator. Poor outreach of the schools and sharply rising expenses after the middle school level of education were also indicated as other important considerations that influenced the decision of the parents on whether to send their children to school (Jeffrey, C., Jeffery, R., & Jeffery, P., 2004). It is a vicious cycle for low-income groups since they have: less income ⟶ no or fewer role models ⟶ no social networks ⟶ limited exposure ⟶ less income. All of these factors have the effect of lowering expectations, motivation, and awareness of the value of education.

Many casual workers do not find year-round gainful employment, which is a cause for concern. For instance, the sample population in this occupational group claimed that they only worked six to eight months out of the year and only 15–20 days each month. There may be several plausible explanations for the current scenario. While it is impossible to ignore the cases of poor access to employment opportunities in the farm and non-farm sectors as well as under-reporting of employment days, other tenable explanations include the employment of casual workers in seasonal industries like brick kilns and sugarcane, where they are employed for four to six months of the year. Although not all-inclusive, this list illustrates the daily struggles faced by casual workers.

This issue has been further taken forward by examining the average predicted probabilities of sons, with various types of their father's occupations, entering different occupations than their parents, as presented in Figure 7.2.[6] Intergenerational stickiness exists across occupations, albeit it is more pronounced in categories II, IV and V. Further investigation reveals that a farmer's son has an almost zero average estimated likelihood of entering category II employment (service providers and shop and retail salespeople). Given the rapidly expanding non-farm industry in rural regions, it appears strange. The sector-wise (rural and urban) average predicted probability also represents the expected average likelihood of entering different occupations (Figure 7.2). An urban worker has an edge over a rural counterpart when it comes to pursuing these jobs because the majority of category II activities take place in cities. It could be one logical explanation for why the farmer's son stands disqualified from profession category II. Non-farm work is also connected to education, the availability of finance, and social standing, which presents challenges for underprivileged and lower-income groups (Chowdhury, 2017; Jatav & Sen, 2013; Jha, 2006; Kijima & Lanjouw, 2005). According to Figure 7.2's sector-specific average projected probability, urban children outperform their rural counterparts in categories I, II and IV, the reverse is true in categories III and V. In summary, Muslims in rural areas often have it worse than Muslims in urban areas. However, Asher et al. (2018) came to the conclusion that urban Muslims face barriers to upward mobility.

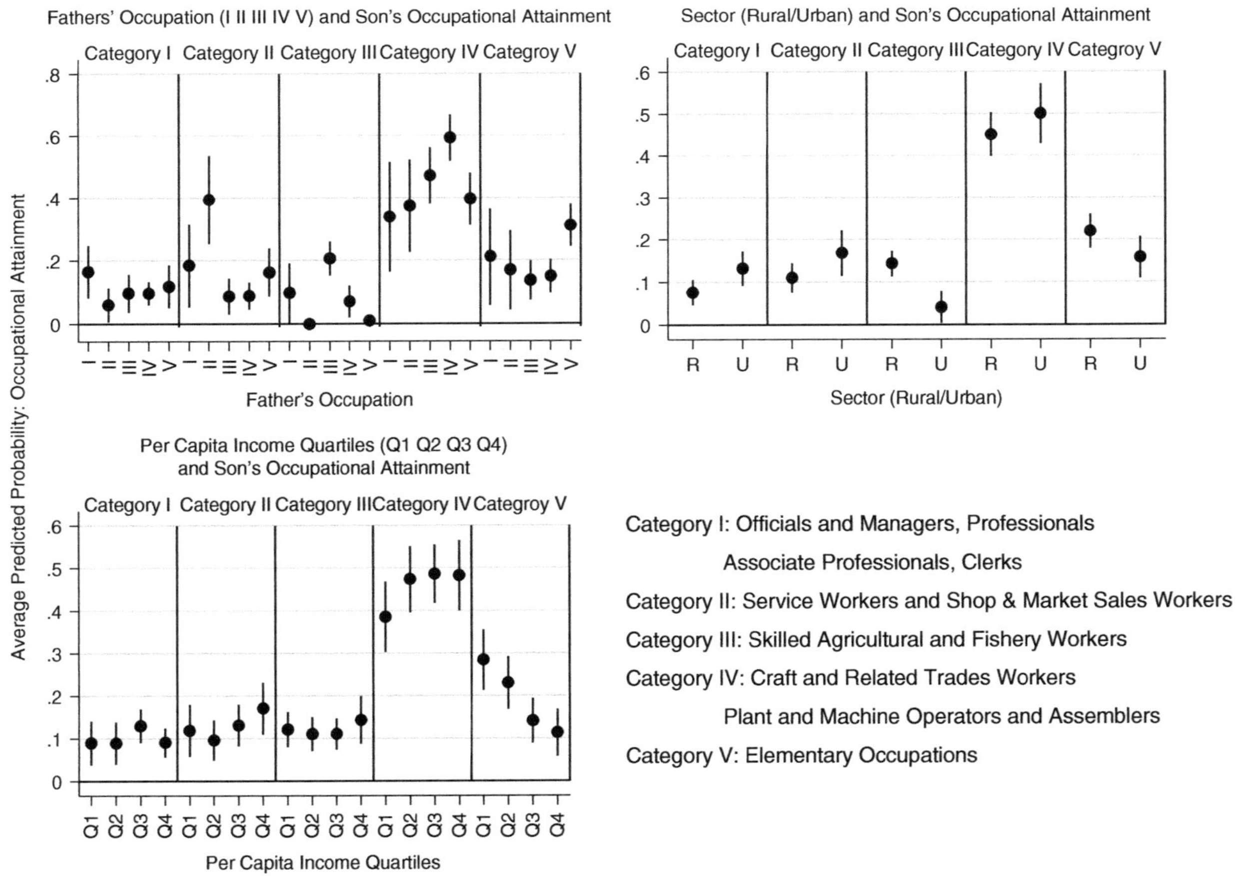

Figure 7.2 Average Predicted Probabilities Based on 590 Father-Son Pairs (as per Other Variables). Note: The Sons Occupation at the y-axis is categorized into five distinct groups, as mentioned in the mobility matrix. Source: Primary Survey-Based Estimates.

Figure 7.2 indicates that the likelihood of a son changing jobs increases as household income rises for category V (laborers). This issue was also addressed earlier with the finding that children's success in the labor market is affected by a variety of factors, including per capita income. For instance, whether the son enters the laborers' rank or receives professional training before accepting any position or starting any business may be determined by the family's financial circumstances. The former scenario occurs when the family's basic earnings are insufficient to pay for the son's professional training expenses. Figure 7.2 demonstrates that sons from middle-class households (Q2 and Q3) are more likely than sons from low-income families to work in category IV occupations (Q1 and Q4). It may be noted that the poverty rate among Indian Muslims is significant (John & Mutatkar, 2005; Panagariya & Mukim, 2014). Arora and Singh (2015) provide projections for West UP, indicating that scheduled castes and Muslims have the highest poverty rates. The high prevalence of poverty suggests that available jobs cannot deliver a minimally acceptable standard of living to the worker and her/his family (Anant et al., 2006), perpetuating their presence in the labor market.

7.9 Missing Muslim Middle Class

The results highlight that children from households with poor levels of education have the lowest educational attainment (intercept term). Furthermore, the labor class's survival battle traps them in a vicious loop of poverty marked by inadequate education, low income and low motivation. However, the entire community as a whole is not performing well in terms of educational attainment. We can observe from secondary data as well that Muslims lag behind other communities, such as Hindu Others, in terms of educational achievement. Since our sample includes members of every Muslim sub-group, a more in-depth examination of the sample population's educational profile should be useful. For this, we mapped respondents who had graduated or at least had some college experience in their preferred stream. Only 73 out of 590 persons (12.37 percent), as shown in Table 7.10, have finished any higher education program. Table 8.7 shows that the majority of Muslim students pursued arts and commerce courses rather than technical education. Because there are not many employment opportunities for those with simple degrees in arts and commerce, this education is unlikely to help them find good ones.

From the secondary data, it was deduced that across other communities, among less educated households, the educational attainment is better than that of the Muslims. All social groupings within the OBCs performed well in both elementary and higher education. It has been noted that among Muslims, upper-middle and middle-class households desire a decent education for their children but do not prioritize professional and quality education. This is likely due to the neighborhood effect or the low perceived value of such education. They have been found to opt for conventional arts, commerce and diploma programs that are somewhat less expensive.

Table 7.10 Types of Courses Taken by Sons in Higher Education

Course	*Frequency*
Graduation in Arts Stream	21
Post-Graduation in Arts Stream	16
Graduation in Commerce Stream	5
Graduation in Science Stream	7
Graduation in Engineering	5
Graduation in Law	3
Master in Law	2
Master of Business Administration	5
Polytechnic	2
Post-Graduation in Commerce	2
Graduation in Medicine (Ayurveda)	2
Bachelor of Business Administration	1
Bachelor of Education	1
Bachelor of Pharmacy	1
Aggregate	73

Source: Based on Primary Data collected by the authors.

It could also be because the size of the class that aspires to higher education and upward mobility is small among Muslims. The missing middle class among Muslims or its diminutive size has been a subject of discussion for a long time (Alam, 2015). Krishnan and Hatekar (2017) have shown that the size of the new middle class in India was constant between 1999–00 and 2004–05 but the same went on to double between 2004–05. The author duo considered the new middle class in India who have their per day per capita expenditure in the range of two to ten dollars. Their findings suggest that the new middle class is heterogeneous in terms of occupations, income sizes and caste groups. And, traditional service and new knowledge-related activities were particularly dominated by the upper-middle class. They further reported that the new middle class, on the one hand, was dominated by the upper castes, while other intermediate and marginalized caste groups, too, had made their way into the new middle class in large numbers. The striking feature is that among Muslims, the size of the lower middle (PCE $2 to $4 per day), middle-middle (PCE $4 to $6 per day), and higher middle (PCE $6 to $10 per day) classes is smaller than that of the "Hindus" as a group and much smaller than the OBCs and Hindu Others. In this scenario, it would be significantly more relevant to provide a historical context that explains why the majority of Muslims lack formal education. According to archival evidence, the partition of India resulted in a very large number of educated upper- and lower-middle-class Muslims migrating to Pakistan, leaving the lower-income class behind (Engineer, 2004; Kamat, 1981). Although the composition has shifted little over time, Muslims continue to fall behind other communities in terms of status. They remain predominantly from the lower middle class, and it would take far longer to reverse the generational impacts of losing the Muslim middle class as a result of India's partition. Due to the requirement for early work for their children so that they may support the family income, the poorer and lower middle classes across all religious groups have typically not considered education to be a viable option or an incentive (Lynch & O'Riordan, 1998; Stivers, 1958). The argument that even if they accept admission for higher education, their likelihood of finishing it is far lower is supported by the high dropout rates and generally sub-par academic achievement of the offspring of these classes. It perpetuates their continued employment in low-paying jobs, which mostly consist of self-employment or manual labor positions where education is not a requirement. Thus, despite the notion that education is basically a community good, participation and outcomes are usually hampered by a range of socio-economic and cultural barriers that the government cannot overcome alone.

7.10 Feminization of Madrasa

Earlier, many scholars have written about this issue, inferring that more and more Muslim girls are opting to attend madrasas for their education (Borker, 2020; Akhtar & Narula, 2010; Jeffery, P., Jeffery, R., & Jeffrey, C., 2005; 28 Sikand, 2005). According to the Sachar Committee's 2006 data, girls account for 45.9 percent of all students enrolled in madrasas. The authors of the present survey also found similar trends in West UP. Some academics contend that enrollment at madrasas is primarily driven by a desire to preserve the unique Muslim identity (Alam, 2003; Saiyed & Talib, 1985). Gupta (2012) presents Madrasa education as a gendered decision by emphasizing the ways in which women's roles within the family limit girls' learning possibilities in madrasas. He based his argument on a field study he conducted in three West Bengal districts. He remarked that at lower levels, there are more girls in Madrasa compared to boys, meaning that parents would choose to send their sons to mainstream, less expensive schools. Several additional studies on Muslim education have similarly recorded the tendency of more females studying Islamic institutions than boys, owing to its relationship with higher marriage chances (Borker, 2020). Some academics examine the same pattern from an economic angle. Their views hover around the contention that people choose Madrasa because it is the only inexpensive option for impoverished Muslims and offers financial advantages including no tuition, free boarding and free accommodation (Sikand, 2005; Engineer, 2001). It is also believed that madrasas grew popular as a result of diminishing or insufficient government schools, particularly in rural regions (Akhtar & Narula, 2010; Jeffery, P., Jeffery, R., & Jeffrey, C., 2005).

7.11 Perception and Discrimination

There is a significant difference between realized discrimination (Figure 7.3 (a) and (b)) and perceived discrimination (Figure 7.3 (c)). The respondents were asked three questions. "Do you think being a Muslim makes you a target of discrimination at work?" the first question asks. Second, "Has any member of your family ever been refused or subjected to discrimination when attempting to get a paid position with a fair salary?". Third, "How frequently do you think a Muslim will be passed over for a job or promotion in favour of a member of a different community who is equally or less qualified?" (Ahmed & Nauriyal, 2021). The low affirmative response to discrimination in the recruitment of regular salaried jobs is attributable to the fact that many people in the Muslim community do not have well-educated family members who are eligible for a regular salaried job in a public or private enterprise. The stark contrast between actual and perceived discrimination may also be because people usually derive their notions about discrimination from their larger personal experiences, such as those with their family and friends or from media reports. The perception of discrimination, however, is far greater than the reality of it. Many respondents claimed that they have grown to believe in prejudice over time as a result of finding few Muslim employees in government agencies, police stations, public institutions and health facilities.

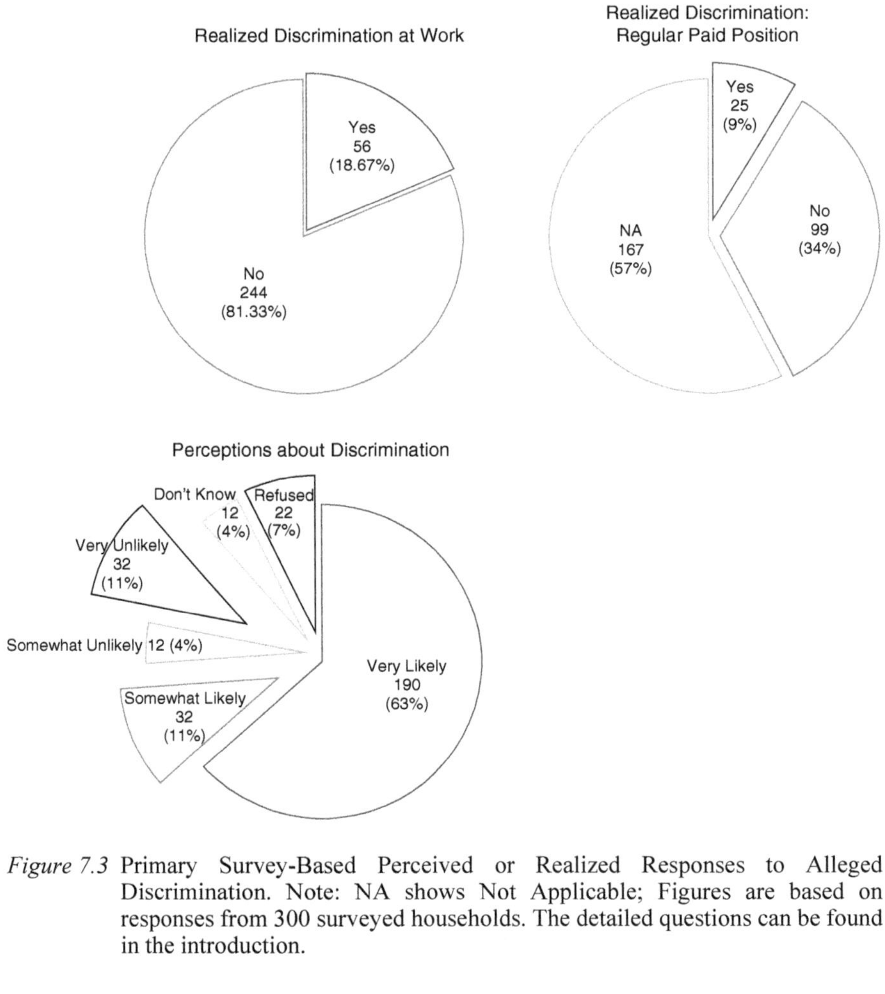

Figure 7.3 Primary Survey-Based Perceived or Realized Responses to Alleged Discrimination. Note: NA shows Not Applicable; Figures are based on responses from 300 surveyed households. The detailed questions can be found in the introduction.

7.12 One Community that Cuts across Religions

In the study area (West UP), a sizable population belongs to the intermediate castes[7] and a landowning social group known as the Jats. This social group is religiously diverse throughout the subcontinent, with Hindu, Muslim and Sikh Jats. As far as West UP is concerned, the Jats are either Hindus or Muslims. A significant amount of political science and political economy research is devoted to the socio-economic and political mobility of Hindu Jats of West UP as opposed to Muslim Jats (Yadav, 2000; Kothari, 1990, Jaffrelot, 2003; Jeffrey, 2001; Brass, 1980a,b). It is possible that this is due to the Hindu Jats' political mobilization and increasing prominence in occupational and educational spheres. This topic piqued the writers' interest, and they decided to investigate it with the locals of district Baghpat, which is home to the majority of West UP's Jat population. In three Baghpat villages (Dola, Oshika and Niwara), a sizable number of individuals have responded to several open-ended questions. However, notable discussions that, to some extent, expounded on the subject occurred with a prominent district lawyer (a Muslim Jat) and a landlord-turned-politician (a Hindu Jat). The senior politician explained in great detail why Muslim Jats have not risen as swiftly as they should. Several of his insights that shed light on the development process are discussed below. "We are Hindus in addition to being Jats. We are neighbors with the Brahmin, Baniya, Kayasth and so on. People with education around us", he said, emphasizing the importance of education and social networks. "We are less focused and less dependent on agriculture now", he added. "We have diversified our occupations; we are in services[8] also, and we are also involved in the interest-based lending business. In cities, we have big shops." Returning to his focus on social networks, he stated, "When two or three people progress in a village, everyone begins to progress." He noted that a community's political representation plays a significant role in upward mobility. He says, "Mantri aur Sansad ka farq padta hai (Ministers and Members of Parliament matter)." On the other hand, the advocate summed up his position by stating, "Hindu Jats place a premium on education. We are equally concerned with education, but, unlike them, we do not make the finest efforts. We leave school too soon without giving it our all." He adds that Muslim Jat villages such as Oshika, Idrispur, Roshangarh, Gauna and Mandi lack intermediate colleges, while in other villages, intermediate colleges are available, from which their Hindu counterparts have benefited. He points out straightaway that the politics of UP have not been favorable to them. He stated, "Jis samaj ko satta mili, chahe jat ho, yadav ho, dalit ho, unko naukri aur sansadhan me labh mila. Musalman keval vote bank ban kar rah gaya (Whichever social group assumed power, be it Jats, Yadavas, or Dalits, every group benefited in terms of public employment and resources)." Muslims have merely become "a vote bank in politicians' hands". Similar sentiments were echoed by several individuals during the field visit. These findings align with earlier studies on patronage and client-based political systems (Zerinini, 2009; Jeffrey, 2002; Verniers, 2016; Kitschelt & Wilkinson, 2007; Brass, 1980a,b; Jaffrelot, 2003). This research question concerning the disparities between Hindu and Muslim Jats brings up new opportunities for ethnographic investigation.

7.13 Conclusions

This study's key finding is that educational mobility is higher than occupational mobility for the younger cohort. It further demonstrates that a sizable proportion of the sons follow in their fathers' footsteps in terms of employment. From the respondents' employment histories, it was found that 70 percent of them continued to work at their first occupation, while the remaining 30 percent switched to other occupations over time. The findings indicate that the father's occupation has a strong influence on the son's academic success. It also emphasizes the likelihood of greater education for sons of fathers in Group I and Group II jobs. Other important markers of how well their children perform in school appear to be the length of the fathers' education and the area of cultivable land they own. It has been discovered that higher landholdings inhibit occupational mobility in agricultural households while boosting it in households with category II employment. It does, however, have the potential to promote educational mobility. Agricultural households with bigger families had increased occupational mobility. Another crucial conclusion of this study is that, due to push and pull pressures, occupational mobility is stronger in rural areas than in urban areas, and that occupational mobility is much greater than educational mobility. In terms of career mobility, urban sample households outperform their rural counterparts.

Notes

1 Qureshi, Lohar, Abbasi, Dhobi,Teli, Salmani, Lohar and Darugir are some major caste groups which comprise other backward class (OBC) among Indian Muslims.
2 *Son's Occupation*= $\delta_0 + \delta_1$ *Son's Years of education*$_i$+δ_2 *Father's occupation*$_i$ + $\delta_3 w_2 + \varepsilon_{i'}$; W_2 is the vector of variables that contains age cohorts, sector (rural/urban), social group (Forward/OBC), monthly per capita income quartiles, landholding in acres and household size. Age cohorts include Cohort I (1954–70), Cohort II (1971–90) and Cohort III (1991–04). The households' self-declared monthly income is classified in four quartiles after converting it into per capita terms. The two continuous variables on the left-hand side of both equations are landholding size in acres and household size (Ahmed & Nauriyal, 2021).
3 Here the margins (average predicted probabilities) are calculated for landholding size after keeping it at 0, 0.5, 1, 1.5, 2, 2.5 and 3 acres. Similarly, for another continuous variable household size, the values for the calculation of margins (average predicted probabilities) are fixed at 4, 6, 8, 10, 12 and 14.
4 *Son's Years of Education*$_i = \gamma_0 + \gamma_1$ *Father's years of education*$_i + \varepsilon_i$
5 R^2= 0.223; Adjusted-R^2 = 0.222; Number of Observations=590
6 For MNL model see footnote 2 of this chapter.
7 Neither upper caste nor the backward caste, but in UP categorized as OBC.
8 He meant regular salaried jobs.

References

Ahmed, N., & Nauriyal, D. K. (2021). Occupational and educational mobility among Indian Muslims: Primary survey-based evidence. *Millennial Asia*, 09763996211044376.

Akhtar, N., & Narula, M. (2010). The role of Indian madrasahs in providing access to mainstream education for Muslim minority students: A West Bengal experience.

Journal of International Migration and Integration/Revue de l'integration et de la migration internationale, *11*(1), 91–107.

Alam, A. (2003). Understanding madrasas. *Economic and Political Weekly*, *38*(22), 2123–2126.

Alam, A. (2015). Emergence of Muslim middle class in post-independence India and its political orientations. *Journal of Muslim Minority Affairs*, *35*(1), 123–140.

Alam, M. S., & Raju, S. (2007). Contextualising inter-, intra-religious and gendered literacy and educational disparities in rural Bihar. *Economic and Political Weekly*, *42*(18), 1613–1622.

Anant, T. C. A., Hasan, R., Mohapatra, P., Nagaraj, R., & Sasikumar, S. K. (2006). Labour markets in India: Issues and perspectives. In J. Felipe and R. Hasan (Eds.), *Labour Markets in Asia: Issues and Perspectives* (pp. 205–300). Asian Development Bank, Manila: Palgrave Macmillan.

Andrew, M., & Hauser, R. M. (2011). Adoption? Adaptation? Evaluating the formation of educational expectations. *Social Forces*, *90*(2), 497–520. https://doi.org/10.1093/sf/sor005

Arora, A., & Singh, S. P. (2015). Poverty across social and religious groups in Uttar Pradesh: An interregional analysis. *Economic and Political Weekly*, *50*(52), 100–109. http://www.jstor.org/stable/44003030

Asher, S., Novosad, P., & Rafkin, C. (2018). Intergenerational mobility in India: Estimates from new methods and administrative data. *World Bank Working Paper*. http://barrett.dyson.cornell.edu/NEUDC/paper_560.pdf

Azam, M. (2015). Intergenerational occupational mobility among men in India. *Journal of Development Studies*, *51*(10), 1389–1408. https://doi.org/10.1080/00220388.2015.1036040

Basu, K., & Tzannatos, Z. (2003). The global child labor problem: What do we know and what can we do? *World Bank Economic Review*, *17*(2), 147–173. https://doi.org/10.1093/wber/lhg021

Bhattacharya, D., & Mazumder, B. (2011). A nonparametric analysis of black-white differences in intergenerational income mobility in the United States. *Quantitative Economics*, *2*(3), 335–379. https://doi.org/10.3982/QE69

Birthal, P. S., Negi, D. S., Jha, A. K., & Singh, D. (2014). Income sources of farm households in India: Determinants, distributional consequences and policy implications. *Agricultural Economics Research Review*, *27*(1), 37. https://doi.org/10.5958/j.0974-0279.27.1.003

Borker, H. (2020). Talim, Dindari aur Shaadi (Education, Religiosity and Marriage): Choosing Madrasa Education for Girls. *Social Change*, *50*(2), 236–253.

Bozick, R., Alexander, K., Entwisle, D., Dauber, S., & Kerr, K. (2010). Framing the future: Revisiting the place of educational expectations in status attainment. *Social Forces*, *88*(5), 2027–2052. https://doi.org/10.1353/sof.2010.0033

Brass, P. R. (1980a). The politicisation of the peasantry in a north Indian state: I. *Journal of Peasant Studies*, *7*(4), 395–426.

Brass, P. R. (1980b). The politicisation of the peasantry in a north Indian state: II. *Journal of Peasant Studies*, *8*(1), 3–36.

Chakravorty, S., Chandrasekhar, S., & Naraparaju, K. (2019). Land distribution, income generation and inequality in India's agricultural sector. *Review of Income and Wealth*, *65*(S1), S182–S203. https://doi.org/10.1111/roiw.12434

Chetty, R., Hendren, N., Kline, P., & Saez, E. (2014). Where is the land of opportunity? The geography of intergenerational mobility in the United States. *Quarterly Journal of Economics*, *129*(4), 1553–1623. https://doi.org/10.1093/qje/qju022

Chevalier, A., Harmon, C., O' Sullivan, V., & Walker, I. (2013). The impact of parental income and education on the schooling of their children. *IZA Journal of Labor Economics*, *2*(1), 1–22. https://doi.org/10.1186/2193-8997-2-8

Choudhary, A., & Singh, A. (2017). Are daughters like mothers: Evidence on intergenerational educational mobility among young females in India. *Social Indicators Research*, *133*(2), 601–621. https://doi.org/10.1007/s11205-016-1380-8

Chowdhury, S. (2017). Microfinance and rural non-farm employment in developing countries. *IZA World of Labor*. https://doi.org/10.15185/izawol.350

Conger, R. D., & Dogan, S. J. (2007). Social class and socialization in families. In J. E. Grusec & P. D. Hast (Eds.), *Handbook of socilalization: Theory and research* (pp. 433–460). Guilford.

Corak, M. (2013). Income inequality, equality of opportunity, and intergenerational mobility. *Journal of Economic Perspectives*, *27*(3), 79–102. https://doi.org/10.1257/jep.27.3.79

Crosnoe, R., Mistry, R. S., & Elder, G. H. (2002). Economic disadvantage, family dynamics, and adolescent enrollment in higher education. *Journal of Marriage and Family*, *64*(3), 690–702.

Davis-Kean, P. E. (2005). The influence of parent education and family income on child achievement: The indirect role of parental expectations and the home environment. *Journal of Family Psychology*, *19*(2), 294–304. https://doi.org/10.1037/0893-3200.19.2.294

Dubow, E. F., Boxer, P., & Huesmann, L. R. (2009). Long-term effects of parents' education on children's educational and occupational success: Mediation by family interactions, child aggression, and teenage aspirations. *Merrill-Palmer Q Wayne State Univ Press*, *55*(3), 224–249. https://doi.org/10.1353/mpq.0.0030.Long-term

Edmonds, E., & Turk, C. (2002). *Child labor in transition in Vietnam* (Policy Research Working Paper, No. 2774). Article Policy Research Working Paper, *NO. 2774*. https://openknowledge.worldbank.org/bitstream/handle/10986/15735/multi0page.pdf?sequence=1

Engineer, A. A. (2004). Reservation for Muslims. *Economic and Political Weekly*, *39*(36), 3984–3985.

Fergusson, D. M., Horwood, L. J., & Boden, J. M. (2008). The transmission of social inequality: Examination of the linkages between family socioeconomic status in childhood and educational achievement in young adulthood. *Research in Social Stratification and Mobility*, *26*(3), 277–295. https://doi.org/10.1016/j.rssm.2008.05.001

Fields, G. S. (2019). Self-employment and poverty in developing countries. *IZA World of Labor*, *60*(March), 1–10. https://doi.org/10.15185/izawol.60.v2

Gregg, P., & Washbrook, E. (2011). The role of attitudes and behaviours in explaining socio-economic differences in attainment at age 11. *Longitudinal and Life Course Studies*, *2*(1), 41–58. https://doi.org/10.14301/llcs.v2i1.142

Gupta, N. (2012). *Reading with Allah: Madrasas in West Bengal*. Routledge.

Hedman, L., Manley, D., van Ham, M., & Östh, J. (2015). Cumulative exposure to disadvantage and the intergenerational transmission of neighbourhood effects. *Journal of Economic Geography*, *15*(1), 195–215. https://doi.org/10.1093/jeg/lbt042

Hitlin, S. (2006). Parental influences on children's values and aspirations: Bridging two theories of social class and socialization. *Sociological Perspectives*, *49*(1), 25–46. https://doi.org/10.1525/sop.2006.49.1.25

Iversen, V., Krishna, A., & Sen, K. (2017). Rags to riches? Intergenerational occupational mobility in India. *Economic and Political Weekly*, *52*(44), 107–114. https://www.epw.in/journal/2017/44/special-articles/rags-riches-intergenerational-occupational-mobility-india.html?0=ip_login_no_cache%3Dd7897b90ac2de4a99546e1e0b51d2eac

Jaffrelot, C. (2003). *India's silent revolution: The rise of the lower castes in North India*. Orient Blackswan.

Jatav, M., & Sen, S. (2013). Drivers of non-farm employment in rural india evidence from the 2009–10 NSSO round. *Economic and Political Weekly*, *48*(26–27), 14–21. http://www.jstor.org/stable/23527236

Jeffrey, C. (2001). 'A fist is stronger than five fingers': Caste and dominance in rural North India. *Transactions of the Institute of British Geographers*, *26*(2), 217–236.

Jeffrey, C. (2002). Caste, class, and clientelism: A political economy of everyday corruption in rural North India. *Economic Geography*, *78*(1), 21–41.

Jeffrey, C., Jeffery, R., & Jeffery, P. (2004). Degrees without freedom: The impact of formal education on Dalit young men in North India. *Development and Change*, *35*(5), 963–986. https://doi.org/10.1111/j.1467-7660.2004.00388.x

Jeffery, P., Jeffery, R., & Jeffrey, C. (2005). The Mother's lap and the civilizing mission: Madrasa education and the rural muslim girls in Western Uttar Pradesh. In Z. Hasan & R. Menon (Eds.), *In a Minority: Essays on Muslim Women in India* (pp. 109–148). New Delhi: Oxford University Press.

Jha, B. (2006). *Rural non-farm employment in India: Macro-trends, micro-evidences and policy options*. Agricultural Economics Unit; Institute of Economic Growth. http://iegindia.org/upload/publication/Workpap/wp272.pdf

John, R. M., & Mutatkar, R. (2005). Statewise estimates of poverty among religious groups in India. *Economic and Political Weekly*, *40*(13), 1337–1345. http://www.jstor.org/stable/4416399

Kamat, A. A. R. (1981). Literacy and education of Muslims: A note literacy and education of Muslims. *Economic and Political Weekly*, *16*(23), 1031–1033.

Khan, I. A. (2016). Muslim education in post-independent India – Issues, factors and prospects. *Journal of Education and Learning*, *10*(1), 63–69.

Kijima, Y., & Lanjouw, P. (2005). Economic diversification and poverty in rural India. *Indian Journal of Labor Economics*, *48*(2), 349–374.

Kitschelt, H., & Wilkinson, S. I. (Eds.). (2007). *Patrons, clients and policies: Patterns of democratic accountability and political competition*. Cambridge University Press.

Kothari, R. (1990). Caste and politics: The great secular upsurge. *Times of India*, *28*.

Krishnan, S., & Hatekar, N. (2017). Rise of the new middle class in India and its changing structure. *Economic and Political Weekly*, *52*(22), 40–48.

Krueger, A. B. (2012). The rise and consequences of inequality Council of Economic Advisers. In *Remarks delivered to the center for American Progress, Washington, DC*.

Lynch, K., & O'Riordan, C. (1998). Inequality in higher education: A study of class barriers. *British Journal of Sociology of Education*, *19*(4), 445–478. https://doi.org/10.1080/0142569980190401

Majumder, R. (2010). Intergenerational mobility in educational and occupational attainment: A comparative study of social classes in India. *Margin*, *4*(4), 463–494. https://doi.org/10.1177/097380101000400404

Mehrotra, S., Parida, J., Sinha, S., & Gandhi, A. (2014). Explaining employment trends in the Indian economy: 1993–94 to 2011–12. *Economic and Political Weekly*, *49*(32), 49–57. https://www.researchgate.net/publication/286723590

Mortimer, J. T., Zhang, L., Wu, C. Y., Hussemann, J., & Johnson, M. K. (2017). Familial transmission of educational plans and the academic self-concept: A three-generation longitudinal study. *Social Psychology Quarterly*, *80*(1), 85–107. https://doi.org/10.1177/0190272516670582

Motiram, S., & Singh, A. (2012). How close does the apple fall to the tree? Some evidence from India on intergenerational occupational mobility. *Economic and Political Weekly*, *47*(40), 56–65. http://www.jstor.org/stable/41720217

Oreopoulos, P. (2003). The long-run consequences of living in a poor neighborhood. *Quarterly Journal of Economics*, *118*(4), 1533–1575. https://doi.org/10.1162/003355303322552865

Panagariya, A., & Mukim, M. (2014). A comprehensive analysis of poverty in India. *Asian Development Review*, *31*(1), 1–52. https://doi.org/10.1162/ADEV_a_00021

Ranganathan, T., Tripathi, A., & Rajoriya, B. (2015). Income and income inequality among Indian rural households. *Institute of Economic Growth (IEG), New Delhi, April*. https://www.researchgate.net/publication/301355952%0AChanging

Ranjan, P. (2001). Dynamic evolution of income distribution and credit-constrained human capital investment in open economies. *Journal of International Economics*, *55*(2), 329–358. https://doi.org/10.1016/S0022-1996(01)00103-9

Razzack, A. (2019). Schooling and the intra-world of Muslim community. *Economic and Political Weekly*, *LIV*(4), 60–65.

Reddy, A. A. (2015). Growth, structural change and wage rates in Rural India. *Economic and Political Weekly*, *50*(2), 56–65.

Reddy, A. B., & Swaminathan, M. (2014). Intergenerational occupational mobility in Rural India: Evidence from ten villages. *Review of Agrarian Studies*, *4*(1), 95–134. http://www.ras.org.in/intergenerational_occupational_mobility_in_rural_india

Reynolds, J. R., & Johnson, M. K. (2011). Change in the stratification of educational expectations and their realization. *Social Forces*, *90*(1), 85–109. https://doi.org/10.1093/sf/90.1.85

Sachar Committee Report. (2006). Social, economic and educational status of the Muslim community of India. In *A Report, Government of India*. http://minorityaffairs.gov.in/reports/sachar-committee-report

Saiyed, A. R., & Talib, M. (1985). Institutions and ideas: A case study in Islamic Learning. *Islam in India*, *2*, 191–209.

Sikand, Y. (2005). *Bastions of the believers: Madrasas and Islamic education in India*. Penguin Books.

Stivers, E. (1958). Motivation for college in high-school boys. *School Review*, *66*(3), 341–350.

Swartz, T. T. (2008). Family capital and the invisible transfer of privilege: Intergenerational support and social class in early adulthood. *New Directions for Child and Adolescent Development*, *119*, 11–24. https://doi.org/10.1002/cd

Taylor, L. C., Clayton, J. D., & Rowley, S. J. (2004). Academic socialization: Understanding parental influences on children's school-related development in the early years. *Review of General Psychology*, *8*(3), 163–178. https://doi.org/10.1037/1089-2680.8.3.163

Thomas, J. J. (2014). The demographic challenge and employment growth in India. *Economic and Political Weekly*, *49*(6), 15–17. http://www.jstor.org/stable/24479252

Torche, F. (2018). Intergenerational mobility at the top of the educational distribution. *Sociology of Education*, *91*(4), 266–289.

Verniers, G. (2016). *The localization of caste politics in Uttar Pradesh after Mandal and Mandir: Reconfiguration of identity politics and party-elite linkages* (Doctoral dissertation, Institut d'études politiques de paris-Sciences Po).

Yadav, Y. (2000). Understanding the second democratic upsurge: Trends of Bahujan participation in electoral politics in the 1990s. In Francine R. Frankel & Rajeev Bhargava (Eds.), *Transforming India: Social and Political Dynamics of Democracy* (pp. 89–119). New Delhi; New York: Oxford University Press.

Zerinini, J. (2009). The marginalisation of the savarnas in Uttar Pradesh?. In C. Jaffrelot & S. Kumar (Eds.), *Rise of the Plebeians? The Changing Face of Indian Legislative Assemblies* (pp. 27–64). Routledge India.

8 Current Evidence and Disagreements

8.1 Introduction

In the different chapters of this work, it has been observed that the ST community lags behind other communities in terms of educational and occupational attainment. SCs, too, have limited mobility when it comes to skill-based professions. Furthermore, SCs' educational mobility improvements are only noticeable during the initial years of schooling. OBCs are one group that has made strides in terms of education and occupational mobility. In this chapter, we analyze the potential issues associated with these trends in light of existing literature.

8.2 Discussion

This section deals with the discussion on aggregate occupational mobility, the movement towards category I occupations, schooling persistence and higher educational attainment.

One of the most intriguing issues is the gaps in the occupational-educational attainment of STs and SCs as compared to the other SRCs, which can be linked to a variety of reasons, including the following:

1) Alleged discrimination: Some studies have documented alleged discrimination in terms of hiring and compensation (Agrawal, 2014; Deshpande & Newman, 2007; Duraisamy & Duraisamy, 2017; Madheswaran & Attewell, 2007; Subramanian, 2001; Thorat & Attewell, 2007). However, the methodologies for assessing discrimination seem to have significant flaws and should be approached with caution.
2) Social network effect: Access to employment-related information is influenced by social structure, social and professional acquaintances, the number of interactions, and the nature of those connections (Andersson et al., 2009; Lin, 1999). In broad heterogeneous labor markets where informality exists, the social network continues to be a critical factor in gaining access to employment (Behtoui, 2008). Members of ethnic enclaves are far more likely than other residents to be employed by their neighbor, implying that the neighborhood plays an important role (Andersson et al., 2009).

DOI: 10.4324/9781003361299-8

3) Job availability: The majority of jobs classified as category I occupations are located in urban areas. The STs, in particular, live in some of the country's most isolated areas (Prakash, 2020). Because high occupational mobility is linked to urbanization and the growth of non-farm activities, as some studies have highlighted (Asher et al., 2020; Emran & Shilpi, 2011), STs' access to such occupations is restricted.
4) Quality of education: Because of the low infrastructure development of schools and colleges in scheduled tribe areas and SC localities, such community members may have earned "graduate and above" degrees, but they face difficulties in occupational mobility due to poor quality of education, a lack of English speaking abilities, and a lack of technical education (Bagde et al., 2016; Borooah et al., 2007; Jeffrey et al., 2005). Furthermore, due to disparities in human resources, primarily formed during schooling, SCs and STs have lower placement rates than students from forward castes after attending higher education institutions (Borooah et al., 2007; Chakravarty & Somanathan, 2008). Earlier research studies have indicated that SCs have higher failure and dropout rates (Chauhan, 2008; Mohanty, 2006). Due to economic and social constraints, they also enroll in government-run schools and academic programs which are not considered to be on par with private schools (Geetha Rani, 2014). The latest NSS 75th round on education reveals that a student from an ST-SC-OBC family is nearly three times less likely to receive an English-medium education. They also continue to be under-represented in medicine, engineering, law and management programs (Kishore & Jha, 2020). It should be noted that the central and state governments' educational affirmative action covers SCs, STs and OBCs. As a result, the cost of education should not be an issue for them. However, government provisions do not cover non-tuition costs, living expenses, and, most importantly, the cost of not working (Jeffrey et al., 2004; Jeffrey & Lerche, 2000; Weisskopf, 2004). Additional relevant factors in this regard include the home ecosystem for education, career guidance, social networking, motivation and access to information, where these communities are probably at a disadvantage relative to the rest of the socio-religious communities (Heckman, 1998; Mayer & Jencks, 1989; Stanton-Salazar & Dornbusch, 1995).

However, studies have suggested that affirmative action on the part of the government benefited the target communities, even if the benefits were not distributed evenly among the beneficiaries (Basant & Sen, 2010; Deshpande & Ramachandran, 2019; Hnatkovska et al., 2013; Howard & Prakash, 2010; Prakash, 2020; Sinha, 2018). These affirmative actions encouraged the formation of regional interest groups and political parties, which adopted affirmative action provisions that benefited their political constituencies more, resulting in an unequal distribution of benefits. Thus, despite the ongoing debate about the efficacy of affirmative action in terms of improving the target population's living conditions on the ground, it undoubtedly empowered them politically, with the effects visible in the Indian body politic (Jaffrelot, C., 2006).

We found that STs and SCs have begun to perform well in terms of educational attainment, even when the father is illiterate. As the education systems have evolved further, the likelihood that people in both communities will pursue secondary or higher education has gone up. However, none of them moves about much in their occupations, and their prospects of finding category I employment are slim. Also SCs have lower mobility than OBCs but higher mobility than STs. In terms of education and employment, the SCs have made some strides. They, along with STs, have been subject to affirmative action since the Indian constitution came into force in 1950, but their growth has been slower than that of OBCs, despite the fact that affirmative action for the latter has a history of fewer than 25 years. This study presents two arguments in this regard: First, STs alone—not the ST-SC combination—face deprivation. Therefore, studies that have indicated improvement in ST-SCs together need to be revisited or re-evaluated. Second, notwithstanding the educational advancements made by STs and SCs, no corresponding improvements can be shown in terms of occupation.

Recent scholarship on this topic has centered on educational benefits, as the majority of professional-technical jobs are in the private sector, and the public sector continues to shrink (Bagde et al., 2016; Deshpande & Ramachandran, 2019; Frisancho & Krishna, 2016). Some studies have inferred that discrimination apart, the job disparity between SC-STs and forward castes is due to significant gaps in their higher educational attainments, as well as noticeable differences in the quality and content of schooling (Basant & Sen, 2010; Borooah et al., 2007). Numerous socio-economic-religious-psychological factors contribute to children dropping out of school or opting out of their secondary education prior to completing it (Basant & Sen, 2010). The literature on the issue of affirmative actions (AAs) is summarized in Table 8.1.

As far as the Muslim community is concerned, they have demonstrated educational backwardness at various occupational-educational levels of fathers. Though the poor performance of Muslims in the lowest educational families is understandable, even the educational achievement of highly educated and decently employed families falls short of that of other groups. The general belief is that children of more educated parents will have stronger educational outcomes. Studies have shown that the continuation of educational backwardness may persist as a result of the absence of role model effects, a depressive neighborhood environment, and disengagement from common public life (Elliott & Sims, 2001; Kao & Thompson, 2003).

8.3 Conclusion

The discussion in this chapter focuses on the success of affirmative actions in light of the evidence presented in the different chapters of the book. This discussion on education and occupation further proves the point of the critical combination of both variables in the analysis. If education or occupation had been discussed in an isolated attempt, we would never be able to make sense of the comprehensive picture of the relative progress made by the STs, SCs and OBCs. The present

Table 8.1 Some recent studies on the impact of AAs in India

Author(s)	*Study period*	*Outcome variable*	*IG perspective*	*ST-SC combined Or separated*	*Findings*
Borroah et al. (2007)	NSS 55th round (1999-00)	Employment in Regular Wages Salaried (RWS) Jobs	NO	Separated	Without the job quota, the modest increase in RWS job representation would not have occurred. There is no discernible discrimination against Hindu OBCs in the hiring process. The disparity between SC and ST education is more pronounced in higher education. Poor education is to blame for the higher education gap. Elementary schools should be the starting point for these efforts.
Basant and Sen (2010)	NSS 61st round (2004-05)	Higher Education	No	Separated	Higher educational deficits for Hindu OBCs have not been large, and higher educational deficits for Hindu-STs have decreased significantly in recent years, particularly when considering the currently studying or qualified population. Reservations in higher education are arguably an inducement to cross the threshold, just as job reservations are a strong inducement to pursue higher education.
Frisancho and Krishna (2016)	EEI data for one institute 2008	Higher Education in elite engineering education	No	Separated	One of the results of AA policies in India is that there are considerable differences in admission standards. The lowest section of SC-ST students is catching up to general students in terms of grades by the end of their degrees. No caste-based wage differentials within occupations; still the placement of minority students more in lower-paying jobs compared to general category students.

(*Continued*)

Table 8.1 Continued

Author(s)	*Study period*	*Outcome variable*	*IG perspective*	*ST-SC combined Or separated*	*Findings*
Deshpande and Ramachandran (2019)	NSS based 2000–12	Occupation, education, wages and public employment	Yes for education	Combined	The study's findings indicate that absolute caste inequalities in years of education and prestigious white-collar occupations have remained static, despite the fact that log incomes below the median have converged and log incomes above the median have diverged. Examining the 1993 expansion of job quotas to OBCs, it was concluded that affirmative action had a beneficial effect on the likelihood of obtaining government jobs and completing secondary school.
Howard and Prakash (2010)	NSS 1983–99	Occupation	No	Separated	The findings indicate that job quotas have a sizable impact on the occupational structure of marginalized groups. The study also suggests that job quotas increase the likelihood of SC individuals to choose high-skill occupations and decreases the likelihood of choosing low- and middle-skill occupation. For STs quite the opposite is true. Their chances of high-skill occupations are less and high for low-and middle-skill occupations. Second, the impact of work quotas is strongly linked to an individual's schooling years. Overall, the findings suggest that the job quota program influences individuals' career choices and leads to their higher socio-economic status within the targeted populations.

Prakash (2020)	NSS 1983–99	Salaried employment, Education, Living Standard,	No	Separated	The study finds that in rural areas the chances of joining salaried jobs increase by 0.6 percent for SCs in response to a 1-percentage point increment in the employment quota. The STs are totally unaffected from the benefit of employment quota. The study reports that the policy improved the well-being of SC individuals in rural areas who had completed less than secondary education. Finally, the impact of the employment quota policy varies by state characteristics.
Hnatkovska et al. (2013)	NSS 1983–05	Occupation, Education and Wages	Yes	Combined	Using survey data from successive rounds of the National Sample Survey, the study finds that intergenerational education and income mobility rates of SC/STs have converged to non-SC/ST levels between 1983 and 2005. Furthermore, SC/STs have equaled non-SC/STs in terms of occupational versatility. It concluded that over the last 20 years, India's systemic reforms have coincided with the removal of caste-based barriers to socio-economic mobility.
Bagde et al. (2016)	State engineering entrance exam data	Education	NO	Separated	At relatively higher-quality institutions affirmative policies increase program attendance. The study finds no evidence that affirmative action places marginalized students in programs for which they are ill-prepared.

Note: EEI refers to Elite Engineering Institutions; Source: Compiled by the author.

discussion also leaves an option for future researchers for micro-level exploration of the effectiveness of affirmative actions and occupational-educational success.

References

Agrawal, T. (2014). Educational inequality in rural and urban India. *International Journal of Educational Development*, *34*(1), 11–19. https://doi.org/10.1016/j.ijedudev.2013.05.002

Andersson, F., Burgess, S., & Lane, J. (2009). *Do as the neighbors do: The impact of social networks on immigrant employment* (IZA Discussion Paper No. 4423; Institute for the Study of Labor, Bonn). http://ftp.iza.org/dp4423.pdf

Asher, S., Novosad, P., & Rafkin, C. (2020). Intergenerational mobility in india: New methods and estimates across time, space, and communities. Unpublished manuscript. https://paulnovosad. com/pdf/anr-india-mobility. pdf..

Bagde, B. S., Epple, D., & Taylor, L. (2016). Does affirmative action work? Caste, gender, college quality, and academic success in India. *American Economic Review*, *106*(6), 1495–1521.

Basant, R., & Sen, G. (2010). Who participates in higher education in India? Rethinking the role of affirmative action. *Economic and Political Weekly*, *45*(39), 62–70.

Behtoui, A. (2008). Informal recruitment methods and disadvantages of immigrants in the Swedish labour market. *Journal of Ethnic and Migration Studies*, *34*(3), 411–430.

Borooah, V. K., Dubey, A., & Iyer, S. (2007). The effectiveness of jobs reservation: Caste, religion and economic status in India. *Development and Change*, *38*(3), 423–445. https://doi.org/10.1111/j.1467-7660.2007.00418.x

Chakravarty, S., & Somanathan, E. (2008). Discrimination in an elite labour market job placements at ii m-ahmedabad. *Economic and Political Weekly*, *43*(44), 45–50.

Chauhan, C. P. S. (2008). Education and caste in India. *Asia Pacific Journal of Education*, *28*(3), 217–234. https://doi.org/10.1080/02188790802267332

Deshpande, A., & Newman, K. S. (2007). Where the path leads: The role of caste in post-university employment expectations. *Economic and Political Weekly*, *42*(41), 2133–2140.

Deshpande, A., & Ramachandran, R. (2019). Traditional hierarchies and affirmative action in a globalizing economy: Evidence from India. *World Development*, *118*, 63–78. https://doi.org/10.1016/j.worlddev.2019.02.006

Duraisamy, P., & Duraisamy, M. (2017). Social identity and wage discrimination in the Indian labour market. *Economic and Political Weekly*, *52*(4), 51–60.

Emran, M. S., & Shilpi, F. (2011). Intergenerational occupational mobility in rural economy: Evidence from Nepal and Vietnam. *Journal of Human Resources*, *46*(2), 427–458. https://doi.org/10.1353/jhr.2011.0009

Elliott, J. R., & Sims, M. (2001). Ghettos and barrios: The impact of neighborhood poverty and race on job matching among blacks and Latinos. *Social Problems*, *48*(3), 341–361.

Frisancho, V., & Krishna, K. (2016). Affirmative action in higher education in India: Targeting, catch up, and mismatch. *Higher Education*, *71*(5), 611–649. https://doi.org/10.1007/s10734-015-9927-1

Geetha Rani, P. (2014). Disparities in earnings and education in India. *Cogent Economics and Finance*, *2*(1). https://doi.org/10.1080/23322039.2014.941510

Heckman, J. J. (1998). Detecting discrimination. *Journal of Economic Perspectives*, *12*(2), 101–116. https://doi.org/10.1257/jep.12.2.101

Hnatkovska, V., Lahiri, A., & Paul, S. B. (2013). Breaking the caste barrier: Intergenerational mobility in India. *Journal of Human Resources, 48*(2), 435–473. https://doi.org/10.1353/jhr.2013.0012

Howard, L. L., & Prakash, N. (2010). Do employment quotas explain the occupational choices of disadvantaged minorities in India? *International Review of Applied Economics, 26*(4), 489–513. https://doi.org/10.1080/02692171.2011.619969

Jaffrelot, C. (2006). The impact of affirmative action in India: More political than socioeconomic. *India Review, 5*(2), 173–189.

Jeffrey, C., Jeffery, P., & Jeffery, R. (2005). When schooling fails young men, education and low-caste politics in rural North India. *Contributions to Indian Sociology, 39*(1), 1–38. https://doi.org/10.1177/006996670503900101

Jeffrey, C., Jeffery, R., & Jeffery, P. (2004). Degrees without freedom: The impact of formal education on Dalit young men in North India. *Development and Change, 35*(5), 963–986. https://doi.org/10.1111/j.1467-7660.2004.00388.x

Jeffrey, C., & Lerche, J. (2000). Stating the difference: State, discourse and class reproduction in Uttar Pradesh, India. *Development and Change, 31*(4), 857–878. https://doi.org/10.1111/1467-7660.00180

Kao, G., & Thompson, J. S. (2003). Racial and ethnic stratification in educational achievement and attainment. *Annual review of sociology, 29*(1), 417–442.

Kishore, R., & Jha, A. (2020, August 1). Mapping education inequalities. *Hindustan Times*. https://www.hindustantimes.com/india-news/mapping-education-inequalities/story-xhTIlYty7kF7MNqxnOyGtO.html

Lin, N. (1999). Building a network theory of social capital. *Connections, 9*(6), 28–51. https://doi.org/10.3217/jucs-009-06-0501

Madheswaran, S., & Attewell, P. (2007). Caste discrimination in the Indian urban labour market: Evidence from the National Sample Survey. *Economic and political Weekly, 42*(41), 4146–4153.

Mayer, S. E., & Jencks, C. (1989). Growing up in poor neighborhoods: How much does it matter? New Series, *243*(4897), 1441–1445.

Mohanty, M. (2006). Social inequality, labour market dynamics and reservation. *Economic and Political Weekly, 41*(September 2), 3777–3789.

Prakash, N. (2020). The impact of employment quotas on the economic lives of disadvantaged minorities in India. *Journal of Economic Behavior and Organization, 180*, 494–509. https://doi.org/10.1016/j.jebo.2020.10.017

Sinha, R. (2018). Closer, but no cigar: Intergenerational mobility across caste groups in India. In *Policy research working paper WPS8401, World Bank Group, development research group* (Issue April). https://doi.org/10.1596/1813-9450-8401

Stanton-Salazar, R. D., & Dornbusch, S. M. (1995). Social capital and the reproduction of inequality: Information networks among Mexican-origin high school students. *Sociology – The Journal of the British Sociological Association, 68*(2), 116–135.

Subramanian, S. (2001). On an index of discrimination. *Journal of Social and Economic Development, III*(2), 199–207.

Thorat, S., & Attewell, P. (2007). The legacy of social exclusion: A correspondence study of job discrimination in India. *Economic and Political Weekly, 42*(41), 4141–4145.

Weisskopf, T. E. (2004). Impact of reservation on admissions to higher education in India. *Economic and Political Weekly, 39*(39), 4339–4349. http://www.jstor.org/stable/4415591

Index

For Product Safety Concerns and Information please contact our EU representative GPSR@taylorandfrancis.com
Taylor & Francis Verlag GmbH, Kaufingerstraße 24, 80331 München, Germany

www.ingramcontent.com/pod-product-compliance
Ingram Content Group UK Ltd.
Pitfield, Milton Keynes, MK11 3LW, UK
UKHW020002200926
475702UK00015B/2428
* 9 7 8 1 0 3 2 4 2 1 2 3 0 *